THE
U.S.
HISTORY
HIGHWAY

THE U.S. HISTORY HIGHWAY

A GUIDE TO INTERNET RESOURCES

Dennis A. Trinkle and Scott A. Merriman
Editors

M.E. Sharpe
Armonk, New York
London, England

Library of Congress Cataloging-in-Publication Data

Trinkle, Dennis A., 1968–
    The U.S. history highway : a guide to internet resources / [edited by] Dennis A. Trinkle
and Scott A. Merriman.
        p. cm.
    Includes index.
    ISBN 0-7656-0907-X (pbk. : alk. paper)
        1. United States—History—Computer network resources—Directories. 2. Web
sites—Directories. 3. Internet. I. Merriman, Scott A., 1968– II. Title.

    E175.88.T75 2002
    025.06′973—dc21   2001049789

Printed in the United States of America

The paper used in this publication meets the minimum requirements of
American National Standard for Information Sciences
Permanence of Paper for Printed Library Materials,
ANSI Z 39.48-1984.

BM (p)   10   9   8   7   6   5   4   3   2   1

For Betty Merriman, David Merriman, Holly Merriman Gamage, Judy Merriman Nadzam, and Susan Merriman

Contents

Acknowledgments

We cannot possibly thank everyone who has played a small or large role in the writing of this book, so we hope that you know that your efforts and support are recognized and appreciated.

Dennis A. Trinkle would like to thank the faculty, staff, and students of DePauw University for their many tangible and intangible contributions to *The U.S. History Highway*. DePauw is a lively learning community, and I want to thank President Robert Bottoms and Vice President Neal Abraham for their support and encouragement of my many activities. I also want to especially thank several faculty and staff colleagues who daily make my teaching, research, and work better and more successful: John Schlotterbeck, Barbara Steinson, John Dittmer, Julia Bruggemann, Glen Kuecker, Aaron Dzuibinskyi, Lou Miller, Sue Balter, Bob Hershberger, Carol Smith, Julianne Miranda, Dan Pfeifer, Scott Cooper, Ken Owen, and Bob Bruce. I would also like to thank the members of my other professional family—the American Association for History and Computing. In particular, my sincere appreciation is extended to Ken Dvorak, Charles Mackay, Jeffrey Barlow, Kelly Robison, Jessica Lacher-Feldman, Steve Hoffman, and Deborah Anderson. It is a genuine pleasure to work with so many creative and passionate teachers and scholars. Finally, but certainly not least, special thanks to my wife, Kristi, my brother, Keith, my mother, Gayle, and all the members of my extended family. Your constant energy and care are a great inspiration.

Scott A. Merriman would like to thank his family, friends, and teachers, both past and present, for their support and guidance. Special thanks to my wife, Jessie, for her assistance, both in this writing effort and many others. I would also like to recognize the History Department of the University of Kentucky, faculty, staff, and fellow graduate students alike, for their support and encouragement. Especially deserving of gratitude for serving as mentors are Robert Ireland, Eric Christianson, David Hamilton, and Robert Olson. My years at UK have been enriched by my friendships with Holly Grout, John Patrick Mullins, Tom Riley, Erin Shelor, Jules Sweet, and Jennifer Walton. In my larger travels, I have been ably assisted by many people, far too many to mention, and I would be remiss if I did not thank at least some of them here. I am truly grateful for my continuing friendships and professional relationships with Jeffrey Barlow, Rowly Brucken, Randal Horobik, Charles Mackay, Jen McGee, Kelly Robison, David Staley, Amy Staples, and Paul Wexler. I am thankful to my family for their perpetual support. Finally, for all those who have supported me, but who are not specifically mentioned, thanks!

Introduction

More than 60 percent of American households now report that they regularly access the Internet. This figure represents a stunning historical transformation. The number of Web pages is increasing so rapidly that no reliable estimate exists, though best guesses suggest more than a billion pages and climbing. The growth rate and proliferation are staggering and is historically unprecedented. Radio, television, and the telephone became part of American daily life at a comparatively glacial pace. Such dizzying expansion and alteration make the Internet a tremendously exciting phenomenon, but also unsettling and unwieldy.

To novices and even seasoned users, the Information Superhighway can be information overload at its worst, often more intimidating and frustrating than exciting. For anyone interested in history, however, the Internet simply cannot be ignored. The resources are richer and more valuable than ever. There are nearly fifty thousand sites dedicated to World War II alone. Students can find the complete texts of hundreds of thousands of books, work with previously inaccessible primary documents, and explore thousands of first-rate sites dedicated to historical topics. Publishers can advertise their wares, and professors can find enormous databases devoted to teaching suggestions, online versions of historical journals, and active scholarly discussions on a wide variety of research topics. The Internet is quite simply the most revolutionary storehouse of human knowledge in history.

For most of us, however, whether we are students, professors, librarians, editors, or just lovers of history, there are not enough hours in our already busy days to go chasing information down an infinite number of alleyways, no matter how useful or interesting that information might be. This is especially true for those of us who have never logged on to a computer network or who have only a basic acquaintance with the Internet. The aim of this book is to provide a general introduction to the skills and tools necessary to navigate the Information Superhighway and to offer detailed information about the thousands of quality resources that are out there and how to find them.

Part I is a short primer for those with little or no experience using the Internet. It discusses what exists and what you can do with it. It explains how to gain access to the Internet and outlines what types of software are necessary. There is also an important section on the manners and rules that govern the Internet—"netiquette," as seasoned users call it. A valuable new section on evaluating Internet resources has been added to the chapter as well.

Part II is the heart of the book. It lists hundreds of sites that will appeal to anyone interested in history and that our specialist section authors have determined to be reliable and useful for the serious study of history. This section will allow you to avoid the helter-skelter databases, such as Yahoo!, Excite, and DogPile, that take you to information regardless of quality and utility. You will not find sites created by first graders in Indianapolis or by biased, ahistorical groups like the Holocaust Deniers of America. Bon Voyage!

THE
U.S.
HISTORY
HIGHWAY

Part I

Getting Started

Chapter 1

The Basics

History of the Internet

Since this book is directed at those interested in history, it seems sensible to begin with a brief history of the Internet itself. The story of the Internet's origins is as varied, complex, and fascinating as the information the Net contains. Ironically, the Net began as the polar opposite of the publicly accessible network it has become. It grew out of the Cold War hysteria surrounding the Soviet launch of *Sputnik*, the first man-made satellite, in 1957. Amidst paranoia that the United States was losing the "science race," President Eisenhower created the Advanced Research Projects Agency (ARPA) within the Department of Defense to establish an American lead in science and technology applicable to the military. After helping the United States develop and launch its own satellite by 1959, the ARPA scientists turned much of their attention to computer networking and communications. Their goal was to find a successful way of linking universities, defense contractors, and military command centers to foster research and interaction, but also to sustain vital communications in case of nuclear attack. The network project was formally launched in 1969 by ARPA under a grant that connected four major computers at universities in the southwestern United States—UCLA, Stanford, the University of California, Santa Barbara, and the University of Utah. The network went online in December 1969. The age of computer networks was born.

In the early 1970s, it became clear to the initial developers of the ARPANET that the system was already stretching past its Cold War origins. Non-military research institutions were developing competing networks of communication, more and more users were going online, and new languages were being introduced all of which made communication difficult or impossible between net-

5

works. To resolve this problem, the Defense Advanced Research Projects Agency (which had replaced ARPA) launched the Internetting Project in 1973. The aim was to create a uniform communications language that would allow the hundreds of networks being formed to communicate and function as a single meganetwork. In an amazing display of scientific prowess comparable to the Apollo Program, this crucial step in the development of the Information Superhighway was accomplished in a single year when Robert Kahn and Vinton G. Cerf introduced the Transmission Control Protocol/ Internet Protocol (TCP/IP). This protocol (as the rules governing a computer language are termed) made possible the connection of all the various networks and computers then in existence and set the stage for the enormous expansion of the Internet.

Over the next decade, the Department of Defense realized the significance and potential of the Internet, and non-military organizations were gradually allowed to link with the ARPANET. Shortly after that, commercial providers like CompuServe began making the Internet accessible for those not connected to a university or research institution. The potential for profiting from the Internet fueled dramatic improvements in speed and ease of use.

The most significant step toward simplicity of use came with the introduction of the World Wide Web (WWW) which allows interactive graphics and audio to be accessed through the Internet. The WWW was the brainchild of Tim Berners-Lee of the European Laboratory for Particle Physics, who created a computer language called "hypertext" that made possible the interactive exchange of text and graphic images and allowed almost instantaneous connection (linking) to any item on the Internet. Berners-Lee was actually developing this revolutionary language as the Internet was expanding in the 1970s and 1980s, but it was only with the introduction of an easy-to-use Web browser (as the software for interacting with the Web is called) that the Web became widely accessible to the average person. That first browser—Mosaic—was made available to the public by the National Center for Supercomputing Applications at the University of Illinois, Urbana–Champaign in 1991. Three years later, Mosiac's creator, Marc Andreessen, introduced an even more sophisticated browser that allowed the interaction of sound, text, and images—Netscape Navigator. The next year Microsoft launched a browser of its own—Internet Explorer.

Today, there are many software options for exploring the Internet, and access can be purchased through thousands of national and local service providers. One need no longer be a military researcher or work at a university to "surf the Net." There are now more than one hundred million users logging onto the Internet from the United States alone. Tens of thousands of networks now are connected by TCP/IP, and the Internet forms a vast communication system which can legitimately be called an Information Superhighway.

Uses of the Internet

This section of Part I will explain the most useful features of the Internet for those interested in history. It will discuss sending and receiving e-mail, reading and posting messages to Usenet newsgroups and discussion lists, logging on to remote computers with Telnet, transferring files using the File Transfer Protocol, and browsing the WWW. The next section will discuss in greater detail the software packages that perform these tasks and explain exactly how to get online.

Sending and Receiving E-mail

E-mail (electronic mail) is the most popular feature of the Internet. It offers almost instantaneous communication with people all over the world. The Nora Ephron film *You've Got Mail* has made e-mail as widely known as the United States Post Office, and e-mail functions very similarly, allowing users to send and receive messages or computer files over the Internet. Rather than taking days or weeks to reach their destination, however, e-mail messages arrive in minutes or seconds. A professor in Indianapolis, Indiana, can correspond with a student in Delhi, India, in the blink of an eye. A publisher, editor, and author can exchange drafts of a history book they are preparing with no delay. And, e-mail does not involve the high costs of international postage, fax charges, or long-distance telephone premiums. E-mail is always part of the basic service arrangement provided with Internet access, and it is quite easy to use with the software packages discussed later.

A Note on E-mail Addresses

E-mail addresses are very similar to postal addresses. Like a postal address, an e-mail address provides specific information about where the message is to be sent along the Internet. For example, a friend's address might be something like

Gkuecker@depauw.edenvax.edu.

If you look at the end of the address, you will notice the .edu suffix. This means the e-mail message is going to an educational institution. In this case, it is DePauw University, as the second item indicates. Edenvax shows that the message is traveling along the Net to someone on a Vax computer designated as Eden at DePauw University. Finally, the address reveals that the recipient is your friend Glen Kuecker (Gkuecker). This is just like providing the name, street address, city, state, and zip code on regular mail.

The names that individual institutions choose for their Internet address vary widely, but to help make e-mail addresses a little easier to understand, all addresses in the United States are broken down into the computer equivalent of zip codes. We already noted that the .edu in the above message indicates that the recipient's account is at an educational institution. There used to be six key three-letter designations that provided a clue as to where your e-mail was going to or coming from. Seven additional designations have recently been approved. The thirteen designations are

Category	Meaning
.com	commercial organizations
.edu	educational institutions
.gov	government organizations (non-military)
.mil	military institutions
.net	network service providers
.org	miscellaneous providers and nonprofit organizations
.aero	air-transport industry
.biz	businesses
.coop	cooperatives
.info	unrestricted
.museum	museums
.name	individuals
.pro	accountants, lawyers, and physicians

A common naming system for American primary and secondary schools has also recently been introduced. This system uses the school name, the k12 designation, and the state where the school is located in the address. A typical address might read

KeithTrinkle@howe.k12.in.us.

This indicates that a student, teacher, or administrator at Howe High School in Indiana sent the e-mail. The k12.in.us will always be present in e-mail coming from a primary or secondary school.

These designations do not apply to e-mail addresses for accounts located outside the United States, but an equally simple system exists for identifying foreign messages. All mail going to or coming from foreign accounts ends with a two-letter country code. If you have a colleague in France, you might receive an e-mail message ending with .fr. You may receive an e-mail message from an editor in Canada ending in .ca. Or, if you met a historian with similar interests

on that last trip through Tanzania, you might soon receive mail ending with .tz.
These extensions are:

AF	Afghanistan
AL	Albania
DZ	Algeria
AS	American Samoa
AD	Andorra
AO	Angola
AI	Anguilla
AQ	Antarctica
AG	Antigua and Barbuda
AR	Argentina
AM	Armenia
AW	Aruba
AU	Australia
AT	Austria
AZ	Azerbaijan
BS	Bahamas
BH	Bahrain
BD	Bangladesh
BB	Barbados
BY	Belarus
BE	Belgium
BZ	Belize
BJ	Benin
BM	Bermuda
BT	Bhutan
BO	Bolivia
BA	Bosnia-Herzegovina
BW	Botswana
BV	Bouvet Island
BR	Brazil
IO	British Indian Ocean Territory
BN	Brunei Darussalam
BG	Bulgaria
BF	Burkina Faso
BI	Burundi
KH	Cambodia
CM	Cameroon
CA	Canada
CV	Cape Verde

KY	Cayman Islands
CF	Central African Republic
TD	Chad
CL	Chile
CN	China
CX	Christmas Island
CC	Cocos Islands
CO	Colombia
KM	Comoros
CG	Congo
CD	Congo, Democratic Republic
CK	Cook Islands
CR	Costa Rica
CI	Côte d'Ivoire
HR	Croatia
CU	Cuba
CY	Cyprus
CZ	Czech Republic
DK	Denmark
DJ	Djibouti
DM	Dominica
DO	Dominican Republic
TP	East Timor
EC	Ecuador
EG	Egypt
SV	El Salvador
GQ	Equatorial Guinea
ER	Eritrea
EE	Estonia
ET	Ethiopia
FK	Falkland Islands
FO	Faroe Islands
FJ	Fiji
FI	Finland
FR	France
GF	French Guiana
PF	French Polynesia
TF	French Southern Territories
GA	Gabon
GM	Gambia
GE	Georgia
DE	Germany

GH	Ghana
GI	Gibraltar
GB	Great Britain
GR	Greece
GL	Greenland
GD	Grenada
GP	Guadeloupe
GU	Guam
GT	Guatemala
GN	Guinea
GW	Guinea-Bissau
GY	Guyana
HT	Haiti
HM	Heard and McDonald Islands
HN	Honduras
HK	Hong Kong
HU	Hungary
IS	Iceland
IN	India
ID	Indonesia
IR	Iran
IQ	Iraq
IE	Ireland
IL	Israel
IT	Italy
JM	Jamaica
JP	Japan
JO	Jordan
KZ	Kazakhstan
KE	Kenya
KI	Kiribati
KP	Korea (North)
KR	Korea (South)
KW	Kuwait
KG	Kyrgyz Republic
LA	Lao People's Democratic Republic
LV	Latvia
LB	Lebanon
LS	Lesotho
LR	Liberia
LY	Libyan Arab Jamahiriya
LI	Liechtenstein

LT	Lithuania
LU	Luxembourg
MO	Macau
MK	Macedonia
MG	Madagascar
MW	Malawi
MY	Malaysia
MV	Maldives
ML	Mali
MT	Malta
MH	Marshall Islands
MQ	Martinique
MR	Mauritania
MU	Mauritius
YT	Mayotte
MX	Mexico
FM	Micronesia
MD	Moldova
MC	Monaco
MN	Mongolia
MS	Montserrat
MA	Morocco
MZ	Mozambique
MM	Myanmar
NA	Namibia
NR	Nauru
NP	Nepal
NL	Netherlands
AN	Netherlands Antilles
NT	Neutral Zone
NC	New Caledonia
NZ	New Zealand
NI	Nicaragua
NE	Niger
NG	Nigeria
NU	Niue
NF	Norfolk Island
MP	Northern Mariana Islands
NO	Norway
OM	Oman
PK	Pakistan
PW	Palau

PA	Panama
PG	Papua New Guinea
PY	Paraguay
PE	Peru
PH	Philippines
PN	Pitcairn
PL	Poland
PT	Portugal
PR	Puerto Rico
QA	Qatar
RE	Réunion
RO	Romania
RU	Russian Federation
RW	Rwanda
SH	Saint Helena
KN	Saint Kitts and Nevis
LC	Saint Lucia
PM	Saint Pierre and Miquelon
VC	Saint Vincent and the Grenadines
WS	Samoa
SM	San Marino
ST	São Tomé and Principe
SA	Saudi Arabia
SN	Senegal
SC	Seychelles
SL	Sierra Leone
SG	Singapore
SK	Slovakia
SI	Slovenia
SB	Solomon Islands
SO	Somalia
ZA	South Africa
ES	Spain
LK	Sri Lanka
SD	Sudan
SR	Suriname
SJ	Svalbard and Jan Mayen Islands
SZ	Swaziland
SE	Sweden
CH	Switzerland
SY	Syria
TW	Taiwan

TJ	Tajikistan
TZ	Tanzania
TH	Thailand
TG	Togo
TK	Tokelau
TO	Tonga
TT	Trinidad and Tobago
TN	Tunisia
TR	Turkey
TM	Turkmenistan
TC	Turks and Caicos Islands
TV	Tuvalu
UG	Uganda
UA	Ukraine
AE	United Arab Emirates
UK	United Kingdom
US	United States
UM	United States Minor Outlying Islands
UY	Uruguay
UZ	Uzbekistan
VU	Vanuatu
VA	Vatican City State
VE	Venezuela
VN	Vietnam
VG	Virgin Islands (British)
VI	Virgin Islands (U.S.)
WF	Wallis and Futuna Islands
EH	Western Sahara
YE	Yemen
YU	Yugoslavia
ZM	Zambia
ZW	Zimbabwe

A Note on E-mail Security

Because sending e-mail is so similar to sending a letter by postal service, many
people forget that there is a major difference—federal laws discourage anyone
from looking at (or intercepting) your mail, and sealed packaging provides a
fairly reliable way to detect tampering. Unfortunately, e-mail is not protected in
the same ways. As your electronic message passes through the Internet, it can
be read, intercepted, and altered by many individuals.

Some security measures have been developed to protect e-mail just as an envelope secures letters. The latest versions of many programs that process e-mail now include the ability to encrypt messages. Encryption converts your e-mail into a complex code that must be deciphered by an e-mail program or Web browser that is designed to convert the encoded message back into regular text. The latest versions of Netscape, Internet Explorer, Eudora, and Pegasus include the ability to code and decode encrypted e-mail, but no e-mail program automatically converts a message into a secured code. If you want your messages or files encrypted, you will have to follow the directions provided with your e-mail package for doing it. If you purchase products and services over the Internet, you will also want to be certain that your account or credit card numbers are insured by some sort of encryption. Nevertheless, it is prudent to keep in mind that no security measure is completely reliable.

Reading and Posting Messages on Usenet Newsgroups

For anyone interested in history, Usenet newsgroups are another rewarding feature of the Internet. They are the electronic equivalent of the old New England town meetings at which anyone could pose a question or make an observation and others could respond to it. At present, there are more than ten thousand newsgroups dedicated to thousands of different topics, and many of these relate to history. Each is regulated by a moderator who, like the editor of a newspaper, sets the quality and tone of the posts. There are groups that regularly discuss the Holocaust, the American Revolution, historical publishing, library concerns, and cartography, just to mention a few areas.

The software that allows one to easily locate and participate in these newsgroups will be discussed later. Before passing on to the next topic, however, you should note that there are several clues to determining the content and nature of groups that will help down the road. Like e-mail addresses, the addresses of newsgroups provide some insight into the nature of the group. Take the newsgroup

alt.civilwar.

This address indicates that the group discusses the alternative topic—the Civil War. Each newsgroup will have a similar address revealing its type and topic. The following categories will aid in determining which of the more than ten thousand newsgroups are worth investigating:

Category	Meaning
alt.	alternative themes (Most groups relating to history carry the alt. designation)
comp.	computer related topics
misc.	miscellaneous themes
news.	posts about newsgroups
rec.	recreational topics
sci.	scientific discussions
soc.	social concerns
talk.	talk radio style format

Reading and Posting Messages on Discussion Lists

Discussion lists are a hybrid mixture of e-mail and newsgroups. With discussion lists, the posts and replies that anyone can access in newsgroups are sent by e-mail only to those who have subscribed to the list. As with most newsgroups, there is an editor who screens the posts before they are sent to subscribers, maintaining quality and decency. There are discussion lists that target students, professors, editors, publishers, librarians, and general readers. Almost any historical topic imaginable has a list devoted to it. How open the discussion lists are to subscribers is determined by the moderators. Some limit membership to those with a special interest, while others permit anyone who wishes to join. Chapter 2 discusses the lists focusing on history and explains their qualifications for subscription in more detail.

Chapter 2 will also provide more specific instructions on how to subscribe to each group. All discussion lists share a basic subscription format, however. To subscribe (or to unsubscribe), you simply send an e-mail message to the computer that receives and distributes the messages. This computer is called the listserver (or listserv) because it serves the list. For example, to send a message to a list discussing the history of dogs (H-Dog), you would send the e-mail message

Subscribe H-Dog yourfirstname yourlastname

to the e-mail address

Listserv@ucbeh.san.uc.edu.

The listserv would quickly acknowledge your registration as a member, and e-mail posts from the other list members would begin arriving in your box.

A Word of Warning about Discussion Lists

You should be careful to join only subscription lists that are truly of interest and be certain to read your e-mail several times a week. Most discussion lists are very active, sending out fifteen or more messages per day. If you get carried away at first, you may find yourself buried under an avalanche of several hundred e-mail posts awaiting your eager attention. So be careful to subscribe only to those lists that most interest you until you gain a feel for how much mail you are likely to receive.

Multi-User Virtual Environments

Unlike discussion lists, multi-user virtual environments (MUVEs) allow real-time conversations between participants anywhere in the world—that is, they can speak to each other at the same time as if on a conference telephone call. The most popular and widely known version of a multi-user environment is the chat room. There are now thousands of "rooms" on the Internet where people come together daily to discuss philosophy, politics, or the latest NBA game. Chat rooms are generally informal arenas. Another type of MUVE, the Multi-User Domain, Object Oriented, or MOO as they are commonly called, has been widely adopted for educational and serious use. MOOs allow the same real-time conversation of chat rooms, but the participants interact within a textually described world created by other participants. MOOs offer every user the opportunity to construct and describe the spaces and objects of this textual world.

Many universities and scholarly societies now sponsor MOOs that are open to the public. On some of these MOOs you can take a virtual class, engage in historical re-creations, or simply converse about historical issues. The MOOs related to history are discussed in more detail in Part II. A good directory to educational MOOs and to tutorials for those who would like more guidance can be found at: http://www.itp.berkeley.edu/~thorne/MOO.html.

Logging onto a Remote Computer with Telnet

Anyone who has ever used an electronic library catalog is familiar with the computerless screens and keyboards that allow patrons to access the library's catalog. These machines do not have their own microprocessors, but are linked to a central computer that shares information with all of the terminals connected to it. Telnet is a program offered by all Internet service providers that permits your home or office computer to act just like the terminals at the library. It enables you to temporarily connect to a remote computer and access its information as if it were on your own computer. Those interested in history will find Telnet particularly important because almost every major library in the world now allows Telnet access to its catalogs. You can do subject searches or find out which libraries possess a specific work you are looking for.

Transferring Files with File Transfer Protocol (FTP)

File Transfer Protocol (or FTP) is similar to Telnet. Like Telnet, it is a program that connects you to a remote computer. FTP does not allow you to read the material on the remote machine; rather, it actually allows you to copy the files or programs and transfer them to your own computer. You can use FTP to get a copy of the United States Constitution or to download (as retrieving information with FTP is called) a program that teaches you the history of the Vietnam War. Thousands of sites with downloadable files, programs, and historical information are out there waiting to be tapped. Many of the best and most useful FTP sites will be discussed in Part II.

As with Telnet, there are many packages that permit FTP access. For now, we will mention only that there are three main types of FTP access. There is anonymous FTP, identified FTP, and restricted FTP. Anonymous FTP allows you to connect to a computer and download information without identifying yourself. Identified FTP also allows you to copy materials, but it requires you to give your e-mail address and name, so that the sponsors of the site can maintain statistical information about the use of their site. Restricted FTP is used by some commercial and private institutions that only allow FTP for a fee or for authorized users. The sites mentioned in Part II specify which of these categories the sites fall into and explain how to gain access when a fee or password is required.

Browsing the WWW

For most computer users, time on the Internet will mean exploring the WWW and working with a Web browser (as the programs that allow access to the WWW are called). The Web is the most popular and fastest growing section of the Internet because it combines text, sound, and graphics to create multimedia sites. History buffs can find everything from an audio track of the *Battle Hymn of the Republic* to short film clips of JFK's assassination to a complete version of the French *Encyclopédie*. The most powerful Web browsers also perform all of the other Internet functions such as e-mail, Telnet, and FTP, so new users need only master one basic software package.

The Web and Web browser packages owe much of their popularity and potential to their multimedia format, but they also profit from their ability to link information. With the WWW, Web page developers can create links to any other page on the Web so that, when you use your mouse to point at a highlighted image or section of text and then click the correct mouse button, your computer can almost instantly bring up that information. Thus, a link on a home page (the first page of information that you see when you connect to a Web site) can connect you to any other site, just as a cross-reference in a textbook sends you to other related information. This makes the WWW an amazingly easy-to-use source of information or recreation (for those who become Web junkies).

Chapter 2 discusses the software that makes connecting to the Web possible, but as with e-mail, you will need to understand Web addresses to find information on the WWW. These addresses are called URLs—uniform resource locators—which is simply techno-talk for addresses. Every page on the Web has a unique URL. This makes it very easy to go directly to the information you need. They look something like this:

http://mcel.pacificu.edu/JAHC/JAHCiv2/index.html

Some addresses are longer than this. Some are shorter. All contain three basic parts. Looking from right to left, the first designation you notice is index.html. This tells you that you are retrieving a file called index in the html format. HTML (Hypertext Markup Language) is the standard language of the Web for saving multimedia information. Other possibilities include .gif and .jpeg, which indicate graphic image files; .avi and .wav, which indicate audio files; and .mov, which signals a movie. XML is a new markup protocol like HTML that also allows metatags or descriptive tags that describe the content without appearing on the page. Software can then do more sophisticated searches. Another common protocol is .asp. This means that the page is being created via a database. ASP refers to active server pages, which are a language for getting information from databases.

The middle part of the address, mcel.pacificu.edu/JAHC/JAHCiv2, is just like an e-mail address, specifying what network and computer stores the information so that your software package can find it on the Internet. The .edu extension tells you the information is at an educational institution; as with e-mail, there will always be a three-letter code revealing the type of institution that sponsors the site.

The http:// lets you know that the browser is using the Hypertext Transfer Protocol to get the information. This is the standard language that governs the transfer and sharing of information on the Web. If you were using your browser to Telnet or FTP, the http:// would be replaced by ftp:// or telnet:// and then the address, showing which function your computer is performing.

Of course, you can use the Internet and profit from the WWW without spending hours studying their technical background, history, and terms. The next chapter tells you how to get on the Internet and what software you need.

Chapter 2

Signing On

Getting on the Internet

Once upon a time, getting connected to the Internet was the hardest part of going online. In the early days, if you did not work for the military or a research institution, you were out of luck. The introduction of commercial providers in the 1980s made access easier to obtain, but it might cost you as much as a new car. Today, there are thousands of local and national Internet service providers, and the competition has made Internet access amazingly inexpensive. In most markets, you can now get almost unlimited access for $10 or $15 per month. For those fortunate enough to work for a library, college, university, or publisher, the price is often even better—free. Getting on the Internet has never been easier or less expensive.

Internet access is offered by three basic categories of service providers—corporate/institutional, national commercial, and local commercial providers. For those who work at companies or institutions offering Internet access to their employees, the best way to learn about your options is to speak directly to your system manager or computer support staff.

For those who do not have access to the Internet at work or school, there are several factors to consider in choosing a provider. Perhaps most important is finding a service that offers a local phone number or a toll-free number, so that you need not pay long distance charges for your Internet access. The attractiveness of the Internet vanishes quickly in the presence of a $400 phone bill. Fortunately, there are now so many service providers it is usually easy to find a provider that offers a local phone number in your area. Cable and satellite providers are also scurrying to offer other access options besides telephone connections.

The second consideration is the type of service you desire. Many national and local service providers in your city or state will offer almost unlimited access to the WWW, e-mail, FTP, and other basic services for very affordable rates ($5 to $20 a month). (Local service providers can be found by looking in your local phone book under "Internet Service Providers" or "World Wide Web Service Providers.") There are also several national service providers, such as America Online and CompuServe, which provide special services in addition to basic Internet access. These services include access to electronic versions of national newspapers, up-to-the-minute stock market reports, and special discussion lists and newsgroups available only to subscribers. Because these national service providers offer features you cannot find elsewhere, they are more expensive. The best way to decide if any of the national service providers feature packages you want is to contact each of them directly, keeping a record of the benefits and limitations of each service.

The Hardware

Convenient use of the Internet and its many tools is governed by speed. The faster your computer can send and process information, the more pleasurable and productive your time on the Net will be. Thus, a simple rule of thumb guides the purchase of computer equipment for use on the Internet: Buy the best machine you can realistically afford. This does not mean to mortgage your house just to get better equipment. All new computers sold today are more than adequate for exploring the resources described in this book. For those with older computers, machines with the minimum configurations listed in Tables 2.1 and 2.2 will allow you to easily access the resources of the Internet. More memory (RAM), a faster processor, and a speedier modem will all enable you to interact with the Net more quickly, however. If you want to start with the basic system described below and gradually upgrade, make sure the first addition you make is more RAM. Upgrading from 32 megs to 64 or 128 megs of RAM or more will make the most noticeable difference in the performance of your computer. Improving your processor should be second and trading in your old modem should be done last. At present, the speed of phone lines restricts the effectiveness of modems, so you will get the least improvement in your system from the purchase of a faster modem.

The Software

While many educational institutions and the national service providers such as AOL and CompuServe offer their own software packages with directions and

Table 2.1

Windows-Based Configurations

Processor	486 or higher
RAM	32 MB with Windows 95, 98, or NT
Modem	28.8 KBS or faster recommended
Hard drive	35 MB free space recommended
Sound card and speakers	Recommended for multimedia
VGA monitor	Required
Network or dial-up connection	Required

Table 2.2

Apple Configurations

Processor	PowerPC with OS 7.6.1 or higher
RAM	24 MB or higher
Modem	28.8 kbs or faster recommended
Hard drive	35 MB free space recommended
Sound card and speakers	Required
VGA monitor	Required
Network or dial-up connection	Required

tutorials, those who choose local service providers can select the software they wish to use to access the Internet. Most local service providers will also give new users software needed to access the Internet along with detailed instructions. In principle, however, you can use any package you wish to connect to the Internet through a local provider. This section will present brief descriptions of some of the best packages and explain where to obtain them.

Web Browsers and E-mail Programs

Netscape Communicator and Microsoft Internet Explorer

The two powerhouse packages (Web browsers, as they are called) that most Internauts use are Netscape Communicator and Microsoft Internet Explorer.

They combine all the tools for accessing the Web, sending e-mail, Telnetting, and using FTP. Both can display the combinations of graphics and text that make the Internet a lively and exciting resource. They are simple to use, come with tutorials and a help feature, and are good choices for all users from novices to experts.

Netscape Communicator and Microsoft Internet Explorer also can both be downloaded on the Internet. You can download Netscape at the following address (please note, addresses are case sensitive):

> http://www.netscape.com/computing/download/

Microsoft Internet Explorer can be downloaded at

> http://www.microsoft.com/windows/ie/default.htm

Both Netscape and Internet Explorer are currently available free.

Eudora and Pegasus

Netscape and Internet Explorer perform all of the functions you need to explore the Internet, including e-mail. However, those who send and receive a lot of electronic correspondence, or who plan to send long files along with their messages, may prefer to use a package designed specifically to handle electronic mail. Qualcomm's Eudora and Pegasus are currently two of the best packages for handling e-mail that are available on the Internet at no cost to students, faculty, and staff. Both packages can send messages to lists of recipients, permit the use of special filters to sort and screen e-mail, allow secure protection of files, send files in addition to or along with text, and feature attractive graphic environments and menus that make them easy to use. Eudora is available via FTP at

> http://www.eudora.com/

Pegasus is available via FTP at

> http://www.pmail.com/

Netiquette and Copyright

Because electronic communication is still new, the rules governing online expression are still evolving. There are already, however, some basic courtesies that keep the free and open communication of the Internet polite and enjoyable.

With this goal in mind, here are some Netiquette hints that can keep you from accidentally offending someone.

General Netiquette

The most important thing to remember is that Internet communication is just like writing a letter. Electronic messages can be seen by many individuals other than the intended recipient. They can be forwarded to countless people. They can even be printed and posted in public areas. Thus, the golden rule of Internet communication should never be forgotten:

Never write anything you would not want a stranger to read.

It is also important to remember that e-mail is judged by the same standards as other written communication. Sometimes, the ease and speed of electronic communication lull users into forgetting to check grammar and spelling. This can lead to your e-mail being forwarded to thousands of individuals, and you do not want people all over the Internet laughing because you innocently asked if it was Vasco de Gama who circumcised the world with a forty-foot clipper.

There are also several special grammatical conventions that govern the Internet. One important rule is not TO WRITE EVERYTHING OUT IN CAPITAL LETTERS, to underline everything, *to italicize everything*, or **to put everything in bold**. Seasoned e-mail readers consider these the equivalent of shouting at the top of your lungs—the mark of a "newbie," or someone who has not yet learned to behave properly on the Internet.

Because e-mail lacks a convenient way to convey emotion through text, you will often encounter special symbols in e-mail correspondence. For example, a :) or :(is often put after a sentence to express happiness or sadness. A :0 may be added to express surprise. A :; may be inserted to indicate confusion, and history buffs who think they are Abe Lincoln may include a =|:-)= somewhere in their messages. These symbols add a bit of charm to Internet communication, but it is important to remember that they are only appropriate in informal correspondence. They also should not be overdone. Using too many emotive symbols is considered to be another mark of a newbie.

Rules for Newsgroup and Discussion List Posts

Besides the Netiquette governing general Internet communication, there are also some rules for those who wish to participate in newsgroups and discussion lists.

1. Before you make a post to a group or list, it is wise to follow the group's posts for a while. This will help you to know what has already been asked and what type of questions/statements are considered appropriate. Asking repetitive or uninformed questions can get you off to a bad start.

2. Think before you write. Do not send off emotional or ill-considered responses to posts. (This is called "flaming" in Internet parlance.) Take time to consider criticisms, sarcasms, and insults carefully. Remember the Internet is not an anonymous frontier, and online remarks can be just as hurtful to a person as any others.

3. Do not send private correspondence to groups or lists. If you just want to thank someone, send the message to the person directly. And be very careful in replying to a message. You do not want to accidentally tell several thousand readers about your date last night because you replied to the wrong address.

4. Do not post advertisements to groups or lists. This is considered extremely rude and intrusive, and it is the surest way to become the victim of vicious flaming. Internauts are being careful to avoid the spread of junk mail to the Internet.

Copyright

The question of copyright is an important one for students, teachers, librarians, publishers, and all those on the Internet. Everyone wants to know what the laws are governing copying and sharing information on the Internet, and lawyers and lawmakers are working to develop clear rules that govern electronic mediums. For now, the issues of copyright as they pertain to the Internet are still somewhat hazy, but there are some certainties that can guide your steps.

Most importantly, all online correspondence, files, and documents are handled like other written documents. They are automatically held to be copyrighted in the individual author's name. When an Internet item is copyrighted by some other party, the copyright holder generally identifies him or herself at the end of the document.

Students, teachers, and general users will be glad to know that a judge ruled in 1996 that Internet documents can be copied according to the fair use rules that govern printed sources. You can make personal copies of online documents and images, and you can incorporate them in instructional packages (if you are a student, teacher, or librarian) as long as the package is in no way intended to generate a profit. Other more precise rules governing copyright will undoubtedly be developed in the near future. For now, the safest course seems to be treating Internet sources just like other written documents.

Evaluation of Internet Content

Jessica Lacher-Feldman

It is often said that the WWW places the world on your desktop. From the comfort of your home, your office, a cybercafé, or any computer with Internet access, you can access vast amounts of valuable information. But how do you know as an information consumer what information is accurate, true, or legitimate?

Human history and educational experience give researchers an urge to rely on the accuracy of everything they see in print. The act of publishing lends a sense of legitimacy that is not necessarily justifiable. Simply because something has been published, whether online or in print, does not allow you to conclude that the work is accurate.

Traditionally, academic publishing involved a great deal of editorial control, and the distribution of scholarly works was greatly limited. Electronic publishing has leveled the playing field, making it much easier to produce and distribute works to a broad audience. A wealth of information exists on the WWW, information that can answer questions, further research, spark an interest, and put people in contact with others with similar interests and agendas on the other side of the world. But in terms of publishing to the WWW, we must ask if all Web resources are created equal.

The Web offers convenience, speed, and variety that are unprecedented. Many students and other information consumers view the Web as the first and only stop that needs to be made when doing any kind of research. This is a dangerous assumption. Researchers and others who use the Web who believe that "everything you need is on the Web" are invariably hindering their scholastic potential. That certainly is not to say that there is not a vast amount of very valuable information on the Web. Useful information can be found in the form of self-published articles and Web sites by historians and scholars. Course syllabi from other colleges and universities shed light on a particular subject and provide still more resources both in print and online. Web sites of archival repositories and other cultural institutions identify and describe their collections online, providing users with digital surrogates and context for some of their holdings. The WWW offers an incredible bounty of information, but as with any type of research, the user must exercise good judgment in evaluating its value, authority, verity, and validity.

Information literacy is a set of abilities that allows individuals to "recognize when information is needed" and to "locate, evaluate, and use effectively the needed information."[1] Information literacy is a critical skill in the era of the WWW. With the ease and access of the WWW, anyone with the ability to use an HTML editor and access to a bit of Web space can place any material at all on the Web. This accessibility can create numerous problems for researchers who fail to evaluate the information provided.

The U.S. History Highway presents a broad range of history-related Web sites that have been evaluated and recommended by scholars in their respective fields. This text provides direction for information seekers that has been evaluated by respected scholars. The fallibility of any work concerned with the WWW remains that of the Web itself. In such a volatile environment, a site can disappear overnight, leaving frustrated researchers behind. Unless a Web site has been archived on a hard drive or CD-ROM, if it disappears, it could disappear permanently. Sites are constantly being added and deleted from the WWW. Sites that were once free might begin charging a fee for use, limiting access, or the search tool might change and interfere with previous work.

The speed, breadth, and availability of online resources have changed the way that libraries do business, as well as the way a researcher might approach a project. For many researchers, serendipitous browsing of library stacks has been replaced by surfing the Web. There is room in this world for both approaches, and it is certain that one approach is not better than the other.

Over the years, users have developed a degree of trust in regard to print sources. Editors review books and journals, and publishers are committed to printing and distributing these works. The process of publishing an article in an academic journal or a scholarly monograph through a commercial or university press is long and tedious. Copy editors carefully scrutinize these print materials. A panel of peers reviews and edits them long before the material is presented to the public. Then these print sources are often reviewed in other journals. These peer-reviewed sources are traditionally deemed reliable and accurate.

The WWW has democratized the distribution of information by offering a means to self-publish material without necessarily benefiting from scrutiny and peer review. Web sites are almost never reviewed or refereed, certainly not to the extent that scholarly print materials are. This freedom has opened up new opportunities to those with very specialized interests and a desire to make that information available to the world. At the same time, this information explosion has created a much greater need to learn to evaluate these online materials. The danger of finding faulty information on the WWW increases as additional sites are added. By taking a Web source at face value without first trying to verify the information and the source, users run the risk of perpetrating an untruth, not to mention the possibility of embarrassment. Many Web sites indicate on the index page that they are endorsed by a particular group or evaluating body. While this endorsement does not necessarily hold the same weight as a review in a scholarly journal, depending on the endorsing body, this information offers evidence of the validity and value of a Web site.

With the ability to do research online at any time from any place comes the responsibility to understand and evaluate online materials to make certain that these resources are accurate, unbiased, and of high quality. With practice and a few skills, it isn't difficult to become a good information consumer. You must develop critical thinking skills and an understanding of how to evaluate online sources—that is, you must gain a degree of information literacy. The ability to evaluate online resources when doing research is an extension of the ability to evaluate print sources and primary source materials. Drawing upon analytical skills and common sense, and incorporating some guidance from information professionals and others, the evaluating of online resources becomes a critical step in the research process.

There are several questions that you need to ask when viewing a site for the first time. First, look at the **content**. Are the title and the author of the site easily identified? Is the author credible? Does the author have experience and expertise on the subject? Does the site represent a specific group or organization that is clearly indicated? If a corporate entity or a political or religious body sponsors a site, there might be a hidden agenda, despite the organization's attempt to present clear and unbiased information. Clues to the kind of site are present in the URL. If the Web address ends with a .com, then it is a corporate site. A site with the .edu suffix is from an educational institution, probably a college or university. However, an .edu site such as www.ua.edu/~esmith.html should be considered a personal page that, although hosted by an educational site, may not be officially sanctioned by the college or university and therefore could be biased. Information on a site with the suffix .gov indicates a government Web site. The information on .gov sites and .edu sites is among the most reliable information on the WWW with relation to history and history-related sources.

When looking at the content, you must also seek out the **purpose** of the material. Does the material appear to be scholarly or popular? Who is the intended audience? Is it written for students, scholars, or peers? Also consider the **tone** of the material. Is it written in a comic or satirical fashion? As with print material, the researcher needs to be able to recognize the fundamental differences between a scholarly work and a nonscholarly work. A scholarly work is intended for a narrow audience and is usually serious in both content and the overall appearance of the work. Popular works are written for a broader audience and therefore have a broader appeal—the Web sites will have more graphics and color, and the topics will be broader and of a more popular interest. This is true of both Web and print materials. For example, compare these sites:

http://people.aol.com/people/index.html

and

http://mcel.pacificu.edu/JAHC/jahcindex.htm

The first site is full of images, bright colors, and blinking graphics. The second site is a sober white page with black and blue text. The second site, while it is full of valuable information, is not meant for as broad an audience as the first.

Other types of Web sites should be duly noted. The first is the general interest site or publication. These sites, while they do provide valuable information, are not geared toward the scholar or expert in a given field. Another type of site is the sensational site, which plays upon the gullibility and curiosity of its readers by using inflammatory language and humor.

Compare these two sites:

http://www.scientificamerican.com/

and

http://www.weeklyworldnews.com/index.cfm

While these may be obvious examples of the differences in types of online publications, comparing the style, content, and language serves as a useful exercise in understanding the broad range of publications. While we may never consider using the *Weekly World News* in a research project, information that is just as inaccurate and inflammatory exists in other, more subtle guises.

Even the simple question of the **date** and **edition** of material should be noted. You should also consider the **scope** of the material presented. Does the site intend to be narrow or broad in discussing the subject matter? If the creator omits important events, dates, or aspects of a particular issue, this would indicate a problem with the site. Does the site provide a list of related resources? Does this list appear to be complete or selective? Does the list appear biased in any way?

Also be aware of the **uniqueness** of a site. Is the material presented at this site available in print or elsewhere online? If the information on the site has been published elsewhere, that fact should be noted on the site. If the researcher is seeking out general information on a specific topic, is the Web site the best place to seek out this information?

Images on the Web provide historical evidence and valuable tools for research. Images of handwritten letters, photographs, art, and other materials can be extremely interesting and valuable to the historical researcher. But you should be aware that images can be altered in order to provide evidence to support a controversial belief. Such alterations have been especially common in sites created by hate groups, most notably Holocaust deniers, who proliferate on the WWW. Altered aerial photographs are presented as "evidence" that the Holocaust never happened. Because the WWW is so accessible, both to the end user and to the publisher or creator, it has become an easy way to publish materials that are subversive and perpetrate hate or falsehoods. Some Web sites are blatant in that regard, but others are very cleverly orchestrated to manipulate the user. This can be done with both images and text. Look for evidence of

bias by investigating the creator of the site and their agenda. This information may not be obvious to the user. Be aware that a legitimate nonprofit organization can have an .org Web site, but an .org site is not necessarily an indicator of reliable information.

When controversial information is presented to an audience in a slick and manipulative fashion, the novice researcher could easily be fooled. When using digitized surrogates of primary sources, including images of photographs, letters, or other correspondence, it is critical to take note of the Web address and trace its origin. Verify the source!

For example, the URL

http://rmc.library.cornell.edu/frenchrev/Lafayette/Images/Screen/2_11.JPG

is an image of a handwritten recipe for Martha Washington's lip salve, transcribed by Eleanor Parke Custis, adopted daughter of George and Martha Washington, for Natalie, Mathilde, Clementine, Oscar, and Edmond Lafayette, written December 17, 1824. By looking at the URL in its entirety, we can see that it is from a library at Cornell University, from a grouping related to the French Revolution and to Lafayette. We also know that this is a .jpg image. Without this URL, and just looking at the page, all we see is a digitized handwritten page, with no identifying information from the creator. Using a software program such as Adobe PhotoShop, the creator of a Web site could alter a photograph or a document with relative ease. While there is no great controversy about a recipe for lip salve, remember to look for a hidden agenda and for inconsistencies in an image itself.

Digitized primary sources in the form of online exhibits and collections have increased dramatically in the past few years. Libraries and archives are creating digital surrogates of collections and presenting this material on the WWW. These exhibits and digital collections are excellent opportunities to gain access to materials that, without the advent of the WWW and its graphics capabilities, would be nearly impossible to see. It is important to remember that these collections are made of digitized copies of the originals. Whether they are being accessed as preservation copies or from a location halfway across the world, you should look at the URL to determine where these images are from and how they are being used.

When researching on the WWW, you must always look for the **sources** used in creating a site. All of this information should be clearly stated, either on a bibliography page or on the index page of the site. Are there accurate and clear **citations**? Can you verify these citations? If this information is not readily available, this may indicate a problem. Check the **links** provided. Are the sites listed appropriate and useful? Is the site **current**? Are the links current? While a Web site that was mounted in 1996 may have the best information available online about a particular event, it is the responsibility of the researcher to verify this information and make certain that the site is the best possible source for the purpose.

When it comes to Web sites, **style** is not just a question of aesthetics but can often indicate if the creator of the site is skilled and serious about the information presented. An attractive Web site suggests to the researcher accuracy and authority, but this certainly is not always the case. In this information age, we must learn to be good *information consumers*. You should take note of the navigability, structure, and usability of the site. Is there search capability on the site? If not, how does the lack of a search function interfere with the functionality of the site? How does the writing style correspond to the information in the site and the site's intended audience? All of these factors should be noted when considering a Web site for use in research. All information is not created equal.

It is also essential to remember **copyright** and **fair use**. Copyright laws are complicated and confusing to everyone. Even if copyright information on the Web site is not made clear to the user, the material still falls under copyright law. While access may be free on the WWW, you must still adhere to copyright laws just as you would with print media.

When doing a search for online sources, it is very important to understand the **types of sources** you are looking for. A user doing historical research needs to seek out sites that are best suited for the project at hand, such as material presented by experts in the subject matter or cultural agencies that specialize in that particular area. While the Web site of a regional chamber of commerce might offer current demographics information, that may not be the best material to use when you are writing on the geographic area as it was in the mid-nineteenth century. Before you begin to search the Web, you must define your research and gain an understanding of what kinds of sites will be helpful. The sources need to match your purpose.

Searching the Web is a task that many have grown accustomed to and comfortable with in just the past few years. How do you know if you are doing an **effective search**? Use a good search engine such as google.com or northernlight.com, paying attention to its instructions on how to search effectively. It is useful to try the same search terms with several different search engines and compare your results.

When choosing a search engine, there are some important factors to consider:

- Is the interface clear and easy to use?
- How large is the database? (This should be evident on the main page of the engine.)
- How is the material indexed (by a machine, or by people)?
- How well do the search capabilities (Boolean searching, advanced searching) work?
- Are the results ranked?

You can also take advantage of workshops and instruction in your local academic or public library. Brief courses in online search skills are offered frequently at educational institutions. Don't hesitate to **ask a librarian** for advice and instruction with online searching. A few minutes spent receiving a few good tips can be extremely valuable, ultimately quite time-saving.

If you have a strong interest in a particular topic, it is a good idea to frequently check the Web for information on that topic. Some Web sites offer alerts to new sites in your particular area of interest.

If you keep a few basic principles in mind, developing the skills needed to evaluate online resources is not a difficult task. *The U.S. History Highway* has done some of this work for the researcher by providing online sources that have been scrutinized by scholars in their respective fields. As the WWW grows and changes, the researcher must be prepared to interpret and access the very best that the WWW has to offer without risking the use of inaccurate, subversive, or inappropriate information. By asking the right questions and approaching online research with a critical eye and an open mind, the history researcher can reap the bounty of the WWW.

Note

1. American Library Association, *Presidential Committee on Information Literacy: Final Report* (Chicago: American Library Association, 1989), available at http://www.ala.org/acrl/nili/ilit1st.html.

Part II

Internet Sites for Historians

The history sites on the Internet present an astounding amount of information. No one could ever hope to examine and read everything that is now online. Of course, no one could ever read every book in the Library of Congress either. This is why the Library of Congress is meticulously organized and cataloged. When you need to find a book or fact, you can go to an index or turn to a librarian for assistance. There is no Internet librarian, but the subject-area specialists who have written the following sections offer the same guidance and assistance one gets from a knowledgeable librarian or seasoned teacher. Part II of *The U.S. History Highway* is designed to help you find specific information when you are looking for it and guide you to interesting and useful sites that are worth examining for pleasure or serious study.

As you read this guide, you will notice that the historical sites on the Internet have been created by a wide variety of people, ranging from history professors and students to publishers and history buffs. There is also a broad range of content on the Internet. Some sites are scholarly; others are more informal. Some are composed entirely of links to other sites. The resources described in *The U.S. History Highway* have been screened for quality, utility, and reliability. In an age of information superabundance, however, it is important that everyone become a skilled critic of electronic information. To help you make personal determinations about each site, whenever possible the names and sponsoring institutions or organizations are clearly indicated. The contributors have identified, with a checkmark (✓), the sites that they feel are exemplary. Nevertheless, we urge you not to assume that every argument or resource that you encounter on the following pages is credible or valid. Just as many excellent books contain some errors and misinterpretations and every library contains fallacious books, so some of the sites mentioned here contain a mixture.

33

Part II

Internet Sites
for Historians

Chapter 3

General History

Dennis A. Trinkle and Scott A. Merriman

A Walk Through Time

http://physics.nist.gov/GenInt/Time/time.html

A Walk Through Time is an interesting look at the history of timekeeping. Beginning with an explanation of various ancient calendar systems, the site then discusses early clocks such as sundials and waterclocks, modern time keeping methods, and time zones. The National Institute of Standards and Technology maintains the site.

ArchNet

http://archnet.asu.edu/

ArchNet is sponsored by the University of Connecticut and contains field reports, images, conference information, electronic exhibits, fieldwork opportunities, and more. It covers archaeology throughout the world, and the site is an excellent way to learn about field practices and the scholarship of historical archaeology.

Arctic Circle

http://www.lib.uconn.edu/ArcticCircle/index.html

Arctic Circle presents information on the history and culture of the Arctic regions. The site focuses on the people of the Arctic, but there is also much information on the natural resources and environment of the area. Norman Chance, a cultural and environmental anthropologist at the University of Connecticut, manages the site.

ArtServ: Art and Architecture

http://rubens.anu.edu.au/

ArtServ provides access to 16,000 images relating to the history of art and architecture around the world. The site is maintained by Michael Greenhalgh, Professor of Art History at the Australian National University.

Best Witches

http://www.rci.rutgers.edu/~jup/witches/

Best Witches contains information on witchcraft trials from around the world; some historical diaries, letters, and testimonials; and links to other sites of interest.

Bill Douglas Centre for the History of Cinema and Popular Culture

http://www.ex.ac.uk/bill.douglas/

This archive houses the Bill Douglas and Peter Jewell Collection at the University of Exeter, which contains over 60,000 items, including 25,000 books and thousands of films.

A College Web Index of Significant Historians and Philosophers

http://www.scholiast.org/history/histphil.html

This is a site with many links to significant historians and philosophers, including George Berkeley and Thomas Paine. It is the effort of Peter Ravn Rasmussen, a history doctoral student at the University of Copenhagen.

Eighteenth-Century Resources

http://andromeda.rutgers.edu/~jlynch/18th/

Eighteenth-Century Resources contains a wide variety of material on the eighteenth century, from electronic texts to calls for papers. There is a large collection of digitized primary sources and many links to other sites. These pages are the labor of love of Jack Lynch, an English professor at Rutgers University.

Galaxynet

http://www.galaxy.com/cgi-bin/dirlist?node=53033

Galaxynet is a large, searchable database of links to sites on all subjects. This address takes you to Galaxynet's list of links to history sites.

Great Books of Western Civilization

http://www.mercer.edu/gbk/index.html

This site is arranged around eight "great books" courses offered by Mercer University. Each section has a course description.

History Departments Around the World

http://chnm.gmu.edu/history/depts/

This is an alphabetical listing of links to history department home pages in the United States and foreign countries. It is managed and updated by the Center for History and New Media at George Mason University.

History of Money from Ancient Times to the Present Day

http://www.ex.ac.uk/~RDavies/arian/llyfr.html

This is an interesting collection of essays by Glyn and Roy Davies of the University of Exeter on a range of topics dealing with money and currency. The topics include: "Warfare and Financial History," "The Significance of Celtic Coinage," "The Third World and Debt in the Twentieth Century," and "Origins of Money and Banking."

History/Social Studies Web Site for K-12 Teachers

http://www.execpc.com/~dboals/boals.html

This is a large annotated metasite aimed at K-12 teachers and students. The site is maintained by Dennis Boals.

H-Net Home Page

http://h-net2.msu.edu/

H-Net is a project sponsored by the National Endowment for the Humanities to bring the humanities into the twenty-first century. H-Net's home page contains links to the more than one hundred discussion lists they sponsor, to the Web pages of each of those discussion lists, to their extensive book review project, and to hundreds of other resources for historians.

The Horus' History Links

http://www.ucr.edu/h-gig/

Created and maintained by history faculty members at the University of California, Riverside, Horus History Links is one of the best general gateways to historical Web sites. The Horus project contains links to more than 1,000 sites, and it features excellent interactive graphics and a multimedia format.

HyperHistory Online Project

http://www.hyperhistory.com/

The HyperHistory Project attempts to present world history as a flowing, illustrated timeline. In ten-year increments, major figures and events are presented with clickable biographies and descriptions. The project is still under construction.

Maritime History on the Internet

http://ils.unc.edu/maritime/home.shtml

The Guide to Maritime History Web page provides general information on all aspects of maritime history, including ships, music, art, and nautical archaeology. Peter McCracken of the University of North Carolina, Chapel Hill's School of Information and Library Science maintains the pages.

Professional Cartoonists Index

http://www.cagle.com/teacher

This site offers the largest collection of newspaper editorial cartoons on the Web. Current cartoons from seventy-one newspaper editorial cartoonists are presented with the permission and participation of the creators, who include the top names in the field, such as Pulitzer Prize winners Michael Ramirez, Jeff MacNelly, Jim Borgman, Mike Luckovich, Steve Breen, Dick Locher, Jim Morin, and Mike Peters. Along with the cartoons is a rich network of resources for students and teachers, including lesson plans for using the editorial cartoons as a teaching tool in the social sciences, art, journalism, and English at all levels. The goal is to help teachers and students use cartoons for interactive learning.

Tennessee Technological University History Resources

http://www2.tntech.edu/history/

Created by the Department of History at Tennessee Technological University, this is a good general starting point for resources on the Internet, including Gopher resources and essays on why one should study history and what careers are available for historians.

University of Kansas History Resources

http://www.ukans.edu/history/VL/

This site, sponsored by the University of Kansas, is one of the oldest and largest collections of links to sites on all topics of history. It is an excellent starting point for research.

World Rulers

http://rulers.org/

World Rulers lists the past and present leaders of every state in the world. Birth and death dates are provided, as well as pictures for some. Monthly updates are posted.

Chapter 4

General United States History

Ken Kempcke

Metasites

Academic Info: United States History

http://www.academicinfo.net/histus.html

A subject directory of Internet resources tailored to a college or advanced high school audience.

American and British History Resources on the Internet

http://www.libraries.rutgers.edu/rul/rr_gateway/research_guides/history/history.shtml

Produced at Rutgers University, this site provides a structured index of scholarly resources available online. Its contents include Reference Resources, History Gateways and Text Sites, Titles by Historic Period, and Archival and Manuscript Guides.

The Digital Librarian: History ✓

http://www.digital-librarian.com/history.html

Maintained by Margaret Vail Anderson, a librarian in Cortland, New York, this page provides links to hundreds of fascinating Web resources on American history.

Index of Resources for United States History

http://www.ukans.edu/history/VL/USA/index.html

This Web page from the University of Kansas offers links to over 1,200 sites of interest to students of United States history.

Internet Public Library: United States Resources ✓

http://www.ipl.org/ref/RR/static/hum30.55.85.html

Site hosted by the University of Michigan School of Information.

Links for the History Profession

http://www.oah.org/announce/links.html

This site, maintained by the Organization of American Historians, furnishes a wide variety of links to professional societies, associations, centers, and resources.

The TimePage: American History Sites

http://www.seanet.com/Users/pamur/ahistory.html#us

A general directory with links to hundreds of U.S. history sites.

United States History ✓

http://www.tntech.edu/www/acad/hist/usa.html

A list of links to history sites arranged chronologically and by subject from the History Department at Tennessee Technological University.

Voice of the Shuttle: American History Page

http://vos.ucsb.edu/shuttle/history.html#us

Constructed by Alan Liu at the University of California, Santa Barbara, this site provides links to U.S. history resources, academic departments, conferences, journals, discussion lists, and newsgroups.

Yahoo: U.S. History

http://dir.yahoo.com/Arts/Humanities/History/U_S__History

The well-known Web directory's list of American history sites categorized by region, subject, and time period.

Regular Sites

About.com: American History

http://americanhistory.about.com/homework/americanhistory/

A guide for American history, with feature articles, Web site links, and discussion forums. Topics covered include the Civil War, colonial America, government, immigration, biographies, and more.

An Abridged History of the United States ✓

http://www.us-history.info/home.html

An online textbook produced by William M. Brinton. The text includes photographs and hypertext links to various court cases and other historical documents.

AMDOCS: Documents for the Study of American History ✓

http://history.cc.ukans.edu/carrie/docs/amdocs_index.html

Part of the Electronic Library at the University of Kansas, this site provides access to hundreds of important documents vital to the study of American history. The materials date from the fifteenth century to the present.

American History Online ✓

http://longman.awl.com/history/default.htm

From Longman Publishing Company, this bank of resources includes interactive practice tests, downloadable maps, primary sources, Web activities, and reference links.

American Memory ✓

http://lcweb2.loc.gov/ammem

American Memory is the online resource compiled by the Library of Congress's National Digital Library Program. With the participation of other libraries and archives, the program provides a gateway to rich primary source materials relating to the history and cultural developments of the United States. The site provides multimedia collections of digitized documents, photographs, maps, recorded sound, and moving pictures.

The American Presidency

http://www.grolier.com/presidents/preshome.html

A history of presidents, the presidency, politics, and related subjects. Provides the full text of articles from the *Academic American Encyclopedia* and includes an online exhibit hall, historical election results, presidential links, and a trivia quiz.

American Studies Electronic Crossroads

http://www.georgetown.edu/crossroads

Maintained at Georgetown University, ASEC contains pedagogical, scholarly, and institutional information for the international American Studies community. Includes a collection of resources and tools for use by teachers, administrators, and students as well as indexes to online courses and projects.

A Chronology of U.S. Historical Documents

http://www.law.ou.edu/ushist.html

Provides hundreds of important documents related to American history from pre-Colonial times to the present. From the University of Oklahoma Law Center.

Douglass: Archives of American Public Address ✓

http://douglass.speech.nwu.edu

Douglass is an electronic archive of American oratory and related documents. It is intended to serve general scholarship and courses in American rhetorical history at Northwestern University.

Historic Audio Archives

http://www.webcorp.com/sounds/index.htm

Audio files containing the voices of famous Americans.

Historical Text Archive

http://historicaltextarchive.com/links.php?op=viewlink&cid=6

The Historical Text Archive provides links to Native American history, U.S. historical documents, the Colonial period, the Revolution, the early republic, the nineteenth and twentieth centuries, U.S. wars, and more.

History Buff's Home Page

http://www.discovery.com/guides/history/historybuff/historybuff.html

Produced by the Newspaper Collectors Society of America, this site is devoted to press coverage of events in American history. It includes an extensive, searchable library with the categories Civil War, Baseball, Engravings, Journalism Hoaxes, Old West including Billy the Kid, Jesse James, Crime Figures such as Bonnie and Clyde and Lizzie Borden, and over a dozen other categories. The Presidential Library includes the inaugural addresses of all U.S. presidents. There is also a primer and price guide for historic newspapers.

History Matters: The U.S. [History] Survey Course on the Web ✓

http://historymatters.gmu.edu

Designed for high school and college teachers of U.S. History survey courses, this site serves as a gateway to Web resources and offers unique teaching materials, first-person primary documents, and threaded discussions on teaching U.S. history. From the American Social History Project/Center for History and the New Media.

The History Net

http://www.thehistorynet.com

Provides access to discussion forums and hundreds of full-text articles on American history from selected journals. Also includes a picture gallery and a list of events and exhibits taking place around the United States. Produced by the National Historical Society.

History's Best on PBS

http://www.pbs.org/history/american.html

Links to American history programs that have appeared on public television.

A Hypertext on American History: From the Colonial Period until Modern Times

http://odur.let.rug.nl/~usa

The main body of this hypertext comes from a number of United States Information Agency publications: *An Outline of American History*, *An Outline of the American Economy*, *An Outline of American Government*, and *An Outline of*

American Literature. The text is enriched with hypertext links to relevant documents, original essays, other Internet sites, and to other *Outlines*.

Making of America

http://www.umdl.umich.edu/moa

Making of America (MOA) is a digital library of primary sources in American social history from the antebellum period through Reconstruction. The collection is particularly strong in the subject areas of education, psychology, American history, sociology, religion, and science and technology. The collection contains approximately 1,600 books and 50,000 journal articles with nineteenth-century imprints.

The National Archives and Records Administration

http://www.nara.gov

The NARA site furnishes electronic access to historical records of government agencies, as well as an online exhibit hall, digital classroom, and genealogy page. The site also includes multimedia exhibits, research tools, and NARA publications.

The National Portrait Gallery

http://www.npg.si.edu

A searchable site that contains photographs, portraits, and biographical information on thousands of prominent Americans.

An Outline of American History

http://usinfo.state.gov/products/pubs/history/toc.htm

A book-style outline produced by the U.S. Information Agency.

Presidents of the United States

http://www.ipl.org/ref/POTUS

This resource contains background information, election results, cabinet members, notable events, and some points of interest on each of the presidents. Links to biographies, historical documents, audio and video files, and other presidential sites are also included to enrich this site. From the Internet Public Library at the University of Michigan.

The Smithsonian Institution ✓

http://www.si.edu

The Smithsonian Institution's Web page provides access to a fascinating array of historical resources in many subject areas. Its offerings include Smithsonian collections, exhibits, photographs, and publications, as well as links to sites hosted by the institution's museums and organizations. The Smithsonian's Online Research Information System allows browsers to search the institution's various online catalogs.

Talking History

http://www.talkinghistory.org/

This site provides audio files of the weekly radio program *Talking History*, a coproduction of the History Department of the State University of New York at Albany, the History Department of Creighton University (Omaha, Nebraska), and WRPI-FM, Troy, New York.

United States Historical Census Browser ✓

http://fisher.lib.Virginia.EDU/census

The data presented here describe the people and the economy of the United States for each state and county from 1790 to 1970.

United States History

http://www.usahistory.com

Information on presidents, history trivia, statistics, wars, states, the Constitution, and more.

U.S. Diplomatic History Resources Index

http://faculty.tamu-commerce.edu/sarantakes/stuff.html

Created by Nicholas Evan Sarantakes, a professor at Texas A&M University, Commerce, this Web page is an index of resources available to historians of U.S. foreign policy. Geared toward scholars in history, political science, economics, area studies, international relations, and journalism, it provides an extensive list of historical archives and papers indexed alphabetically and by subject.

Chapter 5

African-American History

Mary Anne Hansen

Metasites

Academic Info: African-American History: An Annotated Resource of Internet Resources on Black History

http://academicinfo.net/africanam.html

This resource links to numerous categories of quality sites on African-American history for researchers, university students, and teachers; categories include Digital Library, Important Men and Women, Civil Rights, Teaching Materials, and more. This is a valuable site for locating primary materials. The directory is created and kept updated by Academic Info, a private organization compiling subject indexes for respected Web sites on a wide range of topics.

African-American Civil War Memorial

http://afroamcivilwar.org/

The African-American Civil War Memorial site links to a variety of informative resources, including the database of soldiers and sailors created by the United States National Park Service and the Civil War Soldiers and Sailors.

African-American Literature

http://curry.edschool.virginia.edu/go/multicultural/sites/aframdocs.html

Created as part of the Multicultural Paths Project at the University of Virginia, this resource links to numerous classic African-American documents, some of which are historical in nature, and some literary.

African-American West

http://www.wsu.edu:8080/~amerstu/mw/af_ap.html#afam

Created and maintained by the American Studies Program at Washington State University, this metasite links to a variety of resources dealing with blacks in the history of the American West.

American Identities: African-American

http://xroads.virginia.edu/~YP/ethnic.html

One of several valuable African-American history sites created and maintained by the University of Virginia's American Studies Program, with links to numerous other sites, some of which are historical.

A-Z of African Studies on the Internet

http://docker.library.uwa.edu.au/~plimb/az.html

This resource lists a vast array of links to African and African-American sites. Dr. Peter Limb of the University of Western Australia, who has a Ph.D. in African Studies, created and maintains it.

Historical Text Archive: African-American History

http://historicaltextarchive.com/

This metasite, created by Don Mabry, a professor at Mississippi State University, provides links to sites in several categories: Africa, African-American, genealogy, and teaching materials, to name a few. Although Mississippi State University hosts this site, the institution takes no responsibility for it.

Social Studies School Services: Black History

http://www.socialstudies.com

This commercial site offers a variety of helpful resources, such as lesson plans, student exercises, RealVideo clips of products for sale, and product catalogs. It also offers reviews of other sites and links. A helpful site for historical information, as well as for purchasing teaching materials.

General Sites

Aboard the Underground Railroad

http://www.cr.nps.gov/nr/travel/underground/

This site introduces travelers, researchers, historians, and preservationists, to the people and places associated with the Underground Railroad. Descriptions and photographs of fifty historic places listed in the National Park Service's National Register of Historic Places are included, along with a map of the most common directions of escape taken on the Underground Railroad and maps of individual states marking the location of the historic properties.

African-American Census Schedules Online

http://www.prairiebluff.com/

A private project, this site is a compilation of the special slave and free black manuscript census data compiled by the U.S. government before the Civil War. Twenty-eight states are represented, with the rest to be added in the future. A valuable resource for genealogical research.

African-American Heritage: Our Shared History

http://www.cr.nps.gov/aahistory/

This National Park Service resource lists an extensive array of sites for learning about individual African-Americans and significant places in African-American History. Photographic archives are included.

African-American Heritage Preservation Foundation, Inc.

http://www.preservenet.cornell.edu/aahpf/homepage.htm

Created by the AAHPF, a nonprofit foundation dedicated to the preservation of African-American history, this site provides information, photographs, and archaeological reports on preservation projects with which the organization is involved.

African-American Mosaic: A Library of Congress Resource Guide for the Study of Black History and Culture

http://lcweb.loc.gov/exhibits/african/intro.html

This Library of Congress Resource Guide was created to bring the study of black history and culture to the Web community. The site includes comprehensive text and images from nearly 500 years of the black experience in the Western Hemisphere. Coverage of a variety of topics is included: Liberia, abolitionists, western migration, and documents from the Works Progress Administration, the Federal Writers Project, and the Daniel Murray Pamphlet collection, to name a few.

African-American Resources at the University of Virginia

http://etext.lib.virginia.edu/rbs/rbs16–95.html

Assembled by the Rare Books Division of the University of Virginia, this site provides the transcribed text of documents and images relating to slavery.

African-American Web Connection

http://www.aawc.com

A private hobbyist's project, this site is a gateway to Afrocentric resources for the African-American Web community and others seeking to learn about the black Web experience.

Africans in America: America's Journey through Slavery

http://www.pbs.org/wgbh/aia/home.html

A PBS production, this resource is presented in four parts, or eras: The Terrible Transformation, Revolution, Brotherly Love, and Judgment Day. Each section offers a Narrative, a Resource Bank of images, documents, stories, biographies, and commentaries, and a Teacher's Guide for using the content of the Web site and television series in U.S. history courses. This resource is problematic with regard to authority; although it was compiled in collaboration with a panel of scholars, there is scant indication of the authorship of the various writings so users may have difficulty placing the various materials in historical context.

Afro-American Sources in Virginia: A Guide to Manuscripts

http://rock.village.virginia.edu/plunkett/

Part of the Carter G. Woodson Institute Series in Black Studies, this site was jointly produced by Michael Plunkett, the University Press of Virginia, and the

University of Virginia's Electronic Text Center. It allows users to search the collections of twenty-four institutions of higher education, museums, and institutes.

American Slave Narratives: An On-Line Anthology

http://xroads.virginia.edu/~hyper/wpa/wpahome.html

From 1936 to 1938, over 2,300 former slaves from across the American South were interviewed under the aegis of the Works Progress Administration. Another creation of the University of Virginia, this site provides a sample of these narratives, as well as some of the photographs taken at the time of the interviews.

Archives of African-American Music and Culture

http://www.indiana.edu/~aaamc/index.html

The AAAMC is a repository of materials covering various musical idioms and cultural expressions from the post-World War II era. A project of the Department of Afro-American Studies at Indiana University, this site gives the details of the vast collections of the AAAMC. An extensive list of links provides a jumping-off point on a variety of topics: the African diaspora, black culture and history, various musical genres, etc. An online reference service is also offered to researchers utilizing this site. A holdings search feature is slated to be added.

The Atlantic Monthly: Black History, American History

http://www.theatlantic.com/unbound/flashbks/black/blahisin.htm

The Atlantic Monthly Web site offers online access to some of the seminal essays by black writers who published in this magazine, including "Reconstruction" by Frederick Douglass and "The Strivings of the Negro People" by W.E.B. Du Bois.

Avery Research Center for African-American History and Culture

http://www.cofc.edu/~averyrsc/

The mission of the Avery Research Center for African-American History and Culture is to collect, preserve, and document the history and culture of African-Americans in Charleston and the South Carolina Low Country. Its site lists its collections, programs, and a calendar of events.

Birmingham Civil Rights Institute

http://bcri.bham.al.us/

This institute is a cultural and educational research center that promotes a comprehensive understanding of civil rights developments in Birmingham, Alabama. The site includes exhibit information, guides to the institute archives, and information about education and public programs.

Black Pioneers of the Pacific Northwest

http://www.teleport.com/~eotic/histhome.html

Part of the Oregon Trail History Library, this site provides historical information about blacks in the Pacific Northwest, including a timeline, biographies and photographs, discussion of the state's exclusion laws, slavery, and a bibliography of recommended reading.

Charlotte Hawkins Brown Memorial

http://www.ah.dcr.state.nc.us/sections/hs/chb/chb.htm

Created by the North Carolina Division of Archives and History, this extensive site provides a history of this founder of the Palmer Memorial Institute, including online texts of documents by and about her. Comprehensive bibliographies provide references to manuscript collections, theses, and primary material about the institute, as well as the history of blacks in the South in general.

The Charlotte-Mecklenburg Story

http://www.cmstory.org/

This site is a project of the Public Library of Charlotte and Mecklenburg County, North Carolina. Numerous photographs and historical information about African-American history are available for perusal.

Civil Rights Oral Histories from Mississippi

http://www-dept.usm.edu/~mcrohb/

This site makes available online the oral histories collected by staff at the University of Southern Mississippi's Center for Oral History and Cultural Heritage and at the Tougaloo College Archives. The online texts of interviews are searchable in a variety of ways, and a bibliography is provided. The Mississippi State Legislature, the Mississippi Department of Archives and History, and the Mississippi Humanities Council funded the project.

A Deeper Shade of Black

http://www.seditionists.org/black/shade.html

A Deeper Shade of Black is one of the premier resources on African-American history, film, and literature. Created and maintained by Charles Isbell of MIT, it is an excellent resource for biographies, with well-developed accounts of figures such as Thurgood Marshall and Paul Robeson. Isbell is also the author of a related site: This Week in Black History (http://www.seditionists.org/black/thisweek.html).

Desegregation of the Armed Forces: Project Whistlestop: Harry S. Truman Digital Archives

http://www.whistlestop.org/study_collections/desegregation/large/desegregation.htm

The Truman Presidential Library has digitized Truman's Executive Order 9981 calling for desegregation, as well as other documents from the study leading up to this decision. A chronology of the Truman administration and the desegregation of the armed forces is included, along with teaching materials.

Digital Classroom of The National Archives and Records Administration (NARA)

http://www.nara.gov/education/teaching/teaching.html

This site contains reproducible copies of primary documents from the holdings of the National Archives of the United States, teaching activities correlated to the National History Standards and National Standards for Civics and Government, and cross-curricular connections. Topics available include the *Amistad* Case, Black Soldiers in the Civil War, and Jackie Robinson. Researchers can locate other historical materials about African-Americans by searching the National Archives Digital Library.

Documenting the American South

http://docsouth.unc.edu/

DAS is an electronic collection sponsored by the Academic Affairs Library at the University of North Carolina at Chapel Hill, providing access to digitized primary materials offering southern perspectives on American history and culture. Intended for researchers, teachers, and students at every educational level, the site provides a wide array of titles. DAS offers five digitization projects, including slave narratives, first-person narratives, southern literature, Confederate imprints, and materials related to the church in the black community. Books, pamphlets, and broadsides written by fugitive and former slaves prior to 1920 are being collected and posted online. It is a project funded by the National Endowment for the Humanities.

W.E.B. Du Bois Virtual University

http://members.tripod.com/~DuBois/

Created and maintained by an African-American/African Studies historian, Jennifer Wager, this extensive site details aspects of Du Bois studies: his life, legacy, and works. It provides links to online texts by and about Du Bois, a bibliography of articles and dissertations in print by and about Du Bois, and a list of Du Bois scholars.

Electronic Text Center: African-American Resources

http://etext.lib.virginia.edu/speccol.html

This site provides online access to a vast collection of original documents about nineteenth-century African-American issues, as well as numerous historical letters from the Special Collections at the University of Virginia Library. A valuable resource for primary research materials.

Exploring *Amistad* at Mystic Seaport: Race and the Boundaries of Freedom in Antebellum Maritime America

http://amistad.mysticseaport.org/main/welcome.html

This Mystic Seaport Museum site explores the *Amistad* Revolt of 1839–1842. Included are a brief narrative, a timeline, and links to other sites. Online historical documents available at the site relate to the capture of the ship and its occupants. A teacher's guide presents numerous activities to be used in the classroom; the site is a powerful teaching resource.

Faces of Science: African-Americans in the Sciences

http://www.princeton.edu/~mcbrown/display/faces.html

This site profiles African-American men and women who have contributed to the advancement of science and engineering; included is a discussion of the present and future of African-Americans in the sciences. The biographies are grouped by scientific discipline and accompanied by an examination of the percentages of doctorates granted to African-Americans in each area of the sciences. Statistical and demographic data from the National Science Foundation are included in easy-to-read graphical format. Researchers will also find links to other related sites.

John Hope Franklin Collection of African and African-American Documentation

http://scriptorium.lib.duke.edu/franklin/collections.html

This site provides online finding aids, subject guides, and digitized materials from selected collections of the Rare Book, Manuscript, and Special Collections Library at Duke University.

Freedmen and Southern Society Project

http://www.inform.umd.edu/ARHU/Depts/History/Freedman/home.html

The editors of this project have selected over 50,000 documents from the National Archives of the United States that they are presently transcribing, organizing, annotating, and presenting online to explain the transition of blacks from slavery to freedom between the beginning of the Civil War in 1861 and the beginning of Radical Reconstruction in 1867. The project is supported by the University of Maryland and by grants from the National Historical Publications and Records Commission and the National Endowment for the Humanities.

Harlem 1900–1940: An African American Community

http://www.si.umich.edu/CHICO/Harlem

Created at the School of Information at the University of Michigan as part of its Cultural Heritage Initiatives for Community Outreach, this site is based on *Harlem: 1900–1940* originally published in 1991 by the Schomburg Center for Research in Black Culture at the New York Public Library. It includes digitized texts and photographs, along with suggestions for teachers using the materials and links to related sites.

Inventory of African-American Historical and Cultural Resources in Maryland

http://www.sailor.lib.md.us/docs/af_am/af_am.html

This site lists by count the structures, historical sites, and collections of materials in Maryland that relate to African-American history. The Maryland Commission on African-American History and Culture supports the project.

The King Center

http://www.thekingcenter.com

The official MLK historical site, this resource provides information both on Martin Luther King, Jr. and on Coretta Scott King, who established the center in 1968 as a living memorial dedicated to the preservation and advancement of the work of her late husband.

Martin Luther King, Jr.

http://www.seattletimes.com/mlk/index.html

Produced by the *Seattle Times*, this site includes editorials, interviews, news columns, and photographs from the newspaper. King is presented in historical context; included are photographs from the civil rights movement. The Study Guide is intended to prompt further discussion about King's life and legacy, in particular how society has or has not changed because of civil rights.

Martin Luther King, Jr. Papers Project of Stanford University

http://www.stanford.edu/group/King/

This project is an effort to assemble and disseminate historical information concerning Martin Luther King, Jr. and the social movements in which he participated. Begun by the King Center for Nonviolent Social Change, the King Papers Project is one of only a few major research ventures that focuses on an individual African-American. Coretta Scott King, founder and president of the King Center, invited Stanford University historian Clayborne Carson to become the project's director and senior editor in 1985. As a result, the project became a cooperative venture of Stanford University, the King Center, and the King estate.

Library Catalogs of African-American Collections

http://www.library.cornell.edu/africana/Library/Catalogs.html

Cornell University Library provides this selected list of libraries that have separate Black Studies collections. In addition to the separate collections, these institutions also maintain integrated general collections that include Black Studies materials.

Montgomery Bus Boycott Home Page

http://socsci.colorado.edu/~jonesem/montgomery.html

Created by a graduate student at the University of Colorado at Boulder, this site provides a chronology and summary of the Montgomery bus boycott, a plan for teaching about the boycott, and numerous essays and links to related sites.

Museum of African Slavery

http://jhunix.hcf.jhu.edu/~plarson/smuseum/welcome.htm

The Museum of African Slavery was created primarily by Pier M. Larson, a professor of African history at The Johns Hopkins University, for primary and secondary students and their teachers. The museum's focus is on the experiences of enslavement in the Atlantic system, Africa and the Americas.

Museum of Afro-American History, Boston

http://www.afroammuseum.org/

This site provides links to historical resources in the Boston area and beyond, including links to numerous other African-American museums, exhibits, and organizations.

National Civil Rights Museum

http://sevier.net/civilrights/

This site's purpose is to support the National Civil Rights Museum's mission to educate and preserve the history of the civil rights movement. Located at the Lorraine Motel, where Dr. Martin Luther King, Jr. was assassinated, the museum houses interactive exhibits that trace the beginnings of the civil rights struggle.

Negro League Baseball Archive

http://www.negroleaguebaseball.com/

This commercial site includes a multitude of information on the history of the Negro Leagues, including team histories and player profiles.

Resources in Black Studies

http://www.library.ucsb.edu/subj/black.html

Created and maintained by the University of California Santa Barbara Library, this site provides links to numerous historical texts and documents, other research institutions focusing on Black Studies, discussion forums, and more.

Schomberg Collection of New York Public Library

http://digital.nypl.org/browse.htm

The New York Public Library's Schomberg Collection is a major research institution for the study of the history and culture of peoples of African descent. This site provides links to digitized collections of photographs and other materials and finding aids to the various collections.

This Is Our War

http://www.afroam.org/history/OurWar/intro.html

Part of the Afro-Americ@ site, this page presents articles written by black war correspondents during World War II for the *Baltimore Afro-American*. Other significant historical resources can also be found at the Afro-Americ@ site (http://www.afroam.org/).

Voices of the Civil Rights Era

http://www.webcorp.com/civilrights/index.htm

Voices of the Civil Rights Era is an audio archive sponsored by Webcorp. It includes speeches made by a variety of historical figures: Malcolm X, Martin Luther King, Jr., and John F. Kennedy.

John H. White: Portrait of Black Chicago

http://www.nara.gov/exhall/americanimage/chicago/white1.html

This National Archives and Records Administration exhibit chronicles photographer John H. White's work photographing Chicago, especially the city's African-American community. White took the photographs for the Environmental Protection Agency's DOCUMERICA project in 1973 and 1974.

Women and Social Movements in the United States

http://womhist.binghamton.edu/index.html

This University of New York, Binghamton, site contains about twenty sets of historical documents dealing with African-American women. Compiled for secondary and higher education studies, this site contains materials by and about black women seldom found elsewhere. The National Endowment for the Humanities funded this project.

Writing Black

http://www.keele.ac.uk/depts/as/Literature/amlit.black.html

Created and maintained at the School of American Studies, Keele University, U.K., Writing Black links to essays, books, and poems about African-American history and culture in the United States up to the present day. Prominent writers include W.E.B. Du Bois, Booker T. Washington, Toni Morrison, and Maya Angelou, to name a few.

Chapter 6

Native American History

J. Kelly Robison

General Sites

American Indian Studies

http://www.csulb.edu/projects/ais/

Created by Troy Johnson at California State University, Long Beach. Johnson maintains a useful list of links to Native American sites. Also contains a large number of images of Native Americans from precontact to the present.

Bureau of Indian Affairs, U.S. Department of the Interior

http://www.doi.gov/bureau-indian-affairs.html

The Bureau of Indian Affairs has information on the tribes, tribal governments, some history, treaties, and documents on current affairs in Native America. The documents make this site important for researchers and teachers delving into the current situation among Native Americans.

First Nations Site

http://www.dickshovel.com/www.html

A very political site maintained by Jordan S. Dill. However, the list of offsite links makes this site a good resource. The onsite links are more generally rants against the system than anything of value.

Images of Native America: From Columbus to Carlisle

http://www.lehigh.edu/~ejg1/natmain.html

Professor Edward J. Gallagher's students at Lehigh University created a series of online essays on how Europeans and Euro-Americans imagined native peoples. The essays are nicely written and contain links to related sites.

MAPS: GIS Windows on Native Lands, Current Places, and History

http://indy4.fdl.cc.mn.us/~isk/maps/mapmenu.html

Paula Giese's site that uses client-side image maps as the gateway to articles on Native American history and culture from precontact to the present. A nice resource for K-12.

Native American Documents Project

http://www.csusm.edu/projects/nadp/nadp.htm

Located at California State University at San Marcos, this site contains primary material related to Allotment, Indian Commissioner Reports of 1871, and the Rogue River War and Siletz Reservation.

Native American Sites

http://www.nativeculture.com/lisamitten/indians.html

A very nice list of sites pertaining to Native America. The topically categorized list contains links to Indian nation Web sites, organizations, and upcoming events. Maintained by Lisa Mitten at the University of Pittsburgh.

NativeWeb

http://www.nativeweb.org/

An extensive collection of links and articles—not just historical, but also political, legal, and social—both for and about indigenous peoples in the Americas. Includes search engines, message boards, and lists of Native events. An excellent site from which to begin research.

On This Date in North American Indian History

http://americanindian.net/

Phil Konstantine's Native American history and culture Web site seems, at first glance, an amateurish attempt by a history buff to have something on the Web. However, despite the somewhat cheesy "Moons," On This Date pages, and other such things, Konstantine has an incredible links page with over 8,000 links. Even On This Date is well worth clicking through.

Perspectives of the Smithsonian: Native American Resources

http://www.si.edu/resource/faq/nmai/start.htm

An excellent starting place for information on Native American history and culture. Includes online Smithsonian exhibits, resources for teachers, parents and students, and an extensive list of readings for various topics. No links, but this site in itself is worth looking into.

Topical Sites

The Avalon Project: Relations Between the United States and Native Americans

http://www.yale.edu/lawweb/avalon/natamer.htm

A superb collection of primary documents relating to Native peoples compiled and digitized by the Yale Law School Avalon Project. The main focus of this site is treaties between the United States government and Native groups. The site also includes statutes, presidential addresses, and a few court cases involving Natives.

The Aztec Calendar

http://www.azteccalendar.com

Done by Rene Voorburg, this nicely done site examines the Aztec calendar. The opening screen depicts the current date in Aztec glyphs. Also contains a calculator that converts any date to its Aztec equivalent. The introduction is a brief but thorough essay on the calendar and its meaning.

Cahokia Mounds State Historic Site

http://medicine.wustl.edu/~mckinney/cahokia/cahokia.html

Run by the Illinois Historic Preservation Agency, Cahokia is the location of a pre-European city across the river from St. Louis, Missouri. The site lists upcoming events at the park and some information on the archaeology and history of Cahokia. This site seems to be a continual work in progress since it has very few new items posted within the past two years.

Native American Authors

http://www.ipl.org/ref/native/

Part of the Internet Public Library, this section of the larger site can be browsed by author, title, or tribal affiliation. There is no search engine or subject browsing, however. Individual title "cards" contain only basic bibliographic information.

Sipapu: The Anasazi Emergence into the Cyber World

http://sipapu.ucsb.edu/

This site not only begs the reader to explore Anasazi architecture and archeology, but also asks for contributions. The research section contains a database of Chaco outliers and a bibliography of related print works. It also links to several scholarly papers on the Anasazi. One interesting item is a wonderful little toy that allows 360-degree viewing of the Great Kiva of Chetro Ketl at Chaco Canyon National Monument. Created by John Kanter at the University of California at Santa Barbara.

Chapter 7

Colonial American History

**Edward Ragan, Scott A. Merriman,
and Dennis A. Trinkle**

Metasites

From Revolution to Reconstruction ✓

http://odur.let.rug.nl/~usa/usa.htm

This metasite, maintained by the Arts Faculty of the University of Groningen, Netherlands, is a massive resource for all aspects of American history. The site is divided into five general sections: outlines, essays, documents, biographies, and presidents. This site is organized around several United States Information Agency publications: *An Outline of American History*, *An Outline of the American Economy*, *An Outline of American Government*, and *An Outline of American Literature*. While the text of these *Outlines* has not been changed, they have been enriched with hypertext links to relevant documents, original essays, and other Internet sites. Currently this site contains over 3,000 relevant HTML documents.

Museums, Libraries, Historical Societies, and Online Organizations

Colonial Williamsburg

http://www.history.org/

The official Web site for Colonial Williamsburg, one of the most extensive historical reconstructions in the United States. The well-illustrated site offers tourist information; educational resources; a Colonial dateline; a historical glossary of names, places, and events in Colonial Williamsburg; photos of buildings and people; articles from the *Colonial Williamsburg Journal*, and an extensive section on Colonial lifestyles.

Common-place ✓

http://www.common-place.org/

Common-place is sponsored by the American Antiquarian Society and the Gilder Lehrman Institute of American History. It bills itself as a "common place for exploring and exchanging ideas about early American history and culture" in a way that is "a bit friendlier than a scholarly journal, a bit more scholarly than a popular magazine." Published quarterly, this online journal includes essays, books reviews, roundtable discussions, and an open forum for commenting on articles that appear in *Common-place*.

H-OIEACH Discussion Network

http://www.h-net.msu.edu/~ieahcweb/

This is the Web site of the H-OIEACH discussion list, which is sponsored by the Omohundro Institute of Early American History and Culture (OIEACH). Affiliated with H-Net, this group focuses on Colonial and Early American history. Its Web pages contain information about the discussion list and allow one to subscribe. They also include calls for papers, conference announcements, bibliographies, book reviews, articles, and links to related sites, including the Omohundro Institute.

Jamestown Rediscovery Project

http://www.apva.org/jr.html

The Jamestown Rediscovery Project, sponsored by the Association for the Preservation of Virginia Antiquities (APVA), is a ten-year comprehensive excavation of Jamestown that began in 1994. This site offers photographs and progress reports on the project to date, two online exhibits, and plans for the future.

The Library of Virginia Digital Library Program ✓

http://www.lva.lib.va.us/dlp/index.htm

The Library of Virginia's Digital Library Program is an internationally recognized effort to preserve, digitize, and provide access to significant archival and library collections. Users can search court records (indexes and guides); births, deaths, marriages, wills, and Bible records; genealogy and biography databases; Virginia military records; newspaper and periodical databases and indexes; photograph collections; business records; and maps, gazetteers, and geographical resources. Perhaps the most stunning accomplishment is the Land Office Patents and Grants Database, which is searchable by keyword and provides links to scanned copies of the original Virginia land patents. To date, the Digital Library Program has "digitized more than 2.2 million original documents, photographs, and maps, and produced more than 80 fully-searchable databases, indexes, and electronic finding aids." All in all, this is a remarkable tool for Virginia historians and genealogists.

Plimoth-on-Web: Plimoth Plantation's Web Site

http://www.plimoth.org/Museum/Pilgrim_Village/1627.htm

The official Web site for the living history museum of seventeenth-century Plymouth. Like the living history museum, the Web site brings 1627 Plimoth back to life.

Society of Early Americanists (SEA) Home Page

http://www.hnet.uci.edu/mclark/seapage.htm

The SEA aims to further the exchange of ideas and information among scholars of various disciplines who study the literature and culture of America up to approximately 1800. The society publishes a newsletter, operates an electronic bulletin board, and maintains the Web site, which contains an excellent list of links on Colonial and Early American history.

Topical Histories

1492: An Ongoing Voyage

http://metalab.unc.edu/expo/1492.exhibit/Intro.html

1492: An Ongoing Voyage is an electronic exhibit of the Library of Congress.

The site weaves images and text to explore what life was like in pre- and post-Columbian Europe, Africa, and the Americas. The site examines the effect that the discovery of America had on each continent and stresses the dark elements of colonization. There are excellent maps, documents, artwork, and supporting text.

Iroquois Oral Traditions

http://www.indians.org/welker/iroqoral.htm

This Web site is part of the American Indian Heritage Foundation's Indigenous Peoples Literature page. The tradition of De-Ka-Nah-Wi-Da and Hiawatha is recounted here along with over twenty other Iroquoian stories about the people of the longhouse and their place in the world. Many of these stories were translated into English and recorded in the late nineteenth and early twentieth centuries.

Salem Witch Museum

http://www.salemwitchmuseum.com/

This site primarily presents travel information, but it also offers an interactive FAQ section on witch trials and local history. Other resources are being added rapidly.

1755: The French and Indian War Home Page

http://web.syr.edu/~laroux/

Created by Larry Laroux, a professional writer, this site serves as a prologue to Laroux's forthcoming book *White Coats*, which will examine the soldiers who fought in the French and Indian War of 1755. The site is presently under construction, but Laroux eventually aims to include histories of important battles, a list of French soldiers who fought in the war, and other statistical records. The site already contains a brief narrative account of the war, along with some interesting information and trivia.

The Thanksgiving Tradition

http://www.plimoth.org/Library/Thanksgiving/thanksgi.htm

The research, education, and public relations departments at Plimouth Plantation's Living History Museum of 17th-Century Plymouth present a cornucopia of information on the American Thanksgiving tradition. Included at this site are relevant primary documents, essays, a sample menu, and a list of alternate claimants for the "first Thanksgiving."

Virtual Jamestown: Jamestown and the Virginia Experiment

http://www.iath.virginia.edu/vcdh/jamestown/

Created by Crandal Shifflett, professor of history at Virginia Tech, the "Virtual Jamestown Archive is a digital research, teaching, and learning project that explores the legacies of the Jamestown settlement." Included are links to primary documents; digitized, 360-degree reconstructions of the fort; discussion of Indian, African, and English life around Jamestown; and timelines that trace the history of the New World. This site has been selected as a top humanities site and included in the NEH EDSITEment Project. If you cannot go to Jamestown in person, this is the next best thing.

Walking Tour of Plymouth Plantation

http://archnet.uconn.edu/topical/historic/plimoth/plimoth.html

This site includes photographs and a narrative description of the living museum at Plymouth Plantation. It addresses many different aspects of early seventeenth-century life in New England, such as housing, cooking, clothing, and tools.

Wampum: Treaties, Sacred Records

http://www.kstrom.net/isk/art/beads/wampum.html

This site offers information on the construction and meaning of wampum to native America. Included are images and descriptions along with links that provide more detail.

Documents and Images

American Colonist's Library: A Treasury of Primary Documents ✓

http://www.universitylake.org/primarysources.html

Compiled by Richard Gardiner, a history instructor at University Lake School (Hartland, Wisconsin), the American Colonist's Library is a comprehensive gateway to the early American primary source documents that are currently available online. Included in the list are links to historical sources that influenced American colonists, online collections of the work of major early American political leaders, the text of the Acts of Parliament concerning the American Colonies, numerous American Revolution military documents, and much more. The hundreds of documents are grouped chronologically from 500 B.C.E. to 1800 C.E. As the site boasts, "if it isn't here, it probably is not available online anywhere."

American Historical Images on File: The Native American Experience

http://www.csulb.edu/projects/ais/nae/

Professor Troy Johnson of California State University, Long Beach, developed this collection of historical images of native peoples. The images span the chronological range of native America, from paleo-Indians to the present. They are presented here with full permission of Facts on File, Inc., but take note of the copyright details before you use them for your own purposes.

A Briefe and True Report of the New Found Land of Virginia

http://wsrv.clas.virginia.edu/~msk5d/hariot/main.html

This Web site includes both facsimiles and transcriptions of the 1588 quarto edition and the 1590 folio edition of Thomas Hariot's *A Briefe and True Report of the New Found Land of Virginia*, "the first original book in English relating to what is now America, written by one of the first Englishmen to attempt new world colonization." Only six copies of the 1588 edition are known to exist, so this site is an important resource for those interested in early English settlement of North America.

Columbus and the Age of Discovery ✓

http://columbus.millersv.edu/~columbus

A searchable database of over 1,100 text articles pertaining to Columbus and themes of discovery and encounter. The site, which has unrestricted access, was built by the History Department of Millersville University of Pennsylvania in conjunction with the U.S. Christopher Columbus Quincentenary Jubilee Commission of 1992.

Theodore De Bry Copper Plate Engravings

http://www.csulb.edu/projects/ais/woodcuts/

This collection of historical images of native peoples is the digitized versions of copper plate engravings made by the Flemish engraver and publisher Theodore de Bry. The engravings are based on the watercolor paintings of the sixteenth-century English explorer John White. Professor Troy Johnson of California State University, Long Beach, developed the site.

Early America

http://earlyamerica.com/earlyamerica/index.html

The focus of Early America is primary source material from eighteenth century America. The site is the public access branch of the commercial American Digital Library <http://www.earlyamerica.com/digital-library/>, which sells reproductions of hundreds of early American documents from the Keigwin and Mathews Collection of eighteenth- and nineteenth-century historical documents, as well as images, maps, and other materials.

The Jesuit Relations and Allied Documents: 1610 to 1791

http://puffin.creighton.edu/jesuit/relations/

This impressive undertaking is the work of Rev. Raymond A. Bucko, a Jesuit priest and professor of anthropology at Creighton University, and Thom Mentrak, a historical interpreter at the Ste. Marie Among the Iroquois Museum in Syracuse, New York. This site contains the scanned and transcribed version of the seventy-one-volume edition edited by Reuben Gold Thwait in the late nineteenth century. *The Jesuit Relations* began as private reports between the Jesuit missionaries in New France and their superiors in Paris. The Jesuits made extensive reports on the native peoples they encountered, making this source a must for serious research into Huron and Iroquoian culture in the seventeenth century.

The Leslie Brock Center for the Study of Colonial Currency

http://www.virginia.edu/~econ/brock.html

This Web site takes some of the confusion out of understanding and working with Colonial currencies. Included here are eighteenth-century pamphlets and other contemporary writings that relate to currency, as well as more recent articles on the various colonies and currencies and links to additional resources covering currency rates and monetary history.

Notes on the State of Virginia

http://etext.lib.virginia.edu/toc/modeng/public/JefVirg.html

Constructed as a series of answers to questions posed by foreign observers, Jefferson's *Notes*, first published in 1787, provide a unique description of the natural and human landscapes of Virginia in the late eighteenth century. This e-text version is sponsored by the University of Virginia Library Electronic Text Center.

The Plymouth Colony Archive Project at the University of Virginia

http://www.people.virginia.edu/~jfd3a/

The Plymouth Colony Archive presents a collection of searchable texts, including seminar analysis of various topics, biographical profiles of selected colonists, probate inventories, wills, *Glossary and Notes on Plymouth Colony*, and *Vernacular House Forms in Seventeenth-Century Plymouth Colony: An Analysis of Evidence from the Plymouth Colony Room-by-Room Probate Inventories 1633–85*, by Patricia E. Scott Deetz and James Deetz. The site itself is maintained by the Deetzes, pioneers in material culture studies.

Chapter 8

American Revolution

Robert M.S. McDonald

Metasites

The American Revolution: National Discussions of Our Revolutionary Origins

http://revolution.h-net.msu.edu/intro.html

This metasite, hosted by the NEH-sponsored H-NET, makes available authoritative essays, archives of interesting discussions, and a bibliography of printed sources on the Revolution. For an extensive array of external links, refer to the section entitled Resources.

Eighteenth-Century Resources

http://andromeda.rutgers.edu/~jlynch/18th

Compiled by Rutgers University English professor Jack Lynch, this metasite of links to Web pages "that focus on the (very long) eighteenth century" and home pages of scholars researching eighteenth-century topics enables students of the American Revolutionary era to view it from a global (and especially trans-Atlantic Enlightenment) perspective. General categories include art and architecture, history, music, philosophy, religion and theology, science and mathematics, and professional journals.

HistoryOnline: American Revolution

http://www.jacksonesd.k12.or.us/k12projects/jimperry/revolution.html

Maintained by the Jackson (Oregon) Education Service District, this metasite provides more than two dozen links. The emphasis here is on colorful sites geared toward students and the general public.

General Sites

American Revolutionary War Timeline: People, Events, Documents

http://www.ilt.columbia.edu/k12/history/timeline.html

Here, Columbia University's Institute for Learning Technologies provides internal links to biographical sketches, historical narratives, and important documents (such as the Albany Plan of Union, the Stamp Act Congress Resolutions, and John Adams's *Thoughts on Government*). Intended for K-12 teachers and students, this site supplies a wealth of information useful to everyone.

The Avalon Project at the Yale Law School: 18th Century Documents

http://www.yale.edu/lawweb/avalon/18th.htm

This reliable, user-friendly site provides unabridged transcriptions of dozens of important Revolutionary era documents, including Colonial charters, state constitutions, Indian treaties, and the Virginia Declaration of Rights. There is also a keyword-searchable version of *The Federalist Papers*. This site is an extraordinary resource for scholars of early American statecraft.

Battles of the American Revolutionary War

http://www.ilt.columbia.edu/k12/history/aha/battles.html

Maintained by Columbia University's Institute for Learning Technologies, this site links users to information on battles and fortifications that figured prominently in the War for Independence. Brief descriptions place these flash points within the context of larger campaigns, describe strategy and important maneuvers, and estimate casualties. Historic illustrations round out the presentations. This site should aid instructors who seek abbreviated but competent descriptions of the military conflict.

Boston National Historical Park: The Freedom Trail

http://www.nps.gov/bost/ftrail.htm

For decades tourists have flocked to Boston's Freedom Trail, the three-mile stretch of historic sites from the Massachusetts State House to Bunker Hill. Now surfers of the Web can also enjoy an enlightening foray into America's Revolutionary past. Valuable information about the significance of the Old South Meeting House, Faneuil Hall, the Old North Church, and the *USS Constitution* gives depth to any student's understanding of the heady, early days of the War for Independence and hints at how urban areas constitute especially fertile fields for political unrest.

Center for Military History: War of American Independence

http://www.army.mil/cmh-pg/online/WAI.htm

This site features several useful resources. Among them is Robert K. Wright, Jr.'s *The Continental Army*, a workmanlike text that recounts the contributions of nonmilitia, nonregular state troops. This site also includes bibliographies and traces the lineages of the units of the Continental Army.

Colonial Williamsburg

http://www.history.org

The official home page of Colonial Williamsburg provides teachers and students with a vivid introduction to the recreated eighteenth-century Virginia capital and the world of imperial Anglo-America. The site offers information on Colonial and Revolutionary Williamsburg's most notable people, places, and events. Teachers will find information on electronic field trips, the Colonial Williamsburg Teacher Institute, and lesson plans for topics such as "Colonial Reaction to the Stamp Act" and "Travel in the 18th Century."

Declaring Independence: Drafting the Documents

http://lcweb.loc.gov/exhibits/declara/declara1.html

An online exhibit on the creation of the Declaration of Independence, this Library of Congress–sponsored site features photographs and transcriptions of Thomas Jefferson's drafts of the 1776 document. In addition, it showcases eighteenth-century printed versions of the text and historic illustrations of its creation and ratification. Brief introductions provide context for these materials. Composition teachers will join history instructors in making use of this site, for it provides a compelling case study of the process of writing and revision.

Documents from the Continental Congress and the Constitutional Convention, 1774–1789

http://lcweb2.loc.gov/ammem/bdsds/bdsdhome.html

Sponsored by the Library of Congress, this invaluable page contains 274 keyword-searchable documents relating to the Continental Congress and the ratification of the Constitution. The texts include treaties, resolutions, committee reports, and extracts from the Congress's journals. This site greatly expedites serious research on Revolutionary era politics.

The Early America Review

http://earlyamerica.com/review

This online historical journal, published since 1996, includes both book reviews and articles (such as "Jefferson and His Daughters," "The Enigma of Benedict Arnold," and "A Conversation with Alan Taylor"). The essays, most of which are footnoted, should interest wide audiences. Accessible and elegantly presented, this is a worthwhile site.

The Heath Anthology of American Literature

http://www.georgetown.edu/bassr/heath/index.html

The Syllabus Builder, listed under Instructor Resources, provides writings by Mercy Otis Warren, Benjamin Franklin, J. Hector St. John de Crèvecoeur, Thomas Paine, John Adams, Thomas Jefferson, Philip Freneau, Timothy Dwight, Phillis Wheatley, Joel Barlow, and other Independence era literati. This virtual library of essential texts, which should ably bolster the resources available to educators at smaller institutions, puts early American classics within reach of everyone.

Historic Mount Vernon: The Home of Our First President, George Washington

http://www.mountvernon.org

Maintained by the curators of George Washington's Potomac River estate, this site provides information about the man who commanded the Continental Army and served as the first U.S. president; in addition, it situates his house within the context of a slave-based plantation labor system. Students of the Revolution will appreciate the authoritative biographical information on Washington, along with the virtual tour of the grounds of Mount Vernon, the pages on George Washington and Slavery, and the narrated image gallery of paintings relating to Washington. A rudimentary George Washington Quiz will challenge children in the primary grades.

Thomas Jefferson: A Film by Ken Burns

http://www.pbs.org/jefferson

The Public Broadcasting System inaugurated this Web site to complement its landmark 1997 documentary series *Thomas Jefferson*, a three-hour televised account (now available on videotape) produced by Ken Burns. Like the film, this site chronicles the multifaceted life of the author of the Declaration of Independence. Student study sheets on political, religious, social, intellectual, and personal freedom and an archive of Jefferson's writings will especially interest educators, as will "Does Jefferson Matter?," an online forum of noted scholars who assess the role of Jefferson (and other "great men") in shaping history.

Thomas Jefferson Online Resources at the University of Virginia

http://etext.virginia.edu/jefferson

The University of Virginia's Electronic Text Center sponsors this extraordinarily useful site concerning its venerable founder. More than 1,700 documents written by Jefferson are accessible, all of them keyword searchable. In addition, electronic versions of Frank Shuffelton's invaluable annotated bibliographies of books and articles about Jefferson (*Thomas Jefferson: A Comprehensive, Annotated Bibliography of Writings about Him, 1826–1980* [New York: Garland Publishing, 1983] and *Thomas Jefferson, 1981–1990: An Annotated Bibliography* [New York: Garland Publishing, 1992]) are also available, sources that truly supersede their printed versions because they, too, are keyword searchable. This is the essential site for individuals seeking to start research on a Jefferson topic.

Liberty! The American Revolution

http://www.pbs.org/ktca/liberty.

This Web site accompanied the 1997 televised PBS documentary (now available on videotape) *Liberty!*, a six-hour account of the causes, course, and consequences of the American Revolution. One especially useful feature is the Chronicle of the Revolution, an illustrated narrative of the independence movement's signal events. This chronological account, which provides a good overview of the era, is supplemented by a number of internal links that give readers more in-depth information about selected topics (such as the Boston Tea Party and Thomas Hutchinson). A timeline, bibliography, index, and listing of external links round out the very useful presentation.

Loyalist, British Songs and Poetry of the American Revolution

http://www.erols.com/candidus/music.htm

The texts of one dozen Loyalist songs and poems, many of them quite obscure, appear on this attractive page. A number of links to other sites focusing on Loyalism can be found here as well.

Monticello: The Home of Thomas Jefferson

http://www.monticello.org

Sponsored by the Thomas Jefferson Memorial Foundation, this exceptional, award-winning site focuses on America's third president and life at his mountaintop home, Monticello. Notable features include A Day in the Life, a richly illustrated narrative, complete with fascinating internal links, of Jefferson's waking moments during a typical day at his plantation. The site includes a clickable index of reports on various subjects prepared by Monticello's research staff; Ask Thomas Jefferson invites youngsters to correspond with the famous Virginian (students' questions and the replies of "Jefferson" are posted on a topically indexed archive). The site also features fresh information on Sally Hemings, the slave with whom—recent DNA testing suggests—Jefferson fathered at least one child. A chronicle of interviews with descendants of Monticello slaves provides a glimpse into the lives of members of Jefferson's extended plantation "family." Teachers will discover online lesson plans that provide technical and pedagogical suggestions for optimizing classroom use of the site.

National Archives and Records Administration: Charters of Freedom

http://www.nara.gov/exhall/charters/charters.html

This online exhibit features materials relating to the Declaration of Independence, the Constitution, and the Bill of Rights. Sponsored by the National Archives, the custodian for these seminal documents, this site enables visitors to view exceptionally clear images of these texts' early manuscript and printed versions; it also includes authoritative essays that consider them in various contexts. See, for example, "The Declaration of Independence: A History," which discusses the drafting and ratification of the Declaration, as well as how different generations treated the physical document as it evolved from state paper to national icon.

Omohundro Institute of Early American History and Culture

http://www.wm.edu/oieahc

Cosponsored by the College of William and Mary and the Colonial Williamsburg Foundation, the Omohundro Institute of Early American History and Culture publishes the highly regarded *William and Mary Quarterly (WMQ)*, a journal of American history prior to 1815. Here, on its official Web site, individuals may browse recent tables of contents from the *WMQ*, see news of upcoming conferences and colloquia, and read *Uncommon Sense*, the institute's newsletter.

Thomas Paine National Historical Association

http://www.mediapro.net/cdadesign/paine

The home page of the Thomas Paine National Historical Association is a good starting point for basic research on the important trans-Atlantic radical whose 1776 *Common Sense* pushed American colonists toward revolution. The site includes information about his life and his New Rochelle, New York home (where the association is based), as well as links to full-text versions of his writings and other Paine-related Web pages.

Philadelphia's Historic Mile

http://www.ushistory.org/tour/index.html

Maintained by the Independence Hall Association, this site allows people in far-flung locales to tour Philadelphia's most historic Revolutionary landmarks. Stops include the old Pennsylvania State House (Independence Hall), where the Continental Congress and Constitutional Convention met; City Tavern; the first and second Bank of the United States; the Liberty Bell; Christ Church; and Franklin Court. Richly illustrated and competently narrated, the tour provides a tantalizing glimpse of not only a young nation's political life but also an old city's streetscape.

From Revolution to Reconstruction: A Hypertext on American History

http://odur.let.rug.nl/~usa/usa.htm

This extraordinarily useful site provides a wealth of reliable information on the American Revolutionary period. Hosted by the University of Groningen in the Netherlands, this page features numerous full-text documents, including thirty written between the 1763 Peace of Paris and the 1783 Treaty of Paris. Internal links to brief biographies of important contributors to the Independence movement appear here as well. While the documents, supplied by the U.S. Information Agency, are reliably transcribed, a few of the biographical sketches, authored by nonnative English speakers, contain spelling and grammatical errors. Quibbles aside, students and teachers of early American history will frequently resort to this massive resource.

Betsy Ross Home Page

http://www.ushistory.org/betsy/index.html

This interesting Web site, sponsored by Philadelphia's Betsy Ross House and the Independence Hall Association, includes a picture gallery of historic American flags, a brief biography of upholsterer/flagmaker Betsy Ross, and information about flag trivia and etiquette. It also includes a section, arranged in a point-counterpoint format, arguing that the story of Ross sewing the first U.S. flag (described by some as a myth) is, in reality, accurate. As a result, this site might be used as a springboard for a discussion on standards of historical evidence and the development of historical memory.

U.S. Army Military History Institute

http://carlisle-www.army.mil/usamhi

Sponsored by the U.S. Army War College at Carlisle, Pennsylvania, the Military History Institute allows historians of the Revolution to use electronic bibliographical databases to search, with keywords, a variety of important primary and secondary sources.

Virtual Marching Tour of the American Revolution

http://www.ushistory.org/march/people.htm

Maintained by Philadelphia's Independence Hall Association, this site, still under construction, currently focuses on the Philadelphia Campaign of 1777. From the landing of British troops at Head of Elk, Maryland, to Brandywine, Germantown, Fort Mifflin, and Valley Forge, this virtual marching tour includes a reliable narrative of events. Photographs, illustrations, and music supplement the text. Several dozen links connect to authoritative, mostly professionally maintained Web pages, from the National Trust for Historic Preservation and the Maryland State Archives to the Friends of the Saratoga Battlefield.

George Washington Papers Home Page

http://www.virginia.edu/gwpapers

The official home page of *The Papers of George Washington*, a documentary editing project based for thirty years at the University of Virginia, makes selected documents relating to Washington's long public career available as keyword-searchable electronic texts. Internal links also provide information about the Washington papers project and staff.

The World of Benjamin Franklin

http://sln.fi.edu/franklin

Sponsored by the Franklin Institute, this site provides a fascinating introduction to Benjamin Franklin for elementary school students. A brief biography and discussions of Franklin as scientist, inventor, statesman, printer, musician, and economist offer an interesting portrayal of this multifaceted individual. Enrichment activities on the Constitution, Franklin's epitaphs, and other subjects supplement traditional lesson plans.

Chapter 9

Early American History (1783–1860)

Edward Ragan

Metasites

From Revolution to Reconstruction

http://odur.let.rug.nl/~usa/usa.htm

This metasite, maintained by the Arts Faculty of the University of Groningen, Netherlands, is a massive resource for all aspects of American history. The site is divided into five general sections: outlines, essays, documents, biographies, and presidents. This site is organized around several United States Information Agency publications: *An Outline of American History*, *An Outline of the American Economy*, *An Outline of American Government*, and *An Outline of American Literature*. While the text of these *Outlines* has not been changed, they have been enriched with hypertext links to relevant documents, original essays, and other Internet sites. Currently this site contains over 3,000 relevant HTML documents.

The Making of America ✓

http://www.umdl.umich.edu/moa/

The Making of America is a digital library of primary sources in American social history from the antebellum period through Reconstruction. Contained in this collection are approximately 8,500 books and 50,000 journal articles on subjects as far-ranging as education, psychology, American history, sociology, religion, and science and technology. The project, sponsored by the University of Michigan, "represents a major collaborative endeavor in preservation and electronic access to historical texts." These texts are searchable by keyword with links to digitized copies of the nineteenth-century imprints. This is an outstanding site for those who need access to nineteenth-century documents.

Nineteenth-Century Documents Project

http://www.furman.edu/~benson/docs/

Lloyd Benson has prepared an extensive collection of primary documents. The period is categorized topically, and all topics seem to emphasize increased sectional differences and the coming of the Civil War. The documents are grouped under the following headings: Early National Politics, Slavery and Sectionalism, the Nebraska Bill, the Sumner Caning, the Dred Scott Decision, John Brown's raid on Harpers Ferry, 1850s Statistical Almanac, the 1860 Election, Secession and War, and the post–Civil War era.

Museums, Libraries, Historical Societies, and Online Organizations

American Treasures of the Library of Congress

http://lcweb.loc.gov/exhibits/treasures/

This is a substantial virtual exhibit from the Library of Congress collections of a variety of items, including letters by Thomas Jefferson and John Quincy Adams's notes from the *Amistad* case. Substantial detail and historical context are provided for each component of the collection. Thomas Jefferson, whose personal library became the core of the Library of Congress, arranged his books into three types of knowledge, corresponding to three faculties of the mind: memory (history), reason (philosophy), and imagination (fine arts).

Amistad: Race and the Boundaries of Freedom in Antebellum Maritime America

http://amistad.mysticseaport.org/main/welcome.html

This site is part of the Mystic Seaport Museum. It contains information on the *Amistad* slave ship, the revolt of its cargo, and the Supreme Court trial of its slave mutineers. The focus of this site is living history. A timeline of events is provided, as are classroom lessons for teachers.

The Early America Review

http://www.earlyamerica.com/review/

Don Vitale edits this electronic "Journal of Fact and Opinion on the People, Issues and Events of 18th Century America." The journal contains wide-ranging articles about the social, political, and military developments of this period. An excellent example of the ways in which modern scholarship seeks to combine traditional formats with technology.

Historic Mount Vernon: The Home of Our First President, George Washington

http://www.mountvernon.org

Visitors to the official Mount Vernon Web site will find information designed to meet a variety of needs. In addition to a virtual tour of the house and grounds, this site contains a biography of Washington written at the fifth-grade level with teaching aids such as quizzes and an electronic image collection.

The Gerrit Smith Virtual Museum

http://www.NYHistory.com/gerritsmith/index.htm

The New York History Net has detailed information about the abolitionist leader. Includes a biographical essay, bibliography, and portrait gallery of Smith and his family. This site was developed in cooperation with the Syracuse University Library Department of Special Collections and Hamilton College, both of whom hold substantial portions of Gerrit Smith's papers.

Topical Histories

Abolition

http://www.loc.gov/exhibits/african/abol.html

The Library of Congress provides information on the history of the antislavery movement in America that led to the formation, in 1833, of the American Anti-Slavery Society. Includes references to Library of Congress holdings such as abolitionist publications, minutes of antislavery meetings, handbills, advertisements, songs, and appeals to women. Demonstrates the tradition of the abolition movement in America before 1833.

African Canadian Heritage Tour

http://www.ciaccess.com/~jdnewby/heritage/african.htm

The African Canadian Heritage Tour celebrates the history of those who made the arduous journey to freedom in Canada via the Underground Railroad. This site is the central Internet presence for a collection of five historical locations that provide information about the Underground Railroad and the African-Canadian settlement of southwestern Ontario: the Buxton Historical Site and Museum, the North American Black Historical Museum, the Sandwich Baptist Church, the Uncle Tom's Cabin–Josiah Henson Interpretive Site, and the Woodstock Institute Sertoma Help Centre.

The American Whig Party (1834–1856)

http://odur.let.rug.nl/~usa/E/uswhig/whigsxx.htm

Essay by Hal Morris that describes the rise of the American Whig Party as an opposition to President Andrew Jackson's king-like tendencies. Included is a history of the Whig Party and links to biographies of Whig presidents and political leaders in America.

John Brown

http://www.pbs.org/weta/thewest/people/a_c/brown.htm

This PBS-sponsored site contains a biography of the radical abolitionist John Brown.

James Fenimore Cooper (1789–1851)

http://odur.let.rug.nl/~usa/LIT/cooper.htm

Kathryn VanSpanckeren has authored this literary biography that evaluates Cooper's role in the development of the American novel. Traces the familial and cultural influences that led Cooper to create Natty Bumppo, his chief protagonist.

Democracy in America: De Tocqueville ✓

http://xroads.virginia.edu/~HYPER/DETOC/home.html

The American Studies program at the University of Virginia maintains this site that explores American democracy in the 1830s, when De Tocqueville traveled across the United States. UVA has combined his itinerary, letters, and journal entries with cultural artifacts from the period to provide a glimpse of American democracy and culture in the early nineteenth century. Among other topics, this site examines issues of gender, race, and religion.

The Donner Party

http://members.home.net/mhaller6/donnerparty.htm

Mike Haller provides a history of the ill-fated Donner Party, which was stranded on its trek across the American West during the winter of 1846–47.

The Founding Fathers

http://www.nara.gov/exhall/charters/constitution/confath.html

The National Archives and Records Administration has compiled biographies of the delegates to the Constitutional Convention of 1787. This is an excellent place to start when studying the U.S. Constitution and the Founding Fathers.

Benjamin Franklin: A Documentary History

http://www.english.udel.edu/lemay/franklin/

J.A. Leo Lemay, the Henry Francis du Pont Winterthur Professor of Colonial American Literature at the University of Delaware, gives visitors a peek into the research that he is doing for a Franklin biography. He offers a detailed chronology of Franklin's life that is divided into three stages: early life, professional interests, and political career. Each event in Franklin's life is verified with citations that are connected to a bibliography of primary documents.

Benjamin Franklin: Glimpses of the Man

http://www.fi.edu/franklin/rotten.html

The Franklin Institute maintains this site, which celebrates the life and work of Benjamin Franklin. It emphasizes his work as a statesman, a printer, a scientist, a philosopher, a musician, an economist, and an inventor.

Horace Greeley (1811–1872)

http://www.honors.unr.edu/~fenimore/greeley.html

David H. Fenimore of the University of Nevada, Reno, offers a detailed biography of Greeley complete with photographs, quotations, a bibliography, and links to related information.

Sarah Grimké, Angelina Grimké

http://www.gale.com/freresrc/womenhst/bio/grimkes.htm

Gale Publishing has created these biographies of Sarah Grimké and Angelina Grimké that focus on their work for abolition and women's suffrage.

Thomas Jefferson: A Film by Ken Burns

http://www.pbs.org/jefferson/

This PBS-sponsored site is the online version of Ken Burns's documentary about Thomas Jefferson. It features selections of Jefferson's writings used in the film, the transcripts of interviews conducted for the film, tips for educators on teaching about Jefferson, and classroom activities for students.

The Thomas Jefferson Memorial Foundation

http://www.monticello.org

The Thomas Jefferson Memorial Foundation has prepared a virtual tour of life at Monticello to demonstrate how Jefferson spent an average day. Included here is a discussion about Jefferson's interests, inventions, family, slaves, and grounds. Lengthy essays seek to explain Jefferson's world to the twentieth-century student. Links connect the reader to additional information about Monticello, its owner, inhabitants, and visitors. "The Jefferson-Hemings DNA Testing: An On-Line Resource" is a valuable link for understanding the current controversy about Jefferson's legacy.

Lewis and Clark ✓

http://www.pbs.org/lewisandclark/

This is the PBS-sponsored online companion to Ken Burns's documentary series on the Lewis and Clark expedition. The site includes biographies for all members of the Corps of Discovery along with equipment lists, timelines, maps, and excerpts from the journals kept. Also included are short histories of the native American tribes that were encountered on the journey. Burns discusses the making of the series, and PBS provides teaching resources. Overall, this is an excellent site.

Manifest Destiny

http://odur.let.rug.nl/~usa/E/manifest/manifxx.htm

This essay by Michael Lubragge traces the history of this concept in America.

Methods of Resistance to Slavery

http://dolphin.upenn.edu/~vision/vis/Mar-95/8677.html

This brief essay by Colette Lamothe examines slaves' responses to slavery, oppression, and exploitation. Lamothe uses a comparative method to explore African slavery in the Caribbean, Latin America, and the United States from the fifteenth to the nineteenth century.

The Mexican-American War (1846–1848)

http://www.pbs.org/kera/usmexicanwar/

This PBS-sponsored site is the online companion to the television documentary. The site provides a detailed analysis of the war from both sides, with the perspective that "there are many valid points of view about a historical event." The war is placed in its larger context as a war for North America. Also included here are a bibliography, a teacher's guide, a timeline of events, historical analysis by experts, and information on the making of the documentary. This site is available in Spanish and English.

The Mexican-American War, 1846–1848

http://www.dmwv.org/mexwar/mexwar.htm

Sponsored by the Descendants of Mexican War Veterans, this site offers a history of the war with sections on the countdown to war, the various conflicts fought across Mexico and California, and the peace that followed. Also provided are maps, documents, images, and links to related resources.

The Mexican-American War Memorial Homepage

http://sunsite.dcaa.unam.mx/revistas/1847/

The Universidad Nacional Autónoma de Mexico sponsors this site. It includes documents, paintings, and a narrative history, presenting the Mexican-American War (1846–1848) from the perspective of participants and observers. The pages are available in English and in Spanish.

Mountain Men and the Fur Trade: Sources of the History of the Fur Trade in the Rocky Mountain West

http://www.xmission.com/~drudy/amm.html

This site is devoted to the mountain men of the Rocky Mountains through 1850. It includes digitized personal and public records and a bibliography for further reading.

New Perspectives on the West ✓

http://www.pbs.org/weta/thewest/

This is the PBS-sponsored online companion to the eight-episode documentary on the American West produced by Ken Burns and Stephen Ives. Burns and Ives introduce the production and provide a timeline with relevant biographies of key figures. Also included are sample primary source documents that were used to create the series and links to related sites.

Orphan Trains of Kansas

http://www.ukans.edu/carrie/kancoll/articles/orphans/

Connie Dipasquale and Susan Stafford present their research about children brought to Kansas from New York on "orphan trains." This site includes first-hand accounts, a timeline, newspaper descriptions, and partial name lists of children on the orphan trains.

Peabody Museum: The Ethnography of Lewis and Clark

http://www.peabody.harvard.edu/Lewis&Clark/

The Peabody Museum of Archaeology and Ethnology at Harvard University has developed this site to examine the cultural implications of the Lewis and Clark expedition. Included here are Native American artifacts (with detailed descriptions), route maps, and a resources page with links.

Politics and Sectionalism in the 1850s

http://odur.let.rug.nl/~usa/E/1850s/polixx.htm

Stephen Demkin has written this essay examining the major political issues of 1850s, such as the Compromise of 1850, the Kansas-Nebraska Act, and the Dred Scott decision. Also included are links to related sites.

Presidents of the United States

http://www.whitehouse.gov/history/presidents/index.html

The official White House Web site provides excellent biographies for each president, along with links to relevant documents and biographies of the first ladies.

Presidents of the United States

http://www.ipl.org/ref/POTUS/index.html

The Internet Public Library has produced a useful collection of presidential Web sites. Sections contain presidential election results, cabinet members, notable events, and links to Internet biographies. The information here is laid out in a very accessible format.

A Roadmap to the U.S. Constitution

http://library.thinkquest.org/11572/?tqskip=1

Jonathan Chin and Alan Stern of ThinkQuest have developed this site on the U.S. Constitution, re-creating the milieu out of which the Constitution emerged. This site provides an annotated copy of the Constitution, explores its origins, examines constitutional "crises" and the relevant Supreme Court decisions, and provides a discussion board for users with specific questions.

Chronology of the Secession Crisis

http://members.aol.com/jfepperson/secesh.html

James F. Epperson charts the chronology of events that culminated with the firing upon Fort Sumter, South Carolina. The site includes links to relevant documents.

The Star Spangled Banner

http://odur.let.rug.nl/~usa/E/banner/bannerxx.htm

Amato F. Mongelluzzo offers an essay that relates the events and dispels several myths surrounding the creation of this poem that became the national anthem.

Henry David Thoreau Home Page

http://www.walden.org/thoreau/

This site, sponsored by the Walden Woods Project, the Thoreau Society, and the Thoreau Institute, is the essential Thoreau site. Emphasized here are Thoreau's biography, images, electronic texts, and scholarly analysis of Thoreau's work.

To the Western Ocean: Planning the Lewis and Clark Expedition

http://www.lib.virginia.edu/exhibits/lewis_clark/ch4.html

The site is part of a map exhibition at the Tracy W. McGregor Room, Alderman Library, University of Virginia. To the Western Ocean is the fourth chapter of a larger exploration of nation building and mapmaking. This site is valuable because it places the Lewis and Clark expedition into a larger historical context.

Two Bloody Days at Buena Vista

http://www.thehistorynet.com/MilitaryHistory/articles/1997/
02972_cover.htm

This article, by Robert Benjamin Smith, details Major General Zachary Taylor's actions at the Battle of Buena Vista in 1847. It includes a full account of the events of the battle along with a map.

Uncle Sam: An American Autobiography

http://xroads.virginia.edu/~CAP/SAM/home.htm

The American Studies program at the University of Virginia has created this site to discuss the origin of this American icon. The forgotten origin of Uncle Sam during the War of 1812 is placed alongside his evolution as a symbol and national icon, including his official adoption and standardization by the U.S. State Department in the 1950s.

The Valley of the Shadow ✓

http://jefferson.village.Virginia.EDU/vshadow2/

Edward L. Ayers, the Hugh P. Kelley Professor of History at the University of Virginia, has developed this massive archive of primary sources that concern the experiences of Franklin County, Pennsylvania, and Augusta County, Virginia, in the years just preceding the Civil War. These two counties were "separated by several hundred miles and the Mason-Dixon line." The document archive includes newspapers, letters, diaries, photographs, maps, church records, population census, agricultural census, and military records. Students can research and write their own histories from the documents provided. The project is primarily intended for secondary schools, community colleges, libraries, and universities. This research is available in CD-ROM form from W.W. Norton Publishers <http://www.wwnorton.com>.

War of 1812

http://www.army.mil/cmh-pg/books/amh/amh-06.htm

This is a discussion of the War of 1812 from *American Military History* (chapter 6). This e-text is sponsored by the Army Historical Series, Office of the Chief of Military History, United States Army. The war is presented as an outgrowth of the Napoleonic Wars. The major battles are narrated in detail, as are comparisons of American and British military capabilities and strategies.

Woman of Iron

http://www.thehistorynet.com/AmericanHistory/articles/0495_text.htm

"In 1825 Rebecca Lukens took over her late husband's iron mill. The company still thrives—a testament to the management abilities of this pioneering woman CEO." The History Net sponsors this article by Joseph Gustaitis.

Documents and Images

"Across the Plains in 1844"

http://www.pbs.org/weta/thewest/resources/archives/two/sager1.htm

Catherine Sager Pringle wrote this account circa 1860. It is reprinted here from S.A. Clarke's *Pioneer Days in Oregon History*, Vol. II (1905).

Across the Plains with the Donner Party

http://www.teleport.com/~mhaller/Primary/VReed/VReed1.html

Mike Haller edited this book of reminiscences by Virginia Reed Murphy about her travel with the Donner party.

The *Amistad* Case

http://www.nara.gov/education/teaching/amistad/home.html

The National Archives and Records Administration provides all documents related to the *Amistad* slave mutiny. This site also includes teaching ideas based on the National Standards for History and the National Standards for Civics and Government.

The Annapolis Convention

http://www.yale.edu/lawweb/avalon/annapoli.htm

The Annapolis Convention assembled to discuss economic issues faced by the states under the Articles of Confederation. It resolved to explore alternatives to the Articles. This site contains the report of the commissioners from the states on September 14, 1786, and links to the Articles of Confederation, the Madison Debates, the *Federalist Papers*, and the U.S. Constitution.

The Articles of Confederation

http://www.yale.edu/lawweb/avalon/artconf.htm

The Articles of Confederation established a central government for the thirteen colonies after the American Revolution. It was a weak system in which the separate states held the balance of power. This site contains a full-text copy of the Articles and links to the Annapolis Convention, the Madison Debates, the *Federalist Papers*, and the U.S. Constitution.

The Bill of Rights

http://www.nara.gov/exhall/charters/billrights/billmain.html

The National Archives and Records Administration provides coverage of the Bill of Rights, including a high-resolution image of the document.

Boundaries of the United States and the Several States

http://www.ac.wwu.edu/~stephan/48states.html

Ed Stephan of Western Washington University has created a charming animated map that depicts the territorial growth of the United States. This site allows students to visualize how national, territorial, and state boundaries changed over time.

Cherokee Nation v. Georgia

http://www.pbs.org/weta/thewest/resources/archives/two/cherokee.htm

This is a full-text copy of the decision handed down by Supreme Court Chief Justice John Marshall in 1831.

The Confessions of Nat Turner

http://docsouth.unc.edu/turner/turner.html

This is the complete text of *The Confessions of Nat Turner* (1831).

The Constitution of the United States

http://www.nara.gov/exhall/charters/constitution/conmain.html

The National Archives and Records Administration maintain this site, where users can read a transcription of the complete text of the Constitution. The Founding Fathers page features the biographies of the fifty-five delegates to the Constitutional Convention and links to biographies of each of the thirty-nine delegates who signed the Constitution. The article "A More Perfect Union" is an in-depth look at the Constitutional Convention and the ratification process. A quiz section gives visitors the chance to test their knowledge.

The *Federalist Papers*

http://www.yale.edu/lawweb/avalon/federal/fed.htm

John Jay, Alexander Hamilton, and James Madison authored these essays, first published in 1787–1788, arguing in favor of constitutional ratification. The collection is searchable by keyword and linked to relevant documents such as the Articles of Confederation, the Annapolis Convention, the Madison Debates, and the U.S. Constitution.

The *Federalist Papers*

http://www.law.emory.edu/FEDERAL/federalist/

The *Federalist Papers* serve as bold statements of American political theory, and this online version makes them more accessible than ever before.

FindLaw: U.S. Constitution

http://www.findlaw.com/casecode/constitution/

This site contains all articles and amendments to the U.S. Constitution, completely annotated with explanations and references. Through hyperlinks, users can access the full-text version of relevant Supreme Court decisions, each placed in its historical context along with pertinent theories of law and government. This is an invaluable resource for legal professionals.

First-Person Narratives of the American South

http://metalab.unc.edu/docsouth/fpn/fpn.html

This site contains an outstanding collection of electronic texts documenting the American South. It includes diaries, autobiographies, memoirs, travel accounts, and ex-slave narratives. The focus is on first-person narratives of marginalized populations: women, African-Americans, enlisted men, laborers, and Native Americans.

A Girl's Life in Virginia before the War

http://metalab.unc.edu/docsouth/burwell/menu.html

This memoir by Letitia M. Burwell describes southern plantation life before the Civil War. It was originally published in 1895.

Godey's Lady's Book

http://www.history.rochester.edu/godeys/

This site includes selections from the popular nineteenth-century women's magazine *Godey's Lady's Book*. Issues from the 1850s include "For the Home," "Nor Just for Ladies," and "Fashion Corner" sections. Visitors to this site will find an informative glimpse into the daily life of the mid-nineteenth-century middle class.

A Grandmother's Recollections of Dixie

http://metalab.unc.edu/docsouth/bryan/menu.html

This is a collection of letters from Mary Norcott Bryan to her grandchildren describing life on a southern plantation before the Civil War. It was published in 1912.

Historical Maps of the United States

http://mahogany.lib.utexas.edu/Libs/PCL/Map_collection/united_states.html

The University of Texas at Austin has digitized the Perry-Castañeda Library Map Collection. This is an excellent source for digitized copies of rare maps.

History of the Donner Party

http://www.teleport.com/~mhaller/Secondary/McGlashan/McGlashanTOC.html

Mike Haller has edited this book by C.F. McGlashan (1879) about the Donner Party.

"The Hypocrisy of American Slavery"

http://www.historyplace.com/speeches/douglass.htm

Frederick Douglass gave this speech on July 4, 1852, in Rochester, New York See elsewhere in this section, Douglass's speech made the following day entitled, "What to the Slave Is the Fourth of July?"

The Jay Treaty

http://odur.let.rug.nl/~usa/D/1776–1800/foreignpolicy/jay.htm

This treaty between Great Britain and the United States, proclaimed in February 1796, was the most controversial issue of George Washington's presidency. Its real significance was that it represented Britain's recognition of American nationality.

Thomas Jefferson on Politics and Government: Quotations from the Writings of Thomas Jefferson

http://etext.virginia.edu/jefferson/quotations/

This site, sponsored by the University of Virginia, contains an extensive collection of Jefferson quotations. The stated goal of this site is to constitute a "fair statement of the complete political philosophy of Thomas Jefferson." Also included are a brief biography of Jefferson and links to related sites.

John Brown: An Address by Frederick Douglass

http://memory.loc.gov/cgi-bin/query/r?ammem/
murray:@field(FLD001+07012896+):@@@ REF

This speech by Frederick Douglass at the Library of Congress Web site is a tribute to John Brown, a radical abolitionist who, in 1859, raided the federal arsenal at Harpers Ferry, Virginia, in a mad attempt to foment a slave revolt, for which Virginia authorities hanged Brown. His last words were: "I, John Brown, am now quite certain that the crimes of this guilty land will never be purged away but with blood." Douglass memorialized Brown as a true hero of the abolitionist cause.

"A Journey to the Seaboard States" (1856)

http://odur.let.rug.nl/~usa/D/1851–1875/olmsted/jourxx.htm

This essay by Frederick Law Olmsted focuses on slavery and the plantation system. It was written in 1856 while Olmsted was on a journalistic assignment for the *New York Daily Times*. Olmsted is critical of slavery as both cruel and inefficient.

Kentucky Resolution (1799)

http://odur.let.rug.nl/~usa/D/1776–1800/constitution/kent1799.htm

This was Thomas Jefferson's republican response to the Federalists' Alien and Sedition Acts. The resolution advanced the state compact theory and argued that states retained the right to notify Congress when it had exceeded its authority.

The Louisiana Purchase Treaty

http://www.nara.gov/exhall/originals/loupurch.html

This online exhibit by the National Archives presents images of the document that was signed in Paris in 1803, along with a transcription of the text.

The Madison Debates

http://www.yale.edu/lawweb/avalon/debates/debcont.htm

The Debates in the Federal Convention of 1787 was created from notes taken by James Madison during the Constitutional Convention held in Philadelphia between May 14 and September 17, 1787. The debates are searchable by keyword or can be accessed according to specific dates. Also contained here are links to the Articles of Confederation, the Annapolis Convention, the *Federalist Papers*, and the U.S. Constitution.

John Marshall

http://odur.let.rug.nl/~usa/D/1801–1825/marshallcases/marxx.htm

Here are the major decisions written by Chief Justice John Marshall, including *Marbury v. Madison* and *Cherokee Nation v. Georgia*. Also included is a biography of Marshall.

The Monroe Doctrine

http://odur.let.rug.nl/~usa/D/1801–1825/jmdoc.htm

The Monroe Doctrine was an early statement on American foreign policy, presented in President Monroe's annual message to Congress on December 2, 1823.

North American Slave Narratives ✓

http://metalab.unc.edu/docsouth/neh/neh.html

This large collection of American slave narratives is part of the Documenting the American South project sponsored by the University of North Carolina at Chapel Hill. This is an excellent resource for better understanding the slaves' world in the antebellum South.

The Prairie Traveler: A Hand-book for Overland Expeditions

http://www.ukans.edu/carrie/kancoll/books/marcy/

This survival guide/handbook, written by Captain Randolph B. Marcy, U.S. Army, was published in 1859.

The Proclamation of Neutrality (1793)

http://odur.let.rug.nl/~usa/D/1776–1800/foreignpolicy/neutr.htm

President George Washington proclaimed American neutrality during the wars of the French Revolution.

Scanned Originals of Early American Documents

http://www.law.emory.edu/FEDERAL/conpict.html

This site includes scanned originals of the Constitution, the Bill of Rights, and the Declaration of Independence.

The Sedition Act of July 14, 1798

http://www.ukans.edu/carrie/docs/texts/sedact.htm

Congress passed this act on July 14, 1798.

"Slavery a Positive Good"

http://douglass.speech.nwu.edu/calh_a59.htm

John C. Calhoun delivered this speech on the floor of the U.S. Senate in 1837.

Treaty of Greenville (1795)

http://odur.let.rug.nl/~usa/D/1776–1800/indians/green.htm

This is the complete text of the American Indian treaty that formally opened the Northwest Territory for settlement.

Uncle Tom's Cabin

http://xroads.virginia.edu/~HYPER/STOWE/stowe.html

The American Studies program at the University of Virginia provides an e-text of Harriet Beecher Stowe's 1852 novel.

Virginia Resolution (1798)

http://www.yale.edu/lawweb/avalon/virres.htm

This was James Madison's republican response to the Federalists' Alien and Sedition Acts. It advanced the state compact theory, which argued that the federal government could operate only within its constitutionally defined limits.

Virginia Statute for Religious Freedom (1786)

http://www.freethought-web.org/ctrl/jefferson_vsrf.html

Thomas Jefferson drafted this act in 1777. An amended version passed the Virginia legislature in 1786. It served as the precedent for the religious freedom article in the Bill of Rights.

"What to the Slave Is the Fourth of July?"

http://douglass.speech.nwu.edu/doug_a10.htm

Frederick Douglass delivered this speech on July 5, 1852. See, elsewhere in this section, Douglass's speech made the day before in Rochester, New York. entitled, "The Hypocrisy of American Slavery."

Chapter 10

The Civil War

James E. Jolly

Metasites

The American Civil War

http://www.homepages.dsu.edu/jankej/civilwar/civilwar.htm

Created by Jim Janke of Dakota State University, this site is an excellent place to begin a search for American Civil War materials. The page is extremely well organized into a wide variety of categories and subcategories that are frequently updated.

The American Civil War, 1861–1865: World Wide Web Information Archive

http://users.iamdigex.net/bdboyle/cw.html

This site contains links to a wide variety of Civil War–related materials such as books, documents, orders of battle, reenactment groups and other historic preservation groups, and e-text versions of Lincoln's First and Second Inaugural Addresses.

The American Civil War Home Page

http://sunsite.utk.edu/civil-war/

The American Civil War Home Page is another excellent place to begin research. It contains links to photographic collections, regimental histories, reenactors, and a host of other materials.

The United States Civil War Center

http://www.cwc.lsu.edu/

The United States Civil War Center, located at Louisiana State University, is dedicated to promoting the study of the Civil War. It has assembled an impressive collection of over 2,400 links to Civil War sites. In addition, the page contains online documents, tips for tracing one's Civil War ancestors, and links to reenactors and vendors.

General Sites

African-American Civil War Memorial

http://www.afroamcivilwar.org/

This site contains a host of information about the design and location of the African-American Civil War Memorial, a photo gallery of the project, and links to African-American Civil War sites.

American Civil War

http://spec.lib.vt.edu/civwar/

Created by the Special Collections Department of the Virginia Libraries at Virginia Tech, this page offers access to a wide variety of letters and diaries of both Union and Confederate soldiers.

Battlefield Medicine in the American Civil War

http://members.aol.com/cwsurgeon0/indexJ.html

Battlefield Medicine in the American Civil War contains a wide variety of information related to medicine in the Civil War. Copies of battlefield reports, eyewitness accounts, and even a copy of General Orders No. 147, which organized the Ambulance Corps in 1862, are included.

Battle Summaries

http://www2.cr.nps.gov/abpp/battles/tvii.htm#sums

Organized by either state or campaign, this site provides Civil War battle summaries, preservation information, and links to the National Park Service.

Captain Richard W. Burt's Civil War Letters from the 76th Ohio Volunteer Infantry

http://my.ohio.voyager.net/~lstevens/burt/

This site, managed by Larry Stevens, includes the letters, poems, and songs of Richard W. Burt of the 76th Ohio Volunteer Infantry, as well as a copy of the 76th's recruiting ad.

Civil War Diaries at Augustana College Library

http://sparc5.augustana.edu/library/civil.html

This page contains two diaries from Illinois soldiers during the Civil War.

Civil War Diary and Letters of David Humphrey Blair

http://netnow.micron.net/~rbparker/diary/index.html

This site, managed by Robert B. Parker, consists of the diary and letters of David Humphrey Blair, a soldier with Company D of the 45th Ohio Volunteers.

Civil War Diary of Bingham Findley Junkin

http://www.iwaynet.net/~lsci/junkin/

This site contains the diary entries of Private Bingham Findley Junkin of the 100th Pennsylvania Volunteer Infantry from March 1864 to June 1865.

The Civil War History of John Ritland

http://members.home.net/jritland1/

This page consists of the narrative of the life of John Ritland, who served with the 32nd Iowa Infantry from 1862 until 1865.

Civil War Letters

http://home.pacbell.net/dunton/SSDletters.html

This site includes a well-indexed collection of twelve letters written by Private Samuel S. Dunton of the 114th New York Infantry between 1862 and 1865.

Civil War Live

http://library.thinkquest.org/2873/data/ref/

This page presents a timeline, an essay outlining causes of the Civil War, and biographical sketches of both Union and Confederate generals.

Civil War Manuscripts at the Southern Historical Collection

http://www.unc.edu/lib/mssinv/exhibits/civilwar/civilwar.html

This site contains a small collection of eleven Union and Confederate letters written between 1861 and 1865. With two exceptions, all the letters come from the eastern theater of the war.

Civil War Resources: Virginia Military Institute Archives

http://www.vmi.edu/~archtml/cwsource.html

Virginia Military Institute's Civil War Resources page includes twenty-three different online manuscript collections. The two most famous are the Stonewall Jackson Papers and the Matthew Fontaine Maury Papers. Maury was an oceanographer, a Confederate States navy commander, and faculty member at VMI. In addition to his Civil War service, topics include his career at the National Observatory in Washington, D.C., his colonization efforts in Mexico, and his professorship at VMI.

Civil War Sites in the Shenandoah Valley of Virginia

http://www2.cr.nps.gov/abpp/shenandoah/svs0–1.html

This site provides a comprehensive study of the battlefields in the Shenandoah Valley. In addition to summaries, the site contains information on the historical context, preservation, and heritage tourism.

Civil War Soldiers and Sailors System

http://www.itd.nps.gov/cwss/

This project is an attempt to build a database of basic information about all those who served in the war.

Civil War Women

http://odyssey.lib.duke.edu/collections/civil-war-women.html

This page offers online information about an archival collection at the Special Collections Library at Duke University. The collection consists of the Rosie O'Neal Greenlow Papers, the Alice Williamson Diary, and the Sarah E. Thompson Papers. It also contains links to other sites containing primary sources related to women and the Civil War.

Dwight Henry Cory Letters and Diary

http://homepages.rootsweb.com/~lovelace/cory.htm

This site contains a collection of letters written by Dwight Henry Cory of the 6th Ohio Volunteer Cavalry.

The John Freeman Diary

http://www.public.usit.net/mruddy/freeman.htm

This site contains the diary of John Henderson Freeman, who served with Company I of the 34th Mississippi Volunteers.

Edward G. Gerdes Civil War Home Page

http://www.couchgenweb.com/civilwar/

This is a good resource for those interested in Arkansas during the Civil War. It includes lists of Confederate cemeteries, burial lists, regimental rosters, and Cherokee Confederate units.

H-Civwar

http://h-net2.msu.edu/~civwar

This site, part of H-Net, contains a discussion list of the Civil War and links to other sites. Eventually the page will also offer links to conferences, grants, and bibliographies.

The Iowa Civil War Site

http://www.iowa-counties.com/civilwar/

The Iowa Civil War Site discusses Iowa in the Civil War. It includes letters, diaries, unit histories, and photos.

Letters from an Iowa Soldier in the Civil War

http://bob.ucsc.edu/civil-war-letters/home.html

This page, by Bill Proudfoot, contains some letters of Private Newton Robert Scott of the 36th Infantry, Iowa Volunteers.

Letters of the Civil War

http://www.letterscivilwar.com/

This site presents a variety of letters from many different sources. Individuals are encouraged to submit letters that they might have for posting to the site. It also contains photos and diaries.

Overall Family Civil War Letters

http://www.geocities.com/Heartland/Acres/1574/

Presented at this site are letters of Isaac Overall, a private with Company I of the 36th Ohio Volunteer Infantry, written between 1862 and his death in 1863.

Pearce Civil War Documents Collection

http://www.nav.cc.tx.us/lrc/Homepg2.htm

Navarro College houses this Web site, which consists of a variety of letters, documents, and diaries.

Poetry and Music of the War Between the States

http://www.erols.com/kfraser/

This site contains wartime and postwar poetry and music from both Union and Confederate sources.

Secession Era Editorials Project

http://history.furman.edu/~benson/docs/

The Secession Era Editorials Project is sponsored by Furman University in South Carolina. Currently, the project provides editorials related to four pre–Civil War events: the Nebraska Bill, the Dred Scott case, Harpers Ferry, and the caning of Charles Sumner. Eventually the project plans to include a complete run of editorials from the major political parties.

Selected Civil War Photographs

http://memory.loc.gov/ammem/cwphtml/cwphome.html

Part of the American Memory project of the Library of Congress, this site presents over 1,100 photographs, most of which were taken by Matthew Brady. It includes a searchable database, a subject index, and links explaining more about Civil War photography.

The Shenandoah 1863 Civil War Museum

http://www.fortunecity.com/victorian/museum/63/index.html

This page contains profiles of Civil War leaders, pictures of battle flags, campaign and battlefield maps, and a list of sources for further research.

Ulysses S. Grant Association

http://www.lib.siu.edu/projects/usgrant/

This site, supported by Southern Illinois University, presents information on Grant's military service, an online version of his personal memoirs, and photographs.

Valley of the Shadow Project

http://jefferson.village.virginia.edu/vshadow2/

A Virginia Center for Digital History project, the original Valley of the Shadow Project, has now been released on CD-ROM. Currently the project is in its second phase, adding to its original collection of primary documents, images, sounds, and discussions. Part One of the Valley of the Shadow Project is titled The Eve of War. Part Two deals with the same communities but concerns itself with The War Years.

Vermont in the Civil War

http://vermontcivilwar.org/index.shtml

This site attempts to document Vermont's participation in the conflict. It contains an index of over 32,000 names of those who served in the war, letters, brief biographies of individuals who served, and a cemetery database of over 3,000 names.

Chapter 11

The Gilded Age and Progressive Era

Kenneth R. Dvorak

Metasites

American Memory

http://memory.loc.gov/ammem/amhome.html

Established by the Library of Congress, this excellent Web research site provides a wealth of information on all topics related to American history. Containing nearly 7 million digital artifacts, the American Memory collection provides search features on print, film, and photographic indexes on all topics of special interest to students and researchers.

The Gilded Age Webquest: Documentating Industrialization in America

http://www.oswego.org/staff/tcaswell/wq/gildedage/student.htm

This award-winning Web site is an excellent resource for K-12 social science teachers looking for innovative and interactive ways to immerse their students in how industrialization transformed American society and culture during the Gilded Age. Students become part of a documentary film crew charged with the responsibility of creating a film about the Gilded Age.

Gilded and Progressive Era Resources

http://www.tntech.edu/www/acad/hist/gilprog.html

This exhaustive Web resource highlights topics central to understanding the Gilded and Progressive Eras. Produced by the History Department at Tennessee Technological University, this Web site should attract anyone interested in learning more about these two important eras in American history.

Populism

http://history.smsu.edu/wrmiller/Populism/Texts/populism.htm

Authored by historian Worth Robert Miller of Southwest Missouri State University, this comprehensive Web resource site offers several gateways for study of the Populist movement. The site contains topical, biographical, and political links that examine the rise of Populism and its appeal to Americans living in the nineteenth century.

The World of 1898: The Spanish-American War

http://www.loc.gov/rr/hispanic/1898/

This Library of Congress Web site titled The World of 1898 provides excellent resources and documents about the Spanish-American War, the period before the war, and some of the fascinating people who participated in the fighting or commented about it. Information about Cuba, Guam, the Philippines, Puerto Rico, Spain, and the United States is provided in chronologies, bibliographies, and a variety of pictorial and textual material from bilingual sources.

The World's Columbian Exposition: Idea, Experience, Aftermath

http://xroads.virginia.edu/~MA96/WCE/title.html

The 1893 World's Columbian Exposition, held in Chicago, Illinois, was the signature event of the decade. This very professional Web research site, created by Julie K. Rose of the University of Virginia, presents the exposition and its importance in an exciting virtual format. This site provides a history of the fair, a virtual tour, written reactions by visitors to the fair, the exposition's historical and cultural legacy, and an extensive bibliographic resource page.

World's Columbian Exposition: Interactive Guide

http://users.vnet.net/schulman/Columbian/columbian.html

Created and maintained by Bruce R. Schulman, this award-winning Web site details the architectural history of the 1893 Chicago World's Columbian Exposition. Divided into four areas of research, the site describes the background, exhibits, art, and architecture of the "white city."

Historical Figures

Presidents of the Gilded Age and Progressive Era

Chester A. Arthur, 1881–85

http://www.whitehouse.gov/history/presidents/ca21.html

Arthur was described by Counterpoise as looking "Presidential"—find out why.

Grover Cleveland, 1885–89 and 1893–97

http://www.rain.org/~turnpike/grover/Main.html

The Grover Cleveland Web resource page provides a complete picture of Cleveland as private citizen and president. Josh Smith of Dos Pueblos High School in Santa Barbara, California, has maintained this site since 1999. Individuals can examine photographs, speeches, family history, and bibliographic sources about Cleveland, including additional links for Cleveland and the tumultuous era in which he lived.

James A. Garfield, 1881

http://www.whitehouse.gov/history/presidents/jg20.html

Did you know that James A. Garfield was the second president shot while in office?

Ulysses S. Grant, 1869–77

http://www.mscomm.com/~ulysses/

This is an exceptional Web resource created by Webmaster Candace Scott. It contains a wealth of information about our eighteenth president, including Grant's family history, his early childhood, and his life as a private citizen, father, husband, soldier, general, and president. This is an extremely important historical resource on a very controversial historical figure.

Benjamin Harrison, 1889–93

http://www.whitehouse.gov/history/presidents/bh23.html

This Web site provides essential information about Benjamin Harrison and his presidency.

Rutherford B. Hayes, 1877–81

http://www.rbhayes.org/

The Rutherford B. Hayes Presidential Center, the first presidential library in the United States, is located in Fremont, Ohio. This Web resource site provides information on Hayes's military career during the Civil War, his personal papers, diaries, and presidential papers. The Hayes Presidential Center, which also contains information on Ohio Civil War soldiers, is sponsored in part by the Ohio Historical Society.

William McKinley, 1897–1901

http://www.cohums.ohio-state.edu/history/projects/McKinley/

One of most outstanding Web resources on the era of William McKinley is this site produced and maintained by Ohio State's history department. This extensive analysis of William McKinley is particularly well suited for students seeking information on Ohio politicians, such as Mark Hanna, McKinley's infamous political campaign manager. The site also contains information on McKinley as president, the Spanish-American War of 1898, and political cartoons and photographs of the period.

White House

http://www.whitehouse.gov/

This site specifically deals with information concerning the presidents of the United States. Managed by the Executive Office staff of the president, this excellent Web resource contains full-text inaugural speeches, information about individual presidential libraries, First Ladies, and links to other relevant historical sites.

Creating Industrial America

American Memory

http://memory.loc.gov/ammem/amhome.html

Andrew Carnegie, 1885–1919

http://www.pbs.org/wgbh/amex/carnegie/
http://www.clpgh.org/exhibit/carnegie.html

The first Web site based on the PBS film documentary *The Richest Man in the World*, provides extensive materials on industrialist and philanthropist

Andrew Carnegie and his personal philosophies, timelines, and an in-depth analysis of the Homestead steel strike. The second, Andrew Carnegie: A Tribute, is an excellent Web resource on Carnegie's true-life rags-to-riches story. Sponsored by the Carnegie Library of Pittsburgh, this ambitious Web resource site contains photographs and audio links honoring Pittsburgh's most famous citizen.

J. Pierpont Morgan, 1837–1913

http://www.jpmorgan.com/CorpInfo/History/overview.html
http://www.nyyc.org/Images/Heritage%20Series/Morgan.htm

Morgan is perhaps the most admired, hated, and despised figure in American financial history. His firm, J.P. Morgan and Company, became the most influential financial center in America, helping to finance the capital needed for the burgeoning post–Civil War economy. The first site, sponsored by the J.P. Morgan Company, provides a brief history of the firm and its founder. The second Web site, sponsored by the New York Yacht Club, showcases J.P. Morgan enjoying one of his many private pursuits.

John D. Rockefeller, 1839–1937

http://www.rockefeller.edu/archive.ctr/bibliog.html#RFB2

The most intriguing Web resource on John D. Rockefeller is this exhaustive bibliographic listing of Rockefeller's family history, sponsored by the Rockefeller Archive Center. This resource also contains a complete listing of published works about John D. Rockefeller.

Industrial Conflict in an Industrializing Age

Coal Mining in the Gilded Age and Progressive Era

http://www.cohums.ohio-state.edu/history/projects/Lessons_US/Gilded_Age/Coal_Mining/default.htm

This extensive Web research site contains valuable information on coal mining in the late nineteenth and early twentieth centuries. Included are photographs, reprinted period articles, and a discussion of the dangers associated with coal mining.

Haymarket Square, 1886

http://www.chicagohs.org/dramas/

The Dramas of the Haymarket earned the 2001 American Association for History and Computing (AAHC) Multimedia Prize for Web Sites. The content is first-rate, well written, and engaging. The resources are well documented and the design includes a nice balance of images and text as well as a consistent layout throughout. The material is expertly arranged. The site is an excellent resource for all audiences from high school to the university to the casual observer interested in Chicago history.

Homestead, Pennsylvania, 1892

http://www.cohums.ohio-state.edu/history/projects/HomesteadStrike1892/
PennMilitiaInField/pennmilitiainfield.htm
http://www.history.ohio-state.edu/projects/HomesteadStrike1892/

The first Web resource site examines the role that the Pennsylvania state militia played in quelling the Homestead steel strike. The second Web resource provides a collection of historical documents pertaining to the strike and the reaction it caused throughout the country.

Inventors for a New Age

Alexander Graham Bell, 1847–1922

http://memory.loc.gov/ammem/bellhtml/bellhome.html

This outstanding Web site maintained by the Library of Congress and its American Memory division contains a multitude of research materials covering the entire life of Alexander Graham Bell, including his written correspondence, photographic images, and a detailed discussion of his invention of the telephone.

Thomas A. Edison, 1847–1931

http://www.hfmgv.org/exhibits/edison/tae.html

Sponsored by the Henry Ford Museum and Greenfield Village, this exciting research site lends itself to revealing the complexities of Edison's personality. Titled Thomas A. Edison and the Menlo Park Laboratory, this site chronicle the efforts by Greenfield Village to preserve and showcase the tremendous accomplishments of Edison.

John Wanamaker, 1838–1922

http://www.srmason-sj.org/council/journal/3-mar/quender.html
http://www.wanamakerorgan.com/

Providing a thorough narrative of the life and times of Philadelphian John Wanamaker, known as "America's Greatest Merchant," this interesting first Web site, produced by *Scottish Rite Journal*, includes photographs and testimonials to America's first successful major retailer. The second site connects with the "Friends of the Wanamaker Organ, Inc.," a historical preservation group interested in preserving the style and substance of Wanamaker's lavish turn-of-the-century department stores.

Frank Lloyd Wright, 1867–1959

http://www.prairiestyles.com/wright.htm

Considered one of America's greatest architects, Wright became world renowned for his stunning private residences and dramatic public buildings. This excellent Web resource provides extensive knowledge of Wright's life, work, and legacy to American architecture.

Writers, Philosophers, and Social Activists

Jane Addams, 1860–1935

http://www.uic.edu/jaddams/hull/hull_house.html

Produced by the University of Chicago Hull House Museum, this excellent narrative essay chronicles the life of social reformer Jane Addams. This Web resource site contains an extensive bibliography and informational links for those wishing to learn more about this famous settlement house pioneer.

Susan B. Anthony, 1820–1906

http://www.susanbanthonyhouse.org/

Susan B. Anthony, regarded as the foremost leader in the early women's rights movement in the United States, advocated that women be given the right to vote and stressed the importance of economic independence for women as a means toward emancipation. The Susan B. Anthony House Web site offers a complete background on this remarkable woman, including a virtual tour of Anthony's residence in Rochester, New York.

William Jennings Bryan, 1860–1925

http://iberia.vassar.edu/1896/1896home.html

Under the rubric "Presidential Election of 1896," Web authors Rebecca Edwards and Sarah DeFeo have created an interesting and through Web resource covering the presidential election of 1896. Here the researcher will find links to topics pertinent to this pivotal national election, including a list of all the key political players and Bryan's famous "Cross of Gold" speech delivered to the Democratic National Convention in July 1896 in Chicago.

Eugene Debs, 1855–1926

http://www.eugenevdebs.com/

Eugene Debs, labor organizer and socialist, worked tirelessly on behalf of American laborers. Long a leader of the American Railroad Union, he led the strike against the Pullman Company of Chicago in 1893, resulting in his arrest and imprisonment for union organizing. This Web site, created by the Eugene V. Debs Foundation, seeks to inform today's audiences of the importance of this nineteenth- and twentieth-century social reformer.

W.E.B. Du Bois, 1868–1963

http://historymatters.gmu.edu/text/1642d-WEB.html

W.E.B Du Bois is considered the leading African-American intellectual of the twentieth century and a man consumed with seeking economic, social, and political justice for African-Americans. He wrote tirelessly about the African Diaspora, especially in his book *Souls of Black Folk* (1903). This Web site features Du Bois's attack on the racial accommodation and gradualism advocated by Booker T. Washington.

Sarah Orne Jewett, 1849–1909

http://www.public.coe.edu/~theller/soj/sj-index.htm

Known as a "regionalist" because her writings captured the flavor of her native New England, Sarah Orne Jewett is most remembered for her book of stories, *The Country of the Pointed Firs* (1896). This excellent Web site is produced by Terry Heller of Coe College and contains an exhaustive collection of Jewett's writings.

Mary Harris (Mother) Jones, 1837–1930

http://www.kentlaw.edu/ilhs/majones.htm

Mother Jones was an enigmatic individual and tireless labor organizer working on behalf of the United Mine Workers of America. She was a free-ranging spirit speaking out against social and political injustices that she felt were damaging to American society. This Web site sponsored by the Illinois Labor History Society provides an excellent narrative of Mother Jones's life.

John Muir, 1838–1914

http://www.yosemite.ca.us/john_muir_exhibit/writings/

John Muir became America's first conservationist and activist for the preservation of wildlife and forest areas, both revered and reviled for his efforts. This informative Web site explores the life of John Muir and provides extensive links chronicling his life and professional contributions.

Frederick Jackson Turner, 1861–1932

http://www.theatlantic.com/issues/qgsep/ets/turn.htm

The American historian Frederick Jackson Turner presented his "frontier thesis" at the American Historical Association's 1893 meeting at the Chicago World's Columbian Exposition, thereby setting the stage for a rethinking of America's historical beginnings. Turner's thesis influenced an entire generation of historians, but most importantly how Americans came to view themselves and their past. This Web site, provided by the *Atlantic Monthly*, reprints an 1896 article by Turner titled "The Problem of the West."

Mark Twain, 1835–1910

http://etext.lib.virginia.edu/railton/index2.html

This excellent Web site, produced by Stephen Railton and the University of Virginia Library, introduces the Web reader to the experience of encountering "Mark Twain in His Times." Featured are online texts of Twain's writings, lesson plans, student projects, archived texts, bibliographies, and featured Mark Twain links.

Walt Whitman, 1819–92

http://memory.loc.gov/ammem/wwhome.html

Author of *Leaves of Grass* (1855), Whitman is best known for a remarkable collection of observations about American life, history, politics, geography, occupations, and speech. The American Memory Web page is an excellent source of information concerning the enigmatic Whitman, his life, and his writings.

Frances Willard, 1839–98

http://www.library.wisc.edu/etext/WIReader/Contents/Pioneer.html

Frances Willard was another of the dynamic women living and working during the Gilded Age. Long a champion of women's rights, she dedicated her life to elevating the status of women. She was one of the founding members of the Women's Christian Temperance Union. This Web site, sponsored by the University of Wisconsin, Madison Library System and the State Historical Society of Wisconsin, is an excellent source of regional Wisconsin history.

American Expansionism in the Gilded Age: Manifest Destiny and the Spanish-American War

The Age of Imperialism

http://www.smplanet.com/imperialism/toc.html

Historians have characterized the actions of the United States during the Spanish-American War as one of overt expansionism fueled by racism. This online history resource of the period examines United States interest in the Pacific Rim especially the Philippines, the Boxer Rebellion in China, and the Spanish-American War of 1898.

Historical Museum of Southern Florida: The Spanish-American War

http://www.historical-museum.org/history/war/war.htm

Florida, lying only sixty miles from Cuba, became a central staging point for American military forces embarking on their invasion of Cuba. This web site pays homage to the Cuban heritage in Florida and for those who fought for independence from Spain.

The Spanish-American War Centennial Web Site

http://www.spanamwar.com/

The Spanish-American War Centennial Web Site is an ambitious site detailing the American military campaigns against the Spanish. This extensive collection of materials includes a chronology of the war; bibliographic sources; back-

ground of the Cuban Revolution of 1895–98; eyewitness reports written by pro-
tagonists on both sides; the role of the American press in promoting the war; music
written about the war; and links to events, exhibits, and Rough Rider activities.

The Spanish-American War in Motion Pictures

http://memory.loc.gov/ammem/sawhtml/sawhome.html

The Spanish-American War was the first war chronicled in the new medium of
motion pictures. This Library of Congress Web site contains sixty-eight motion
pictures produced by Edison Manufacturing Company and the American
Mutoscope and Biograph Company, whose owner was the inventor Thomas
Edison. Many of the films were shot on location in the United States, Cuba, and
the Philippines, depicting soldiers, important personalities, and military parades.
This is a highly recommended resource for those incorporating new materials
into the study of the Spanish-American War.

The World of 1898: The Spanish-American War

http://www.loc.gov/rr/hispanic/1898/

This Library of Congress Web site provides excellent source materials, especially
documenting the people and places that factored into the fighting of the war.

Topical Issues

African-Americans and the U.S. Navy

http://www.history.navy.mil/photos/prs-tpic/af-amer/afam-usn.htm

Produced by the Naval Historical Center in conjunction with the United States
Navy, this interesting Web site contains a wide array of historical documents on
the contributions of African-Americans serving as sailors in the U.S. Navy.
Complete with a wide array of downloadable photographs, this Web site is
highly recommended for high school history courses.

Americans of Asian Indian Origin

http://www-users.cs.umn.edu/~seetala/India/Articles/article001.html
http://www.hist.umn.edu/~erikalee/aahist.html

Produced and written by Srirajasekhar Bobby Koritala, this first Web resource
traces the origins of individuals of Asian Indian origin and their arrival in North
America. Arriving in the United States as a student, the author states that his
intention was to "get a great education" and then return to India. A change in
plans led to this splendid Web site devoted to the history of Asian Indian traders

and immigrants to North America. The second URL is a Web resource on Asian-American history created by assistant professor of history Erika Lee at the University of Minnesota. This site contains a wealth of information surrounding Asian immigration to North America.

Blackface, Blackeye, Racist Images of African-Americans 1890–1940

http://www.authentichistory.com/images/blackface.html

Part of an expansive Web site supported by the Authentic History Center, Primary Sources from American Culture, this selection on racist images found in American advertisements, postcards, and musical sheet music targeting African-Americans is an important resource for cultural historians. Collections include images, collected speeches, and music downloads from antebellum America to the new millennium.

Cartoons of the Gilded Age and Progressive Era

http://www.history.ohio-state.edu/projects/uscartoons/GAPECartoons.htm

Sponsored by the Ohio State History Department, this excellent resource provides some of the best critique of these two eras.

Scott Joplin, 1868–1917

http://www.lsjunction.com/people/joplin.htm

Considered the Father of Ragtime Music, Joplin was a popular figure within the African-American community. This Web site traces the rise of Joplin's career and the continuing popularity of ragtime music.

Native Americans

http://www.americanwest.com/pages/indians.htm

An extensive collection of Native American Web resource links is part of this award-winning Web site supported by The American West organization, which celebrates the heritage and culture of the American West.

Supreme Court: *Plessy v. Ferguson*, 1896

http://www.sgs-austin.org/schoollife/8a/index.htm

In 1892 Homer Plessy, an African-American, refused to sit in a separate railroad car as mandated by the state of Louisiana, which in 1890 had adopted a law proclaiming "equal but separate accommodations for the white and colored races." Created by the eighth-grade Language Arts and Social Studies students at Saint Gabriel's Catholic School in Austin, Texas, this exuberant Web site contains valuable information on the struggle of African-Americans to achieve their equitable share of the American Dream.

Vaudeville

http://memory.loc.gov/ammem/vshtml/vshome.html

Before television, radio, and movies there was vaudeville! This American Memory Web site hosted by the Library of Congress contains a wealth of information on this popular turn-of-the-century entertainment medium. Included are sound recordings, motion picture clips, theater playbills and programs, and much more.

Westward the Empire: Omaha's World Fair of 1898

http://www.unotv.unomaha.edu/wte.html

This interesting Web site, the result of a television documentary produced by the UNO Television Network in conjunction with the Nebraska ETV Network, chronicles the Trans-Mississippi and International Exposition, which debuted on June 1, 1898, in Omaha, Nebraska. This interesting Web narrative explores the celebration of the West's economic and cultural development as seen appropriately enough through personalities such as William Jennings Bryan.

Chapter 12

The Age of Roosevelt

Andrew Kersten and Anne Rothfeld

Metasites

American Memory

http://lcweb2.loc.gov/ammem

This Web site is maintained by the Library of Congress and ought to be the first site visited by anyone interested in American history.

New Deal Network

http://newdeal.feri.org

The Franklin and Eleanor Roosevelt Institute sponsors this Web site, which is the starting point for all issues, historical figures, and events about the Age of Roosevelt.

Historical Figures

Herbert C. Hoover

Herbert C. Hoover Presidential Library and Museum

http://www.hoover.nara.gov

The Hoover Presidential Library and Museum constructed this Web site, which contains information on Hoover's presidency, education modules, and research guides to both the Hoover Presidential Papers and the papers of Rose Wilder

Lane and her mother Laura Ingalls Wilder. Rose Wilder wrote one of the first biographies of Hoover, published in 1919. This site, the best place to start for topics on Hoover, is updated weekly and has links to related sites.

White House: Herbert Hoover

http://www.whitehouse.gov/history/presidents/hh31.html

Maintained by the White House staff, this page has biographies of President Hoover and the First Lady, Lou Henry Hoover, with links to the text of Hoover's inaugural address and to the Hoover Presidential Library.

Huey P. Long

Every Man a King: Excerpts from Huey Long's Autobiography

http://www.ssa.gov./history/huey.html

Constructed by the Social Security Administration, this site contains excerpts from Long's autobiography, *Every Man a King*, published in 1933.

My First Days in the White House: Excerpts from Huey Long's "Second Autobiography"

http://www.ssa.gov./history/hueywhouse.html

The Social Security Administration also maintains this page, in which one can find excerpts from all eight chapters of Long's 1935 book, *My First Days in the White House*.

Anna Eleanor Roosevelt

Eleanor Roosevelt: The American Woman

http://www.geocities.com/CollegePark/Library/4142/index.html

Created by Deborah K. Girkin, this excellent site contains extensive biographical and bibliographical information, documents, pictures, cartoons, and links to other sites on ER. A good place to start a search on Eleanor Roosevelt.

Eleanor Roosevelt Center at Val-Kill

http://www.ervk.org

Val-Kill was Eleanor Roosevelt's cottage along the Hudson River. The Val-Kill Center's purpose is "to preserve Eleanor Roosevelt's home as a vibrant living memorial, a center for the exchange of significant ideas and a catalyst for change and for the betterment of the human condition." The center's Web page provides information, photographs, and an extensive list of useful links to topics and issues concerning her.

Eleanor Roosevelt Resource Page

http://personalweb.smcvt.edu/smahady/ercover.htm

This is a wonderful place to start any Internet search relating to ER. The site, authored by Sherry S. Mahady, contains biographical and bibliographical information, quotes from scholars and peers, documents from ER's newspaper column, newspaper articles, letters from her papers and the National Archives, video clips, and links to other sites with information, pictures, and documents pertaining to Eleanor Roosevelt.

Franklin D. Roosevelt

FDR Cartoon Collection Database

http://www.nisk.k12.ny.us/fdr

At this award-winning site, constructed by Paul Bachorz of Niskayuna High School in Niskayuna, New York, one can find an extensive collection of over 30,000 FDR cartoons taken from newspapers and magazines during the 1930s and 1940s. There are also links to other Web sites, suggestions for school teachers, and Roosevelt's inaugural addresses.

Franklin D. Roosevelt Library and Museum

http://www.academic.marist.edu/fdr

Created by the staff of the Roosevelt Presidential Library, this site provides short biographies of the president and the First Lady. Additionally, the site contains several guides to the collections at the Roosevelt Presidential Library. Increasingly the library is putting documents online. Now accessible is a collection of several thousand documents from the White House safe files during the Roosevelt years. Finally, there is an exceptional, copyright-free, online photograph database.

White House: Franklin D. Roosevelt

http://www.whitehouse.gov/history/presidents/fr32.html

The White House staff maintains this site, which contains short biographies of Franklin and Eleanor Roosevelt. There are links to the texts of FDR's inaugural addresses.

The Great Depression

African-Americans and the New Deal

http://newdeal.feri.org/texts/subject.htm

This location, part of the New Deal Network, contains dozens of documents relating to blacks and the New Deal.

American Memory: FSA-OWI Photographs

http://lcweb2.loc.gov/ammem/fsowhome.html

American Memory, maintained by the Library of Congress, is a wonderful Web site for all topics in American history, with thousands of primary sources that relate to the Age of Roosevelt. This particular location contains over 50,000 (including 1,600 in color) Farm Security Administration and Office of War Information photographs covering the years 1935 to 1945.

The Shenandoah Chapter of the Civilian Conservation Corps

http://pages.prodigy.com/reunion/ccc.htm

The Shenandoah Chapter of the CCC, an organization of former agency workers, scholars, and interested people, maintains this site, which contains pictures, stories, poetry, and links to other sites concerning the CCC.

Dust Bowl Refugees in California

http://www.sfmuseum.org/hist8/ok.html

The Museum of the City of San Francisco maintains a Web page on California history that has this section on Dust Bowl refugees. It contains primary sources and photographs.

The Voices from the Dust Bowl: The Charles L. Todd and Robert Sonkin Migrant Worker Collection, 1940–1941

http://lcweb2.loc.gov/ammem/afctshtml/tshome.html

This page, part of American Memory, contains oral histories, photographs, and dozens of other primary documents relating to the Dust Bowl.

New Deal Art in South Carolina

http://people.clemson.edu/~hiotts/index.htm

This online exhibit of New Deal art in South Carolina, maintained by Susan Giaimo Hiott, has art from the state and links to New Deal art in other states, topics about the Age of Roosevelt, and exhibits from other libraries and museums. A visit to this page is worthwhile even if South Carolinian art is not one's primary topic.

A New Deal for the Arts

http://www.nara.gov/exhall/newdeal/newdeal.html

The National Archives and Records Administration maintains a Web version of this exhibit. The page has several good examples of New Deal art in various forms, including painting, photographs, and posters.

The Trials of the Scottsboro Boys

http://www.law.umkc.edu/faculty/projects/FTrials/scottsboro/scottsb.htm

This location is part of the larger Famous American Trials Web site created by Doug Linder. The page on the Scottsboro boys contains a short history, biographical and bibliographical information, photographs, and trial documents.

Social Security Administration Online History

http://www.ssa.gov/history

The United States Social Security Administration built this page, which contains oral histories, video and audio clips, documents, photographs, brief biographies, and guides to the Social Security Administration archives.

Supreme Court Decisions (Legal Information Institute)

http://supct.law.cornell.edu:8080/supct/

The Legal Information Institute and Cornell University sponsor this Supreme Court decisions Web site, which is an excellent place to gain quick access to decisions from the Wagner Act to Japanese Relocation. The site also contains general information on the Supreme Court.

Works Progress (later Projects) Administration (WPA) Folklore Project and Federal Writers Project

http://lcweb.loc.gov/ammem/wpaintro/

This American Memory site has several thousand WPA folklore and federal writers projects representing over 300 authors from twenty-four states.

WPA Murals and Artwork from Lane Technical High School Collection

http://www.lanehs.com/art.htm

Maintained by Flora Doody, the director of Lane Technical High School's Artwork Restoration Project, this site has lots of WPA artwork, including eleven frescoes, two oil on canvas murals, an oil on steel fire curtain, two carved mahogany murals, and two cast concrete fountain statues. The site also contains artwork created for the General Motors Exhibition at The Century of Progress, Chicago's World Fair (1933–34).

WPA's California Gold: Northern California Folk Music from the Thirties

http://lcweb2.loc.gov/ammem/afccchtml/cowhome.html

This American Memory Web site includes sound recordings, still photographs, drawings, and written documents from a variety of European ethnic and English-and Spanish-speaking communities in Northern California. The collection comprises thirty-five hours of folk music recorded in twelve languages representing numerous ethnic groups and 185 musicians. This collection is well documented and easy to use.

Chapter 13

World War II

Home Front
Anne Rothfeld and Alexander Zukas

German Prisoners of War in Clinton, Mississippi
http://www2.netdoor.com/~allardma/powcamp2.html

Mike Allard's site has minimal text but some interesting pictures of German prisoners at the Clinton, Mississippi, POW camp.

The Homefront During World War II
http://www.gettysburg.edu/~mbirkner/fys120/homefront.html

Professor Michael Birkner of Gettysburg College created this Web site for his first-year seminar class. The site hosts oral histories of the residents of Adams County, Pennsylvania, a photo gallery of Gettysburg College during the war, advertising from the war years, and excerpts from the *Gettysburg Times* concerning everyday life on the home front. The site clarifies how the war affected small-town America.

The Japanese-American Internment
http://www.geocities.com/Athens/8420/main.html
http://www.oz.net/~cyu/internment/main.html (mirror site)

This is a rich and very developed site concerning the internment of Japanese-Americans during World War II. Included are sections on prewar intelligence reports on the loyalty of Japanese-Americans, the politics of internment, the

state of mind and intentions of policy makers, life in the camps, the impact of
the camps on those detained, and firsthand accounts by survivors. The site,
maintained and regularly updated by C. John Yu, contains a large number of
links to other Web sites exploring issues surrounding the internment of Japanese-
Americans.

Japanese-American Internment (Resource Page for Teachers)

http://www.umass.edu/history/institute_dir/internment.html

The History Institute at the University of Massachusetts at Amherst sponsors
this site, which is perhaps the best place to start searching for material on the
internment of Japanese-Americans. Well organized and with dozens of Web
links to documents, pictures, and related camp information, this site, designed
for K-12 teachers, provides rich primary sources for classroom curricula.

Japanese-American Internment at Harmony

http://www.lib.washington.edu/exhibits/harmony/Exhibit/default.html

The University of Washington Libraries created this Web page, which contains
primary source material including letters, the camp newspaper, drawings, pictures, and other documents. It is a useful place to begin an Internet search about
internment; researchers should consult the other sites on internment in this section in order to compare Harmony with other camps.

Japanese American Internment in Arizona

http://dizzy.library.arizona.edu/images/jpamer/wraintro.html

This exhibit, directed by Roger Myers of the University of Arizona, has maps,
photographs, primary documents, such as the text of Executive Order 9066,
and poetry.

Japanese-American Internment and San Francisco

http://www.sfmuseum.org/war/evactxt.html

This site, maintained by the Museum of the City of San Francisco, contain
dozens of newspaper articles about Japanese-American removal, photographs
(including those by Dorothea Lange), contemporary accounts, and related information about internment.

Japanese Internment Camps During the Second World War

http://www.lib.utah.edu/spc/photo/9066/9066.htm

This online photograph exhibit, sponsored by the University of Utah Special Collections Department, displays a sampling of the library's collections concerning the internment of Japanese-Americans, particularly at the Topaz and Tule Lake camps.

The Lions' History: Researching World War II Images of African-Americans

http://www.nara.gov/publications/prologue/burger.html

Barbara Lewis Burger of the National Archives gathered this remarkable series of photos after immersing herself in African-American military history and researching life on the home front in the 1940s. Her intent was to produce a publication that both fills a visual documentation void and stimulates interest in both black history and the holdings of the National Archives. This Web site does achieve both goals.

OWI Photographs

http://lcweb2.loc.gov/ammem/fsowhome.html

This site contains thousands of photographs of the home front taken for the Office of War Information during the war years. It is part of the American Memory project maintained by the Library of Congress.

Pictures of World War II

http://www.nara.gov/nara/nn/nns/ww2photo.html

The National Archives has a treasure-trove of images from World War II. The war was documented on a huge scale by thousands of photographers and artists who created millions of pictures. American military photographers representing all the armed services covered battlefronts around the world. Every activity of the war was photographed. On the home front, the many federal war agencies produced and collected pictures, posters, and cartoons on such subjects as war production, rationing, and civilian relocation. Among the areas covered in this photo ensemble are Leaders, The Home Front, Supply and Support, Rest and Relaxation, Aid and Comfort, and Victory and Peace. If a picture is worth a thousand words, then little more needs to be said.

Rosie the Riveter and Other Women: World War II Heroes

http://www.u.arizona.edu/~kari/rosie.htm

This site contains short vignettes about women's roles in World War II, when women were factory workers, nurses, doctors, soldiers, journalists, prostitutes, and subjects of propaganda art. The site provides a different perspective on the war and some little-known information. A number of World War II propaganda posters illustrate the points in the texts.

Rutgers Oral History Archives of World War II

http://fas-history.rutgers.edu/oralhistory/orlhom.htm

The Rutgers World War II oral history project was funded by the Rutgers class of 1942 and directed by Sandra Stewart Holyoak. Several dozen oral histories from veterans and civilians are available for download (in Adobe Acrobat format).

San Francisco During World War II

http://www.sfmuseum.org/1906/ww2.html

This site, maintained by the Museum of the City of San Francisco, contains information about San Francisco during the war years. Most of the primary sources on this site come from the *San Francisco News*.

Topaz Camp

http://www.millardcounty.com/topazcamp.html

Millard County, Utah, hosts this site, which provides a brief overview of Topaz, a Japanese-American "relocation camp" located in Millard County during World War II. The site explains the background of the relocation of Japanese-Americans, life in the camp, and conditions in the desert. The site also boasts picture postcards of the camp.

What Did You Do in the War, Grandma? Rhode Island Women During World War II

http://www.stg.brown.edu/projects/WWII_Women/tocCS.html

An oral history of Rhode Island women during World War II, written by students in the Honors English Program at South Kingstown High School, this site provides not only information about lesser-known aspects of the war, but also a good model of action for teachers interested in using the Internet for class projects.

World War II Posters: Powers of Persuasion

http://www.nara.gov/exhall/powers/powers.html

The National Archives and Records Administration maintains this page, which has thirty-three war posters and one sound file. The page is divided into two categories representing the two psychological approaches used in rallying public support for the war.

World War II Poster Collection

http://www.library.nwu.edu/govpub/collections/wwii-posters/

The Northwestern University Library's Government Publications division maintains this site. It has a searchable database of 300 wartime posters.

Military History

Alexander Zukas

A-Bomb WWW Museum

http://www.csi.ad.jp/ABOMB/

This online project is a Japanese-hosted Web site designed to inform visitors about the effects of atomic weapons on Hiroshima and Nagasaki and to encourage discussions about world peace. Produced by the Hiroshima City University Department of Computer Science, the site gives a different perspective on the dropping of atomic weapons on Japan from that usually found in the United States. The creators of the Web site state, "The website is neither meant to condemn nor condone the bombing, but is meant as a way for people to express their views on how to achieve peace, on what peace is, and other thoughts about peace." Although the site is a somewhat random collection of material, it will stimulate student discussion of the issues surrounding the use of atomic weapons at the end of World War II and the cultural legacy of the bomb.

Achtung Panzer

http://www.achtungpanzer.com/panzer.htm

One of the many enthusiast sites dedicated to German armor. This one features many illustrations, tables of technical data, and a large number of links to other World War II sites.

Atomic Bomb Decision

http://www.dannen.com/decision/index.html

This site contains full-text documents on the arguments for and against the use of atomic weapons on human targets in the months leading up to the dropping of the atomic bomb on Hiroshima. Most of the originals are in the U.S. National Archives.

The Battle of Britain

http://www.raf.mod.uk/bob1940/bobhome.html

This is a detailed and extensive Web site about the aerial battle over Great Britain in 1940. Hosted by the Royal Air Force, it contains the official reports and a day-by-day account of the four-month battle.

China Defensive, 1942–1945: The China Theater of Operations

http://www2.army.mil/cmh-pg/brochures/72-38/72-38.htm

This account of World War II in China was prepared in the U.S. Army Center of Military History by Mark D. Sherry. In it he explains the differences between the Chinese, European, and Pacific war fronts, what the United States hoped to achieve in China, and the ultimate result of U.S. interventions, supplies, and strategic intentions. The site helps fill out the picture of World War II in this major theatre of the war.

Codebreaking and Secret Weapons in World War II

http://home.earthlink.net/~nbrass1/enigma.htm

This site deals with some of the secret weapons developed by the combatants in World War II and how the Allies found out about the ones the Axis had developed. The site provides a window on the clandestine but militarily significant aspects of the war.

Dad's War: Finding and Telling Your Father's World War II Story

http://members.aol.com/dadswar/index.htm

If you can tolerate the small promotional effort for his works on writing personal history, Wes Johnson has done a service with this index of personal histories and initial instructions for writing your own history for a family member who served in World War II (and, by extension, any war).

East Anglia: The Air War

http://www.stable.demon.co.uk/

Contains a series of informative essays with illustrations concerning various air forces and the aircraft flown during World War II. The site also provides an excellent index of links to related Web pages and a bibliography of print reference works.

Feldgrau.com: A German Military History Research Site 1919–1945

http://www.feldgrau.com/

A detailed Web site developed by an independent scholar working on a number of projects related to German World War II military history. It covers "the history of the units and formations of the various military, paramilitary, and auxiliary forces from 1933–45." Includes discussions of various battles and a bibliography of nearly five hundred titles.

504th World War II Home Page

http://www.geocities.com/~the 504thpir/index.html

An example of the many sites dedicated to military units, this one chronicles the experiences of the 504th Parachute Infantry Regiment during World War II.

Guadalcanal Online

http://www.geocities.com/Heartland/Plains/6672/canal_index.html

Detailed discussion of the first major American offensive in the war in the Pacific.

Hyperwar: A Hypertext History of the Second World War

http://www.ibiblio.org/hyperwar/

A linked anthology of articles related to World War II, many of them discussing specific battles in detail, along with links to other sources.

Imperial Japanese Navy Page

http://www.combinedfleet.com/

Enthusiast Jon Parshall has created a detailed index to links about the Japanese navy during World War II, including detailed histories of individual vessels.

The Luftwaffe Home Page

http://www.ww2.dk/

This site provides data on the *Luftwaffe* and an index of links to *Luftwaffe*-related Web pages.

A Marine Diary: My Experiences on Guadalcanal

http://www.gnt.net/~jrube/index2.html

Entries from the diary of a marine who served at Guadalcanal, with a large set of links to related World War II resources on the Internet.

Midway

http://www.history.navy.mil/photos/events/wwii-pac/midway/midway.htm

This Department of the Navy Naval Historical Center site contains a detailed narrative and excellent photographs of the battle. This is a good place to start gathering information about this important battle, often considered the turning point of the war in the Pacific. The site contains a FAQ section and a list of related resources.

Nanjing Massacre Archive

http://www.cnd.org/njmassacre/index.html

The *China News Digest* hosts this extensive site on the famous Nanjing Massacre in 1937–38 in China, including the war crimes testimony and trial after the war.

Naval Air War in the Pacific

http://www.ixpres.com/ag1caf/navalwar

Photos and paintings of American air combat during World War II.

Normandy: 1944

http://normandy.eb.com/

The *Encyclopedia Britannica*'s multimedia examination of the Normandy invasion.

The Pacific War: The U.S. Navy

http://www.microworks.net/pacific/

This page, a conscious complement and counterpoint to the Imperial Japanese Navy page above, informs visitors of the U.S. Navy's contribution to the overall victory that ended World War II with as much awesome detail as can be mustered. Comparing the information on both Web sites will give the student of World War II naval warfare an excellent overview of the military strength and tactics of these two major Pacific powers. The sites also contain short profiles of naval leaders and personal histories of veterans.

A People at War

http://www.nara.gov/exhall/people/people.html

This site, an online exhibition by the National Archives, focuses much more on the people who served than on a traditional history of the war. It includes a brief discussion of events leading up to the war and links to related sites.

Propaganda Leaflets of the Second World War

http://www.cobweb.nl/jmoonen/

Most of the propaganda shown in these pages is anti-Nazi (airdropped by the U.K./U.S. Allied Air Forces). The Nazis used the same weapon of propaganda and these Nazi leaflets are shown here also. The Web site's author warns that the images and texts of the Nazi propaganda leaflets can be disturbing and offensive on religious, racial, or ethnic grounds. The material, which is produced exactly from the originals, provides visitors with good comparisons on the use of symbols and propaganda during the war.

Red Steel

http://www.algonet.se/~toriert/

Enthusiast Thorleif Olsson's extensive Web site on Russian tanks and armored vehicles.

Return to Midway

http://www.nationalgeographic.com/features/98/midway/

National Geographic has created this multimedia site featuring images and streaming video of the wrecks of the carriers sunk at the Battle of Midway.

The Russian Campaign, 1941–1945: A Photo Diary

http://www.geipelnet.com/war_albums/otto/ow_011.html

This site is the diary of a German soldier along with pictures he took of his experiences on the Russian front with an antitank battalion. It covers the whole span of the

Russian campaign and provides an on-the-ground look at the fortunes of German troops and rare scenes of the fighting between German and Russian forces.

U-Boat Net

http://uboat.net/

A comprehensive study of the German U-boat, including maps, technology, and profiles of more than 1,100 German submarines employed during World War II.

Women Come to the Front: Journalists, Photographers, and Broadcasters During World War II

http://lcweb.loc.gov/exhibits/wcf/wcf0001.html

This Library of Congress site documents the work of eight female war correspondents, most of whom worked overseas while a few documented the home front. The site provides some corrective to the male-dominated discussions of World War II life at the front while documenting continued male prerogative in the periodical business.

The Women's Army Corps

http://www.army.mil/cmh-pg/brochures/wac/wac.htm

The United States Army has developed this online article about the Women's Army Corps during World War II.

The World at War

http://www.euronet.nl/users/wilfried/ww2/ww2.htm

Wilfried Braakhuis has created an extremely detailed timeline of the war, with illustrations, statistics, and a very large number of links, organized by relevant dates. This graphic-intensive site takes a while to load, but is worth looking at.

World War Two in Europe

http://www.historyplace.com/worldwar2/timeline/ww2time.htm

Part of The History Place, a large Web site dedicated to assisting students and educators, this is a World War II timeline with links to illustrations and short articles on specific events.

World War II on the Web

http://www.geocities.com/Athens/Oracle/2691/welcome.htm

An index to more than 400 Web sites concerned with World War II, many of them highly specialized.

World War II Propaganda Posters (U.S.)

http://www.openstore.com/posters/index.html

This is an interesting collection of World War II posters from the United States. They range from recruiting posters to those exhorting greater patriotism, sacrifice, and secrecy. The posters provide an excellent window on wartime culture, at least as officially propagated by the U.S. government.

World War II Resources

http://metalab.unc.edu/pha/index.html

An extensive collection of historical documents from World War II based at the University of North Carolina, Chapel Hill.

World War II Seminar

http://ac.acusd.edu/History/classes/ww2/175.html

Class materials for a World War II history course from the University of San Diego, including an extended bibliography and several timelines created by students.

World War II Sites

http://www.geocities.com/dboals.geo/a-art1a.html#WORLD%20WAR%20II

This is an excellent directory to over 200 Web sites on all aspects of World War II. The major purpose of this directory is to encourage the use of the World Wide Web as a tool for learning and teaching and to provide some help for teachers in locating and using the resources of the Internet in the classroom. This directory is a superb place to start searching for Web sites on World War II.

The World War II Sounds and Pictures Page

http://www.earthstation1.com/wwii.html

Sounds, video, and images of aircraft, warships, propaganda posters, and many other items related to World War II.

The World War II Study: North Africa

http://www.topedge.com/panels/ww2/na/index.html

In this site, many issues regarding the North Africa campaign of the Allies from 1940 to 1943 receive a fresh look. The author examines the importance of North Africa to the Allies and Axis and dispels myths about the campaigns and personalities of the North African theater. He provides a timeline of the conflict and discusses supply issues, troop levels, weaponry, commanders, tactics, and high-command disputes.

World War II Timeline

http://history.acusd.edu/gen/WW2Timeline/start.html

A fairly good and general timeline for World War II that includes a very valuable list of additional links, interesting pictures, maps, and documents, and a good bibliography. Includes some student pages. A first-rate site by Steve Schoenherr of the University of San Diego's History Department.

Chapter 14

The Cold War

Margaret M. Manchester and Alexander Zukas

American Experience: Race for the Superbomb

http://www.pbs.org/wgbh/pages/amex/bomb

This PBS companion site explores a top secret U.S. Cold War program to build a weapon more powerful than the atomic bomb dropped on Japan. The site includes audio clips, a timeline, primary documents, and other educational materials.

The Avalon Project: Documents in Law, History, and Diplomacy

http://www.yale.edu/lawweb/avalon/coldwar.htm

Maintained by the Yale University Law School, this site contains basic documents relating to American Foreign Policy 1941–49; the United States Atomic Energy Commission proceedings in the Matter of J. Robert Oppenheimer; The Warsaw Security Pact: May 14, 1955; State Department Papers Relating to the Foreign Relations of the United States, Vol. X, Part 1, 1958–60; the U-2 Incident: 1960; the RB-47 Airplane Incident: July–September 1960; and the Cuban Missile Crisis.

The Berlin Airlift

http://www.wpafb.af.mil/museum/history/postwwii/ba.htm

This Web site is part of the larger online exhibit entitled U.S. Air Force Museum, Post–World War II History Gallery 1946–50s. The focus is primarily military. The site is a good source of information and images of the aircraft used to airlift provisions to the inhabitants of Berlin.

Chronology of Russian History: The Soviet Period

http://www.departments.bucknell.edu/russian/chrono3.html

The Bucknell University History Department maintains this chronology of Soviet history from 1917 to 1991. The chronology contains numerous links to primary and secondary source materials that provide further information and background.

CIA and Assassinations: The Guatemala 1954 Documents

http://www.gwu.edu/~nsarchiv/NSAEBB/NSAEBB4/index.html

The National Security Archive is an independent, nongovernmental research institute and library located at George Washington University in Washington, D.C. The archive collects and publishes declassified documents acquired through the Freedom of Information Act. On May 23, 1997, the CIA released several hundred records verifying the CIA's involvement in the infamous 1954 coup in Guatemala at the height of the Cold War politics of "brinkmanship." Some of these documents, including an instructional guide on assassination found among the training files of the CIA's covert "Operation PBSUCCESS," are stored on this site.

CNN: Cold War

http://cnn.com/SPECIALS/cold.war/

This Web site was created to accompany the twelve-part series on the Cold War airing on CNN in the winter and spring of 1998–99. The Web site is a valuable resource because it provides an extraordinary diversity of materials, including multimedia and audio clips, interactive maps, primary documents, newspaper and journal coverage of the events, and transcripts of interviews that formed the basis for the series.

Cold War Hot Links: Web Resources Relating to the Cold War

http://www.stmartin.edu/~dprice/cold.war.html

David Price, an anthropologist at St. Martin's College in Lacey, Washington, has compiled an impressive list of links to Web sites that contain primary sources as well as essays and analyses examining the impact of the Cold War on American culture.

Cold War International History Project

http://cwihp.si.edu/default.htm

The Cold War International History Project (CWIHP) Web site was established at the Woodrow Wilson International Center for Scholars in Washington, D.C., in 1991. The project supports the full and prompt release of historical materials by governments on all sides of the Cold War. In addition to Western sources, the project has provided translations of documents from Eastern European archives that have been released since the collapse of communism in the late 1980s. Users may join discussion groups and download issues of the *Bulletin* issued by CWIHP.

The Cold War Museum

http://www.coldwar.org/

In 1996, Francis Gary Powers, Jr. and John C. Welch founded the Cold War Museum to preserve Cold War history and honor Cold War veterans. The Cold War Museum, a Smithsonian Affiliate Museum, endeavors to maintain a historically accurate record of the people, places, and events of the Cold War that will enable visitors to reflect upon the global geopolitical climate of that period (1940s to 1990s). On its Web site, the museum displays artifacts and memorabilia associated with various Cold War-related events, such as the Marshall Plan, the Berlin airlift, the Korean War, the building of the Berlin Wall, the U-2 incident, the Cuban Missile Crisis, the Vietnam War, President Gorbachev's glasnost, the fall of the Berlin Wall, and the collapse of the Soviet Union.

A Concrete Curtain: The Life and Death of the Berlin Wall

http://www.wall-berlin.org/gb/berlin.htm

This site contains a detailed history of the Berlin Wall from its creation to its destruction. Originally it was part of an exhibition comprising a hundred photographs for the Deutsches Historisches Museum in Berlin; this is a good place to start examining the historical and cultural significance of "The Wall."

The Costs of the Manhattan Project

http://www.brook.edu/FP/PROJECTS/NUCWCOST/MANHATTN.HTM

These estimates were prepared by the Brookings Institute and are part of the larger U.S. Nuclear Weapons Cost Study Project.

The Cuban Missile Crisis

http://www.personal.psu.edu/staff/r/x/rxb297/CUBA/MAIN.HTML

This site contains excellent links to primary and secondary source materials on the Cuban Missile Crisis, including the Library of Congress, the Federation of American Scientists, the State Department, the National Security Archive, and Khrushchev's memoirs. The site provides an overview of the crisis and discusses its causes, U.N. and Turkish involvement, and its outcome.

The Cuban Missile Crisis, 1962

http://www.state.gov/www/about_state/history/frusXI/index.html

This is the site for Volume XI of *Foreign Relations of the United States*, the official U.S. Department of State volume of documents dealing with the Cuban Missile Crisis. The entire volume or excerpts can be read online. A very important source for the official documents dealing with this crisis.

The Cuban Missile Crisis, 1962

http://www.fas.org/irp/imint/cuba.htm

The FAS, the intelligence resource program of the Federation of American Scientists, maintains this metasite. It contains links to online State Department documentation, analysis of Kennedy's advisers, the photographic evidence, transcripts of ExComm deliberations, and photographic evidence of the Soviet presence in Cuba until the 1980s.

The Cuban Missile Crisis, October 18–29, 1962

http://www.hpol.org/jfk/cuban/

This Web site contains audio files of a set of tape recordings released by the John F. Kennedy Library in October 1996. These recordings, made in the Oval Office, include President Kennedy's personal recollections of discussions, conversations with his advisers, and meetings with the Joint Chiefs of Staff and members of the president's executive committee. Transcripts of the audio files are included. A rich source of information on the American perspective of the crisis.

Documents Relating to American Foreign Policy: The Cold War

http://www.mtholyoke.edu/acad/intrel/coldwar.htm

The International Relations Program at Mount Holyoke College maintains this Web site. Arranged on a yearly basis from pre-1945 to recent retrospectives on the meaning and significance of the Cold War, this site contains hundreds of links to both primary and secondary source material—especially useful to students and researchers because of the variety of sources available.

Documents Relating to American Foreign Policy: Cuban Missile Crisis

http://www.mtholyoke.edu/acad/intrel/cuba.htm

This collection of links allows researchers and students access to newspaper coverage of the crisis, information relating to Soviet and Cuban perspectives, and essays and books by the most influential historians of this crisis.

Famous American Trials: Rosenbergs Trial, 1951

http://www.law.umkc.edu/faculty/projects/ftrials/rosenb/ROSENB.HTM

Created by Professor Douglas Linder of the University of Missouri, Kansas City School of Law, this Web site contains links to a wealth of firsthand materials, including excerpts from the trial transcript, the judge's sentencing statement, excerpts from appellate court decisions, images, the Rosenbergs' final letter to their sons, and a link to the Perlin Papers, a collection of about 250,000 pages related to the investigation, trial, and execution of Julius and Ethel Rosenberg. The papers were declassified in the 1970s.

Fifty Years from Trinity

http://www.seattletimes.com/trinity/supplement/internet.html

The *Seattle Times* compiled this list of Internet resources relating to the development of the atomic bomb and nuclear energy.

For European Recovery: The Fiftieth Anniversary of the Marshall Plan

http://lcweb.loc.gov/exhibits/marshall

An excellent online exhibit prepared by the Library of Congress, containing primary and secondary source materials on the Marshall Plan and links developed by the Koninklijke Bibliotheek (the National Library of the Netherlands) and other European libraries.

Harvard Project on Cold War Studies

http://www.fas.harvard.edu/~hpcws/

This annotated set of links relating to the study of the Cold War is prepared and maintained by the Davis Center for Russian Studies at Harvard University. The project intends to build on the achievements of the Cold War International History Project and the National Security Archive. The site also contains links to Harvard University's new *Journal of Cold War Studies*.

A History of the Berlin Wall in Text and Pictures

http://members.aol.com/johball/berlinwl.htm

This site was an entry in the Connecticut state competition for National History Day on May 10, 1997. It is a great resource for K-12 students to explore the history of the wall.

The Hungarian Revolution, 1956

http://www.osa.ceu.hu/archives/rip/1956/index.htm

Links are provided to both English-language and Hungarian resources, both primary and secondary.

An Introduction to National Archives Records Relating to the Cold War

http://www.nara.gov/publications/rip/rip107/rip107.html

Hosted by the National Archives, this metasite was compiled by Tim Wehrkamp. It identifies several representative series and data sets of textual, electronic, still picture, and motion picture records that document U.S. government policies, programs, and actions during the Cold War. The compilers have chosen records that illustrate the range and content of National Archives and Records Administration (NARA) holdings relating to this period. These records by no means represent all NARA-held documentation concerning the topic. The intended audience for this publication is graduate students and other researchers new to the field of Cold War history and unfamiliar with NARA records. It would be a good place for them to begin their research.

The National Security Archive Homepage

http://www.gwu.edu/~nsarchiv/

The National Security Archive is an independent, nongovernmental research institute and library located at George Washington University in Washington, D.C. The archive collects and publishes declassified documents gathered through the Freedom of Information Act (FOIA). The archive boasts the world's largest nongovernmental library of declassified documents, including thousands of documents relating to nuclear history, U.S.-Japanese relations, the Cuban Missile Crisis, and other crises of the 1960s and 1970s.

1948: The Alger Hiss Spy Case

http://www.thehistorynet.com/AmericanHistory/articles/1998/698_cover.htm

This site links to a June 1998 *American History* article by James Thomas Gay that examines the Alger Hiss case and the issues that still remain unresolved fifty years later.

The Real Thirteen Days: The Hidden History of the Cuban Missile Crisis

http://www.gwu.edu/~nsarchiv/nsa/cuba_mis_cri/

The National Security Archive has created an extensive Web site on the Cuban Missile Crisis. It includes the essays "Turning History on Its Head" by Philip Brenner, "The Declassified Documents" by Peter Kornbluh and Laurence Chang, "The Most Dangerous Moment in the Crisis" by Jim Hershberg, and "Annals of Blinksmanship" by Thomas Blanton. Visitors can hear audio clips of White House meetings, read the documents exchanged between the White House and the Kremlin, see the U-2 surveillance photos of Russian missile installations, and read a detailed chronology of events relating to the crisis from 1959 to 1992. The site is revisionist and dedicated to dispelling myths about the crisis, especially the myth of calibrated brinkmanship—the belief that if you stand tough you win and that nuclear superiority made the difference in moments of crisis.

Secrets of War

http://www.secretsofwar.com/

This is the companion site to the History Channel's twenty-six-part documentary series entitled *Sworn to Secrecy: Secrets of War*, which was aired in 1998. The site contains transcripts, links to maps, images, and other information relating to the history of espionage.

A Select Bibliography of the U-2 Incident

http://redbud.lbjlib.utexas.edu/eisenhower/u2.htm

This brief bibliography is located at the Dwight D. Eisenhower Presidential Library.

Senator Joe McCarthy: A Multimedia Celebration

http://webcorp.com/mccarthy/

This archive contains film and audio clips from Senator Joseph McCarthy's speeches and appearances on television.

Soviet Archives Exhibit

http://metalab.unc.edu/expo/soviet.exhibit/entrance.html#tour

The Library of Congress developed this online exhibit. Visitors to this site may browse images of documents from the Soviet archives. The two main sections of this exhibit are the Internal Workings of the Soviet System and The Soviet Union and the United States. The section on postwar estrangement includes commentary on Soviet perspectives on the Cold War and the Cuban Missile Crisis.

A Trip Through the Cold War

http://www.bishops.ntc.nf.ca/socstud/coldwar/index.htm

This multimedia project is a product of the History 3201 classes at Bishops College, an urban high school in eastern Canada. The Web site provides an overview of significant people and events of the Cold War era. Its creators hope that students from all over the world will participate in the project. The site includes student essays on various topics of the Cold War, such as the Berlin airlift, the Berlin Wall, the Cuban Missile Crisis, the Korean War, and the Vietnam War, with photos and links to other sites on the Internet. The site provides an imaginative use of the Web for beginning, publishing, and archiving high school history projects.

The U-2 Incident 1960

http://www.yale.edu/lawweb/avalon/u2.htm

The Avalon Project at Yale University developed this Web site, a useful starting place for finding the basic diplomatic documents, including the exchange of notes between the U.S. and Soviet governments, public statements by State Department officials, and the documentation maintained by the State Department in the Foreign Relations of the United States Series.

The VENONA Project

http://www.nsa.gov/docs/venona/index.html

VENONA was the codename used for the U.S. Signals Intelligence effort to collect and decrypt the text of Soviet KGB and GRU messages from the 1940s. These messages provided extraordinary insight into Soviet attempts to infiltrate the highest levels of the U.S. government. The National Security Agency has declassified over 3,000 messages related to VENONA and made them available at its home page.

Chapter 15

Twentieth-Century American History

Scott A. Merriman and Dennis A. Trinkle

The American Experience: America 1900

http://www.pbs.org/wgbh/pages/amex/1900/index.html

This site looks at the PBS program of the same title, which detailed what life was like in 1900. The site includes a detailed description of the program, a teacher's guide, and a timeline.

American Memory Collection

http://memory.loc.gov/ammem/ammemhome.html

Over fifty collections and one million items are now online. Collections in twentieth-century history range from Baseball Cards to Voices from the Dust Bowl to Mapping the National Parks. Includes a FAQ section and a Today in History section, which has links to related collections and sites. Includes information on future initiatives. A must-see for all interested in American history.

American Temperance and Prohibition

http://www.history.ohio-state.edu/projects/prohibition/

A good overview of the move toward prohibition in America. Includes biographies of key figures, an outline of developments, tables of data for alcohol consumption and beer production, and an excellent collection of cartoons.

Anti-Imperialism in the United States, 1898–1935

http://www.boondocksnet.com/ail98–35.html

This site looks at a variety of issues concerned with American imperialism in the first third of the twentieth century. Presents many writings, including Rudyard Kipling's *The White Man's Burden*, and numerous period cartoons. The U.S. intervention in Haiti and the Philippines, along with many writings on related subjects by William Jennings Bryan, are featured. A good site both for people interested in the period and for teachers.

Apollo Lunar Surface Journal

http://www.hq.nasa.gov/office/pao/History/alsj/frame.html

This site examines the lunar landings of the Apollo missions. It includes many photographs and video clips, summaries of the missions, checklists, crew lists, and crew biographies.

Broadcasting in Chicago, 1921–1989

http://www.mcs.net/~richsam/home.html

This site looks at sixty-eight years of broadcasting in America's Second City. Includes an examination of many of the programs aired in Chicago, including *Amos n' Andy*, and *Fibber McGee and Molly*. A virtual tour of the studio facilities is also available.

CIA and Assassinations: The Guatemala 1954 Documents

http://www.gwu.edu/~nsarchiv/NSAEBB/NSAEBB4/index.html

This site reproduces several primary sources dealing with the CIA's involvement in the 1954 coup in Guatemala, including the CIA's plan for assassination. A useful series of documents focusing on the darker side of our nation's past.

Coal Mining in the Gilded Age and Progressive Era

http://www.history.ohio-state.edu/projects/Lessons_US/Gilded_Age/
Coal_Mining/default.htm

This site looks at coal mining in the late nineteenth and early twentieth centuries. It includes many pictures and reprints of stories from the period and a discussion of the dangers of coal mining. A good site for those interested in coal mining of the period.

Coney Island

http://naid.sppsr.ucla.edu/coneyisland/

An engaging popular culture/history site done by a history buff trained in engineering. It discusses the amusement park and presents articles about its history, a timeline, links to related sites, and maps.

Detroit Photos Home Page from the Library of Congress

http://lcweb2.loc.gov/detroit/

This site, part of the American Memory collection, looks at a collection of 25,000 glass negatives and transparencies, taken by the Detroit Photographic Company, that show life at the turn of the century. Includes information on how to order reprints.

Digger Archives

http://www.diggers.org/

This site presents the story of this anarchist counterculture group of the Sixties. Among its activities, centered in San Francisco, were street theater and free stores. The site presents the activities of the organization, pictures, and links to current related groups. An interesting look at an interesting group.

The Digital Classroom

http://www.nara.gov/education/

Presents classroom lessons utilizing resources available in the National Archives. Includes a documentary analysis sheet that helps users analyze and work with documents—a vital resource. Also presents information about summer development workshops for educators. The heart of the site is a set of units, ten on the twentieth century alone, that use primary documents as teaching tools.

Documents from the Women's Liberation Movement

http://scriptorium.lib.duke.edu/wlm/

This site includes a large number of primary source materials on the women's liberation movement. Organized into categories, but also searchable by keyword. Includes links to related resources.

Early Motion Pictures, 1897–1920

http://memory.loc.gov/cgi-bin/query/r?ammem/collections:@FIELD
(SUBJ+@band(Motion+pictures++United+States.)):heading=
Subjects%3a+Motion+pictures—United+States.

A large collection from the Library of Congress's American Memory project. An excellent and very engaging site. Includes films of San Francisco around the time of the Great Earthquake and Fire of 1906, and films of New York around the turn of the century.

Edsitement

http://edsitement.neh.fed.us/

A good resource for teachers. Includes a large number of lesson plans for teaching any century of American history by using Web resources. Also provided are simple directions for those unfamiliar with the Web, including a glossary, commentary on the pluses and minuses of the Internet, and "Tips for Better Browsing." A very useful site.

Famous Trials of the Twentieth Century

http://www.law.umkc.edu/faculty/projects/ftrials/ftrials.htm

This site looks at many famous trials in the twentieth century, including the trials of the Rosenbergs, Leopold and Loeb, and the Scottsboro Boys. It also includes a few from before the twentieth century, including the *Amistad* case, the Salem Witch trials, and the Johnson impeachment. A set of very well-done, very informative pages.

The Fifties

http://www.fiftiesweb.com/fifties.htm

Slightly celebratory look at the Fifties. Aimed at the Boomer generation (this site even includes a claim to be "Boomer Enhanced" and thus have no small print), it includes music, TV, and a list of Burma-Shave slogans. An illuminating example of Fifties culture, though not very analytical.

Films: Research and Resources

http://www.gen.umn.edu/faculty_staff/yahnke/film/cinema.htm

This site contains a great number of resources to learn more about film. It includes a list of the top films of each decade with a commentary; a list of good

recent films; a list (in the site author's opinion) of the best fifty-five films of all
time; and a discussion of intergenerational issues. Although film is not commonly thought of as traditional history, this site provides an interesting look at
another side of history.

For European Recovery: The Fiftieth Anniversary of the Marshall Plan

http://lcweb.loc.gov/exhibits/marshall/

This site, presented by the Library of Congress, discusses the Marshall Plan
that rebuilt Europe after World War II. It presents a detailed chronology of the
plan, explains the reasoning behind it, and provides excerpts from the book *The
Marshall Plan and the Future of U.S. European Relations*, which contains documents from the twenty-fifth anniversary of the Marshall Plan.

The Emma Goldman Papers

http://sunsite.Berkeley.EDU/Goldman/

A good example of how a Web site can promote both primary research and
general learning. This site presents an online exhibit about Goldman, a late
nineteenth/early twentieth-century radical, along with a discussion of the holdings of the Emma Goldman papers. Includes examples from the collection,
images, moving pictures, and other materials to help students learn about
Goldman. This is what an archive collection site should look like.

Guide to the Supreme Court

http://www.nytimes.com/library/politics/scotus/index-scotus.html

This site, from the *New York Times*, provides a good overview of the Supreme
Court at the present time. Includes a list and short description of the "top ten"
cases ever decided by the Court, and articles about the justices currently on the
court, as well as excerpts from recent decisions.

A History of the White House

http://www.whitehouse.gov/history/index.html

This site, a subsite of the official White House site, contains biographies of
every president, First Lady, and family that has lived in the White House. Also
contains a history of the building and a virtual tour.

Kennedy Assassination Home Page

http://mcadams.posc.mu.edu/home.htm

The Kennedy Assassination Home Page is the most balanced and extensive online resource for exploring John F. Kennedy's death. It is maintained by John McAdams, a professor of political science at Marquette University. McAdams's list of links on the Kennedy assassination also offers the best gateway to serious and reliable materials.

Little Rock Central High School Fortieth Anniversary

http://www.centralhigh57.org/1957–58.htm

This site examines the integration of Little Rock Central High School in 1957. Provides pictures and videos, a timeline of events, and a look at the fortieth anniversary celebration in 1997.

Lower East Side Tenement Museum

http://www.wnet.org/archive/tenement/

An interesting museum housed in a restored Lower East Side tenement in New York City. This building had been sealed off for fifty years and now is exactly the way it was in 1935. The site also presents unique dollhouse diorama dramatizations of life at the time, complete with descriptions and explanations. It also includes two Quick Time movies of rooms in the tenements as they might have been in the 1870s and 1930s.

NAACP Home Page

http://www.naacp.org/

This site primarily offers information about the modern NAACP currently, but it also explores the NAACP's past and the struggles it has been involved in.

National Archives

http://www.nara.gov/

Everything you wanted to know about the National Archives and Records Administration. Includes the National Archives Archival Information Locator (NAIL), which allows users to search for records. Also has an online exhibit hall with examples of NARA records including the Declaration of Independence, portraits of black Chicago, and gifts given to presidents from Hoover to Clinton. A necessary stop for all wanting to ride the research train. Includes general information on grants, research facilities, records management, and the Federal Register. It must be noted that only a very small percentage of NARA's

4 billion records are online, so this is a good place both to *find* material and to *find* how to *find* material.

National Civil Rights Museum

http://216.157.9.6/civilrights/main.htm

This is the Web site of the National Civil Rights Museum, located in Memphis, Tennessee. The site discusses the museum, gives hours and other basic information, summarizes the exhibits currently portrayed, and includes an in-depth interactive tour of the museum.

Oyez, Oyez, Oyez

http://oyez.nwu.edu/

This site includes hours of audio of arguments before the Supreme Court of the United States. Site also includes pictures and short biographies of each Supreme Court justice, both past and present, and, for some justices, presents links to related resources, transcripts of decisions, and lists of selected cases they participated in.

The Population Bomb

http://www.pbs.org/kqed/population_bomb/

A look at Paul Ehrlich's book *The Population Bomb* and a PBS show based on the book. The book argues that the world's population is exploding at an unsustainable rate and that more developed countries put an overly large strain on the resource base. This site is a favorable look at one of the more important ecology books of the twentieth century. Includes a population timeline.

Presidential Elections, 1860–1996

http://fisher.lib.virginia.edu/elections/maps/

Contains popular and electoral returns for every election between 1860 and 1996. Includes links to related sites.

Presidential Libraries

http://www.nara.gov/nara/president/address.html

A very useful site for users doing research concerning twentieth-century presidents. All presidents from Hoover to Clinton have (or will have) presidential libraries, and this site contains addresses; phone, fax, and e-mail information; and links to specific sites for each library. Includes a very informative overview of the presidential libraries that explains the background of the system and answers basic questions.

Presidential Speeches

http://odur.let.rug.nl/~usa/P/

In addition to presidential speeches, particularly State of the Union and inaugural addresses, this site includes brief presidential biographies and links to other resources. A good starting point to look for presidential addresses.

Project Whistlestop

http://www.whistlestop.org/index.htm

An online examination of President Truman's actions. Includes a discussion of the Truman Doctrine, the Marshall Plan, and the Berlin airlift.

Redstone Arsenal Historical Information

http://www.redstone.army.mil/history/welcome.html

A site dealing with all aspects of the U.S. Army's aviation and missile command. Includes oral histories, information on specific weapons programs, and chronologies of this command's history. Also presents declassified documents and a history of Warner von Braun.

Retro

http://www.retroactive.com/

Web magazine discussing a variety of subjects, including politics, fashion, and music. Includes feature articles, links to related Web sites, a community discussion board, and a vintage postcard depot, where one can send vintage postcards to a friend.

Jonas Salk, Biography

http://www.achievement.org/autodoc/page/sal0bio-1

The site presents the biography of the developer of the polio vaccine, complete with pictures and the transcript of an oral interview with Salk.

Scopes Monkey Trial

http://www.law.umkc.edu/faculty/projects/ftrials/scopes/scopes.htm

This site relates to the 1925 trial in Dayton, Tennessee, of John Scopes for teaching evolution. The trial loosely became the model for the play and movie *Inherit the Wind*. Cartoons, part of the textbook used by John Scopes, and a discussion of *Inherit the Wind* are included in this very balanced and in-depth look at the case.

The Sixties

http://www.bbhq.com/sixties.htm

This is the Sixties section of the Baby Boomer Headquarters. It includes a quiz to test your knowledge of the Sixties, a list of the events of the Sixties, a gallery of Sixties music, and reflections from a baby boomer.

The Sixties

http://www.geocities.com/SoHo/Studios/2914/

This is a general site on the Sixties. Includes biographies of some of the leading counterculture figures, quotations, the full text of Martin Luther King's "I Have a Dream" speech, and an in-depth timeline for the decade.

Skylighters

http://www.skylighters.org/

This is the official site of the 225th AAA Searchlight Battalion. Although the site is still under construction, it is a great starting point for World War II resources. Includes a chronology of World War II, related links, and oral histories.

The *Time* 100

http://cgi.pathfinder.com/time/time100/index.html

This is a list of the 100 most influential people of the century as decided by *Time* magazine. It presents biographies of the 100 with links to related sites.

The Trial of the Century: The Lindbergh Case

http://www.lindberghtrial.com/index.htm

This site reminds us that the O.J. Simpson trial was not the trial of the century. This site presents an outline of the kidnapping, recaps the events of the trial, and includes a timeline to manifest historical context. It contains a wealth of pictures, both of people connected with the trial and with the period. Finally, it discusses what has happened since the trial and some of the main principles involved. Also contains links to related sites.

Trinity Atomic Web Site

http://nuketesting.enviroweb.org/

This site presents a history of the development of atomic weapons, mostly focusing on the United States. It presents documents, movies, quotations, an annotated bibliography, and links to related sites.

Votes for Women

http://www.huntington.org/vfw/

A very good, comprehensive site on the women's suffrage movement presented by the Huntington Library. Includes biographies of important individuals, descriptions of the important organizations involved, a breakdown of the various eras in the movement, and a long list of related links.

Watergate

http://www.washingtonpost.com/wp-srv/national/longterm/watergate/splash1a.htm

This site, sponsored by the *Washington Post*, looks at the controversy and scandal that toppled President Richard Nixon. Includes a timeline, an examination of where key figures in the scandal are now, and speculation on the identity of "Deep Throat," a key source for the reporters.

Women and Social Movements in the United States, 1830–1930

http://womhist.binghamton.edu/

While not wholly on the twentieth century, this is still a good site to explore for this issue. The codirectors of this project include Kathryn Kish Sklar. The site presents undergraduate and graduate student work and includes related links. Projects of relevance for the twentieth century include Workers and Allies in the New York City Shirtwaist Strike, 1909–1910; Women's International League for Peace and Freedom; and Right-Wing Attacks, 1923–1931. An interesting example of student work posted to the Web.

Writers and Their Works

http://www.pitt.edu/~englweb/weblinks/writers.html

This site examines some of the top nonfiction writers of the postwar era, including Hunter Thompson, Truman Capote, and Joan Didion. Includes links to related sites.

Chapter 16

Modern Military History

Mark Gellis

General Resources

African-American Military History

http://www.coax.net/people/lwf/aa_mh.htm

Bennie J. McRae Jr. has provided this valuable set of indexes to links on the history of black Americans during armed conflict from the Revolution to the Vietnam War as part of his "Lest We Forget" project.

Air Force Historical Research Agency

http://www.au.af.mil/au/afhra/

The United States Air Force's historical agency provides links to various resources on military aviation history.

American History: Wars of the Twentieth Century

http://www.geocities.com/Athens/Academy/6617/wars.html

A short but useful index of military history sites on the Internet.

American Merchant Marine

http://www.USMM.org/

The home page of the United States Merchant Marine includes extensive resources on the history of merchant marine efforts during wartime.

American Wars, Military History, and Military Affairs

http://www.hist.unt.edu/09w-ame4.htm

Professor Lee E. Huddleston has developed a large index of Web sites related to military history, including separate subindexes dedicated to each of the World Wars and another providing links on military affairs and archives.

Article Index

http://www.thehistorynet.com/general/articleindex.htm

Historynet's article index features more than 500 online articles, many of them dealing with various aspects of military history.

BUBL: Military History

http://bubl.ac.uk/link/m/militaryhistory.htm

This index of links, provided by BUBL (BUlletin Board for Libraries) Information Service, includes links to the Battle of Britain History Site and a site dedicated to Britain's small military conflicts during the Cold War.

The Center of Military History

http://www.army.mil/cmh-pg/

The United States Army's Center of Military History provides access to many resources, including a large number of online articles, photographs, and artwork. In addition, one can view and order from the center's catalog of publications on military history.

DefenseLINK

http://www.defenselink.mil/

Offers numerous links to military-related Web sites (including some with sections on military history) and news on defense-related issues—in effect, American military history as it happens.

Department of Defense Dictionary of Military Terms

http://www.dtic.mil/doctrine/jel/doddict/

An online dictionary of military terminology.

Federation of American Scientists

http://www.fas.org/index.html

This remarkable resource, one of the best on the Internet for those interested in military history, provides an enormous set of detailed Web pages with links to military and intelligence operations of the past and present, weapons and military vehicles, arms sales, and related subjects.

Haze Gray and Underway

http://www.hazegray.org

This is one of the best Internet sites in the world for those interested in modern naval warfare. The site includes the World Navies Today page, which provides detailed information on virtually every navy in the world, including the Russian and Chinese navies, and an online version of *The Dictionary of American Naval Fighting Ships*.

The History Guy: Military History

http://www.historyguy.com/Militarylinks.html

Provides links to various Web pages on military history.

History, Reference, and Preservation

http://www.usni.org/hrp/hrp.html

Historical and reference links at the United States Naval Institute's Web site.

Homework Center: Wars and World History

http://www.multnomah.lib.or.us/lib/homework/warwldhc.html

The Homework Center, developed by the Multnomah County Library (Oregon), provides an index of sites oriented around the needs of students learning about military history.

Military History Museums

http://dir.yahoo.com/Arts/Humanities/History/By_Subject/Military_History/
Museums_and_Memorials/

A Yahoo! index of museums dedicated to military history.

Military History Webrings

http://F.webring.com/hub?ring-militaryhistory

Lists Web rings and categories of Web rings dedicated to military history.

Navy Historical Center

http://www.history.navy.mil/

This United States Navy provides this page as a starting point leading to a very large number of links related to naval history. Links include everything from underwater archaeology and information about available research grants to online encyclopedias of naval history and navy ships.

Redstone Arsenal Historical Information

http://www.redstone.army.mil/history/welcome.html

An index to many military history sites, many of them dedicated to the role of missilery in military history.

Responses to War: An Intellectual and Cultural History

http://chomsky.arts.adelaide.edu.au/person/DHart/ResponsesToWar/

David Hart has developed an extensive set of bibliographies and other online resources for students, teachers, and historians.

Twentieth-Century Documents

http://www.yale.edu/lawweb/avalon/20th.htm

Part of the Avalon Project at the Yale University Law School, this index provides links to many online copies of historical documents related to the conflicts of the twentieth century.

Veterans Affairs Canada

http://www.vac-acc.gc.ca/general/

Offers an extensive section—click the history link—on Canada's participation in the conflicts of the twentieth century.

War, Peace and Security WWW Server

http://www.cfcsc.dnd.ca/index.html

This Canadian site, provided by the Information Resource Centre at the Canadian Forces College, offers an extensive list of resources on military history, current conflicts, and modern armed forces.

Warships of the World

http://warships1.com/

A large and very detailed site providing historical and technical data for warships and their weapons, past and present, from virtually every naval power of the modern era.

Wars of the Twentieth Century

http://militaryhistory.about.com/homework/militaryhistory/cs/wars20thcentury/index.htm

Another index of Web sites, this one offers indexes of various topics, including military societies, naval warfare, military aircraft, and modern conflicts like Vietnam and the Gulf War.

The World at War

http://www.fas.org/man/dod-101/ops/war/index.html

Provides an index of links on various contemporary and recent military conflicts.

Conflicts at the Turn of the Century

Anglo-Boer War Centenary

http://www.icon.co.za/~dup42/war.htm

A useful set of links on the Boer War.

Boer War Index

http://users.netconnect.com.au/~ianmac/boermain.html

The Boer War is the focus of this site.

Border Revolution

http://ac.acusd.edu/History/projects/border/page01.html

An illustrated online explication of the Mexican Revolution.

Mexican Revolution

http://www.mexconnect.com/mex_/history/jtuck/jtrevolution11.html

Author Jim Tuck provides an illustrated summary of the Mexican Revolution.

The Philippine-American War Centennial

http://www.phil-am-war.org/

An detailed examination of this conflict, with charts, timelines, illustrated articles, and historical editorial cartoons and quotations.

The Philippine-American War (1899–1902) from Filipino-Americans.com

http://www.filipino-americans.com/filamwar.html

A detailed summary of the conflict, including numerous excerpts from accounts by participants.

The Russo-Japanese War

http://www.navy.ru/history/hrn10–e.htm

Summary of the Russo-Japanese War from a Web site dedicated to the history of the Russian navy.

Russo-Japanese War Research Society

http://www.russojapan.com/

Provides a summary of the war, an image gallery, and other resources.

South African War Virtual Library

http://www.bowlerhat.com.au/sawvl/index.html

Historian Robert Wotton has developed an extensive virtual archive that contains research data related to the Second South African War (1899–1902).

Spanish-American War Page

http://www.ecsis.net/~jrwilobe/

A useful set of links on the Spanish-American War.

The World of 1898: The Spanish-American War Home Page

http://www.loc.gov/rr/hispanic/1898/

A Library of Congress Web site dedicated to the Spanish-American War.

World War I and Its Aftermath

The Aerodrome

http://www.theaerodrome.com/

Provides information on the aces and aircraft of World War I.

America's Secret War

http://secretwar.hhsweb.com/

Amateur historian Dan Leifheit's useful Web site, with government documents and a large collection of images, on American's intervention during the Russian Civil War (1918–1920).

The Australian Light Horse Association

http://www.lighthorse.org.au/

This site contains both historical and current information on famous Australian regiments and battles during the Boer War and World War I.

The First World War

http://www.spartacus.schoolnet.co.uk/FWW.htm

Spartacus, an educational publishing company, is committed to providing free informational resources for the Internet community. This large, illustrated hypertext encyclopedia is dedicated to World War I.

The Great War Series

http://www.wtj.com/wars/greatwar/

A list of links to online books and articles on World War I, including a memoir of the war written by Manfred von Richthofen—the Red Baron—shortly before his death.

The Great War Society

http://www.worldwar1.com/tgws/

This site, from a historical society dedicated to the study of World War I and its effects on human history, includes a list of more than 300 Web sites related to World War I.

History of the British Army in the Great War

http://www.geocities.com/Athens/Acropolis/2354/index.html

Historian and reenactor Jason Griffeth has developed this set of Web pages and list of links on the British Army during World War I.

The Russian Civil War

http://mars.acnet.wnec.edu/~grempel/courses/stalin/lectures/CivilWar.html

One of several lectures placed online by Professor Gerhard Rempel, this one outlines the events of the Russian Civil War that followed the 1917 Revolution.

World War I

http://historicaltextarchive.com/sections.php?op=listarticles&secid=7

Part of the Historical Text Archives Project, this page provides links to articles and multimedia resources about World War I, including a detailed examination of its effects on small European nations and on Arabs.

The World War I Document Archive

http://www.lib.byu.edu/~rdh/wwi/

Developed by scholars at Brigham Young University, this page provides links to a wide range of historical documents related to World War I, ranging from treaties and government proclamations to personal memoirs. The site also includes a biographical dictionary and an image archive.

World War I: Trenches on the Web

http://www.worldwar1.com/

Another Web site providing several links to historical documents and multimedia files.

The Spanish Civil War

Spanish Civil War

http://ac.acusd.edu/History/WW2Timeline/Prelude07.html

Part of a larger project on the history of World War II, this site contains a timeline and links to an image archive.

Spanish Civil War

http://lcweb2.loc.gov/cgi-bin/query/r?frd/cstdy:@field(DOCID+es0031)

A brief summary of the war from a Federal Research Division Country Study of Spain.

The Spanish Revolution and Civil War

http://www.geocities.com/CapitolHill/9820/

Eugene W. Plawiuk's site offers an index of Web resources related to the Spanish Civil War.

World War II

Achtung Panzer

http://www.achtungpanzer.com/panzer.htm

One of many enthusiast sites dedicated to German armor. This one features many illustrations, tables of technical data, and a large number of links to other World War II sites.

The Battle of Britain Historical Society

http://www.battleofbritain.net/bobhsoc/

A detailed site dedicated to the aerial battle over Great Britain in 1940.

Dad's War: Finding and Telling Your Father's World War II Story

http://members.aol.com/dadswar/index.htm

Wes Johnson has done a service with this index of personal histories and initial instructions on writing your own history for a family member who served in World War II (and, by extension, any war).

East Anglia: The Air War

http://www.stable.demon.co.uk/

Contains a series of informative essays with illustrations concerning various air forces and the aircraft flown during World War II. The site also provides a useful index of links to related Web pages and a bibliography of print reference works.

504th WWII Home Page

http://www.geocities.com/~the504thpir/index.html

An example of the many sites dedicated to specific military units, this one chronicles the experiences of the 504th Parachute Infantry Regiment during World War II.

German Armed Forces: 1919–1945

http://www.feldgrau.com/

A detailed Web site covering the German armed forces from the end of World War I until the end of World War II.

Guadalcanal: The First Offensive

http://www.army.mil/cmh-pg/books/wwii/GuadC/GC-fm.htm

A book-length study of this offensive, including maps and charts, one of the many resources provided by the United States Army Center of Military History.

Hyperwar: A Hypertext History of the Second World War

http://metalab.unc.edu/hyperwar/

A linked anthology of articles related to World War II, many of them discussing specific battles in detail, along with links to other sources.

Imperial Japanese Navy Page

http://www.combinedfleet.com/

Another example of the many sites on World War II created by enthusiasts and amateur historians. This one, by Jon Parshall, covers the Japanese navy and provides details about its ships and top officers, along with a useful bibliography of print sources.

The *Luftwaffe* Homepage

http://www.ww2.dk

This site provides data on the *Luftwaffe* and an index of links to *Luftwaffe*-related Web pages.

A Marine Diary: My Experiences on Guadalcanal

http://www.gnt.net/~jrube/indx2.html

Entries from the diary of a marine who served at Guadalcanal, with a large set of links to related World War II resources on the Internet.

Marines at Midway

http://metalab.unc.edu/hyperwar/USMC/USMC-M-Midway.html

Part of the Hyperwar project, this is a detailed, illustrated examination of the Battle of Midway, written by Lieutenant Colonel R.D. Heinl, Jr., USMC.

Naval Air War in the Pacific

http://www.ixpres.com/ag1caf/navalwar/

Photos and paintings of American air combat during World War II.

Normandy: 1944

http://normandy.eb.com/

Encyclopedia Britannica's multimedia examination of the Normandy invasion.

Red Steel

http://www.algonet.se/~toriert/

Enthusiast Thorleif Olsson's extensive Web site on Russian tanks and armored vehicles.

Return to Midway

http://www.nationalgeographic.com/features/98/midway/

National Geographic has created this multimedia site featuring images and streaming video of the wrecks of the carriers sunk at the Battle of Midway.

U-Boat Net

http://uboat.net/

A comprehensive study of the German U-boat, including maps, technology, and profiles of more than 1,100 German submarines employed during World War II.

What Did You Do in the War, Grandma?

http://www.stg.brown.edu/projects/WWII_Women/tocCS.html

An oral history of Rhode Island women during World War II, written by students in the Honors English Program at South Kingstown High School, this site provides not only information about lesser known aspects of the war, but also a good model of action for teachers interested in using the Internet for class projects.

The Women's Army Corps

http://www.army.mil/cmh-pg/brochures/wac/wac.htm

The United States Army has developed this online article about the Women's Army Corps during World War II.

World War II in Europe

http://www.historyplace.com/worldwar2/timeline/ww2time.htm

Part of The History Place, a large Web site dedicated to assisting students and educators, this is a World War II timeline with links to illustrations and short articles on specific events.

World War II in the Pacific's Webring

http://www.geocities.com/guy_conquest/webrings.html

Amateur historian Brian Smith has provided a large and useful index of links on World War II in the Pacific.

World War II Resources

http://www.ibiblio.org/pha/index.html

A large collection of historical documents from World War II.

World War II Seminar

http://ac.acusd.edu/History/classes/ww2/175.html

Class materials for a World War II history course from the University of San Diego, including an extended bibliography and several timelines created by students.

World War II Webring

http://nav.webring.yahoo.com/hub?ring=ww2&list

More than 700 Web pages are listed on this Web ring.

World War II Website Association

http://www.ww2wa.com/

Provides links to various Web pages on aspects of World War II.

The Korean War

Korea

http://tlc.ai.org/korea.htm

This educational site on Korea features an index of links to the Web sites on the Korean War.

The Korean War Museum

http://www.theforgottenvictory.org./

This home page provides an index of links to Internet sites on the Korean War; it also provides information on the museum and its newsletter.

The Korean War Project

http://www.koreanwar.org/

An index to a large set of links (particularly in the Reference section), including other Web sites, articles, images, and maps.

The Korean War Veteran Association

http://www.kwva.org/

This organization's home page provides information on and for veterans of the Korean War.

The Vietnam War

Images of My War

http://www.ionet.net/~uheller/vnbktoc.shtml

One of many personal accounts of Vietnam veterans, this one is a detailed autobiography of a U.S. Army Ranger, focusing on his experiences during the conflict.

Tonkin Gulf Yacht Club

http://nav.webring.yahoo.com/hub?ring=gtyc&list

Large list of Web sites on the naval history of the Vietnam conflict.

U.S. POW/MIAs in Southeast Asia

http://www.wtvi.com/wesley/powmia/powmia.html

An index of online resources related to POW/MIA issues.

Vietnam War Bibliography

http://hubcap.clemson.edu/~eemoise/bibliography.html

Professor Edwin Moïse of Clemson University has developed a large bibliography of print and other sources on the Vietnam conflict.

Vietnam War Internet Project

http://www.lbjlib.utexas.edu/shwv/vwiphome.html

This online project, housed on the Lyndon Baines Johnson Library Web server at the University of Texas, provides links to an extensive list of resources, including bibliographies, images, personal memoirs, documents related to the war, and a complete archive of the Soc.History.War.Vietnam newsgroup.

Vietnam War Webring

http://nav.webring.yahoo.com/hub?ring=vwhring&list

Small but select list of Web sites on the Vietnam War.

Vietnam: Yesterday and Today

http://servercc.oakton.edu/~wittman/

Designed for students and teachers, this site includes a timeline of the war and a large set of related links.

The Wars for Vietnam

http://students.vassar.edu/~vietnam/

This site, developed at Vassar College, provides a historical overview of the war, with links to historical documents and other Vietnam-related Web pages.

Other Cold War Resources

Cold War Hot Links

http://www.stmartin.edu/~dprice/cold.war.html

Professor David Price offers a detailed index of Web resources, mostly articles but some multimedia, on the leading figures and events of the Cold War.

Documents Relating to American Foreign Policy: The Cold War

http://www.mtholyoke.edu/acad/intrel/coldwar.htm

A large list of documents related to the Cold War.

Military History: The Cold War and the Marshall Plan

http://www.nara.gov/alic/milrsrcs/coldwar.html

A list of links related to the Cold War, including online historical texts and bibliographies.

The Israeli-Arab Wars

Arab-Israeli Conflict in Maps

http://www.jajz-ed.org.il/100/maps/

A list of maps detailing the various Arab-Israeli conflicts during the last century.

The Battle of Latakia

http://www.us-israel.org/jsource/History/latakia.html

An online article discussing the historic naval battle—the first involving missile boats—between Israeli and Syrian forces in 1973.

The Battle of Latakia

http://www.geocities.com/SoHo/Coffeehouse/2981/latakia.htm

Another online article on this historic battle, with many photographs of the various types of ships involved.

History of the Israeli Defense Force (IDF)

http://www.idf.il/english/history/history.stm

Detailed historical essays by the Israeli Defense Force outlining the activities of the IDF during the War of Independence, the Six-Day War, and other operations.

Israel

gopher://gopher.umsl.edu:70/11/library/govdocs/armyahbs/aahb6

An Army Area Handbook on Israel, this online book includes discussions of the Arab-Israeli conflicts.

Jewish Virtual Library: Wars

http://www.us-israel.org/jsource/History/wartoc.html

Part of a larger Web site on Jewish history and culture, this is a table of contents for a large set of detailed online articles about the various Arab-Israeli conflicts.

Maps of the Arab-Israeli War

http://www.dean.usma.edu/history/dhistorymaps/Arab-Israel%20Pages/aitoc.htm

Another list of maps showing Arab-Israeli conflicts.

Young Warrior

http://tetrad.stanford.edu/eli/YoungWarrior.html

Memoir of an Israeli soldier fighting in the 1948–1949 war, with many pictures.

The Falklands War

The Falklands Island Conflict

http://met.open.ac.uk/group/cpv/falkland.htm

This site features a data library on military vessels and aircraft, a QuickTime video library, and links to other Falklands-related sites.

Falklands Remembered

http://www.thenews.co.uk/news/falklands/menu.htm

This site, developed by an online Portsmouth, U.K. newspaper, covers many aspects of the Falklands war. The site includes a timeline and a large number of short articles and photographs.

Falklands War

http://www.naval-history.net/NAVAL1982FALKLANDS.htm

Detailed explanation of the 1982 conflict, with maps, photographs, and summaries of the forces involved in the various operations of the war.

The Gulf War

Desert-Storm.com

http://www.desert-storm.com/

An index of sites related to operations Desert Shield, Desert Storm, and Desert Fox.

807th MASH: Operation Desert Shield and Operation Desert Storm

http://www.iglou.com/law/mash.htm

An online account of the experiences of a mobile army surgical hospital's staff during the Gulf War.

Fog of War

http://www.washingtonpost.com/wp-srv/inatl/longterm/fogofwar/fogofwar.htm

Resources on the Gulf War developed by the *Washington Post*, including government documents, images, and video clips.

Operation Desert Storm

http://www.fas.org/man/dod-101/ops/desert_storm.htm

This site provides a brief summary of the Gulf War and a large set of links to articles about the conflict and other military resources.

Persian Gulf War/Operation Desert Storm

http://historicaltextarchive.com/sections.php?op=listarticles&secid=16

This page offers a list of documents related to the Gulf War, including the diaries of an Israeli woman and an Iraqi soldier.

Ronald A. Hoskinson's Gulf War Photo Gallery

http://www.hoskinson.net/gulfwar/

Images and a detailed personal account from a field artillery captain who served in the Gulf War.

Other Recent Conflicts

Blackhawk Down

http://www.philly.com/packages/somalia/sitemap.asp

A Web site detailing one of the battles during American operations in Somalia in 1993.

Conflict Between Ecuador and Peru

http://www.ccm.net/~jsruiz/conflicto.htm

A discussion of the 1995 war, written from an Ecuadorian perspective.

The 1971 India-Pakistan War

http://freeindia.org/1971war/

A detailed online history, from an Indian perspective, of the short but brutal conflict between India and Pakistan in 1971.

Operation El Dorado Canyon

http://www.fas.org/man/dod-101/ops/el_dorado_canyon.htm

A Federation of American Scientists (FAS) Web page on the U.S. attack on Libya in 1986.

Operation Just Cause

http://www.fas.org/man/dod-101/ops/just_cause.htm

A Federation of American Scientists (FAS) Web page on Operation Just Cause, the American invasion of Panama in 1989.

Operation Just Cause

http://www.army.mil/cmh-pg/documents/panama/just.htm

Supplemental documents from the United States Army on Operation Just Cause.

Operation Safe Border

http://www.fas.org/man/dod-101/ops/safe_border.htm

A Federation of American Scientists (FAS) Web page listing Web resources on the Ecuador-Peru conflict of 1995.

Operation Urgent Fury

http://www.specialoperations.com/Operations/grenada.html

This site provides links to Web sites related to the American invasion of Grenada, including a detailed discussion of SEAL operations during the invasion, a bibliography of printed sources, and a video clip of President Ronald Reagan announcing the invasion.

The Soviet Invasion of Afghanistan

http://www.afghan-politics.org/Reference/Soviet_Invasion/soviet_invasion_main.htm

Provides a list of links on the Soviet invasion of Afghanistan.

U.S. Special Operations

http://www.specialoperations.com/Operations/default.html

An index of Web sites on U.S. Special Operations, providing information on many of the conflicts of the last fifty years.

Organizations, International Military Services, and Other Military History Sites

The Australian War Memorial

http://www.awm.gov.au/

Covers the Australian experience in war and includes an online encyclopedia and search engines for exploring the memorial's large collections of war-related photographs and documents.

The Battleship Page

http://www.battleship.org/

This page, hosted by the Iowa Class Preservation Association, a nonprofit organization dedicated to preserving this aspect of America's heritage, provides links to a large number of pages related to the role of the battleship in modern military history.

Institute for the Advanced Study of Information Warfare

http://www.psycom.net/iwar.1.html

Provides links to sites and articles related to the gathering and use of information in warfare.

Military Aircraft Database

http://www.csd.uwo.ca/~pettypi/elevon/gustin_military/

An online encyclopedia dedicated to past and present military aircraft of the world.

Military Woman Home Page

http://www.MilitaryWoman.org/homepage.htm

An index of resources related to issues facing women who serve in the military or who are married to those who serve. Useful for those investigating the history of private lives.

The South African Military History Society

http://rapidttp.com/milhist/

Home page for the organization with various links, including a journal with online articles related to the Boer War and other subjects.

Three-Four-Nine: The Ultimate Reference for the Ultimate F-16 Enthusiast

http://www.f-16.net/index.html

A detailed online encyclopedia dedicated to the F-16 Falcon, one of the most widely exported combat aircraft in the world.

United States Naval and Shipbuilding Museum

http://www.uss-salem.org/

Dedicated to the USS *Salem* (CA-139), the world's only preserved heavy cruiser, and related topics.

Chapter 17

The American West

J. Kelly Robison

The American West is generally thought of as the region of the United States west of the Mississippi River, though sometimes as the area west of the ninety-eighth meridian. Yet historians also study westward expansion, which brings in that area between the Appalachian Mountains and the Mississippi River. In practice, Western American history encompasses a wide scope of place and time. Chronologically, Western History embraces the entirety of human history of the West, from the beginnings in the Neolithic era to the present day. Additionally, historians who study Native American history are usually classified as Western historians, which brings an even larger geographic area and chronological era into the fold. The study of the America West is a diverse field, and the following sites reflect that diversity.

General Sites

America's West: Development and History

http://www.americanwest.com/

Though at first glance this site seems hokey and interested in the much-mythologized "Old West," it does contain useful articles, some images, and links to other sites.

New Perspectives on the West

http://www3.pbs.org/weta/thewest/

The Web site for the PBS special on the American West produced by Ken Burns.

An extensive site with links to a wide range of primary documents, articles on various Western topics, and biographies of Western figures.

Sources for the Study of the Southwest

http://www2.smu.edu/swcenter/links.htm

A well-thought-out and well-organized list of links to sites of interest to those studying the Southwest. Link topics range from the cattle industry to the archaeology of the Southwest. Created by Bob Skinner of Southern Methodist University.

WestWeb: Western History Resources

http://www.library.csi.cuny.edu/westweb/

A growing collection of topically organized links to Western history resources. Created and maintained by Catherine Lavendar of the City University of New York. The site is broken down into thirty-one different chapters, each of which contains numerous links to sites that specialize in that topic. Some of the topic chapters also contain image thumbnails linked to National Archives photographs. The site is also indexed. This site should be the first place anyone interested in Western history sites on the Web should go.

Topical Sites

Borders/*Fronteras*

http://www.si.edu/folklife/vfest/frontera/start.htm

The Smithsonian Institution's online exhibit on the southern U.S. border. Contains essays on music (samples in au form), art, language, and culture, as well as a discussion on what is a border. Also available in Spanish.

California Heritage Collection

http://sunsite.Berkeley.EDU/calheritage/

From the Bancroft Library, this site is a collection of over 30,000 images of California's history and culture. Includes resources for K-12 instructors.

California Mission Studies Association

http://www.ca-missions.org/

Dedicated to the study and preservation of California's missions, this organization's Web site contains articles on the missions, a nice glossary of mission-related terms, and some wonderful photographs. The site also maintains both annotated and unannotated links pages.

Crossing the Frontier: Photographs of the Developing West, 1849 to Present

http://WWW.CalHum.ORG/sfmoma-crossing/

An online version of a traveling exhibition developed by the San Francisco Museum of Modern Art. The site itself contains fifty of the three hundred images in the exhibit, several articles on the West, and teachers' resources. The server is slow, so have patience.

General George A. Custer Home Page

http://www.garryowen.com/

A site dedicated to the study of Custer and the Plains Indian Wars. Contains a plethora of information, including short articles, primary data, and photographs. The site itself is poorly designed and the chosen links are often of dubious quality.

Gallery of the Open Frontier

http://gallery.unl.edu/

In development by the University of Nebraska Press, this site contains a searchable image collection, most of which is derived from the National Archives. Although the Gallery has been around for at least four years, it is still in the demonstration stage.

The Interactive Santa Fe Trail (SFT) Homepage

http://raven.cc.ukans.edu/heritage/research/sft/index.html

Created by Nancy Sween for Kansas Heritage, this site's most interesting feature is its extensive list of other sites related to the Santa Fe Trail. The site takes a long time to load, despite relatively few images.

The Japanese-American Internment

http://www.geocities.com/Athens/8420/main.html

Contains a timeline of the Japanese-American internment, basic information on the camps, and remembrances of internees. Numerous links to other Web sites and to primary documents are also available on this site by John Yu.

Klondike Ho! 1897–1997

http://www.kokogiak.com/klon/

Visually impressive site with basic information on the Klondike gold rush. The site was created by Alan Taylor to commemorate the centennial of the gold rush.

The Lewis and Clark Expedition

http://www.pbs.org/lewisandclark/

The Ken Burns PBS production companion site. Contains excerpts from the Corps of Discovery journals, a timeline of the journey, maps of the expedition, interviews with authorities on the expedition, classroom resources for teachers, and numerous other related materials.

Mormon History Resource Page

http://www.indirect.com/www/crockett/history.html

Dave Crockett's site breaks the history of the Mormon Church into several historical periods, including the trek west and the early days in Utah. The site lists many links and also contains original articles by Crockett.

Mountain Men and the Fur Trade: Sources of the History of the Fur Trade in the Rocky Mountain West

http://www.xmission.com/%7Edrudy/amm.html

This nicely done site contains transcripted primary documents from the fur trade era, digitized business records of the fur trade, and a nice collection of digitized images of period artifacts and art.

Multicultural American West

http://www.wsu.edu:8080/~amerstu/mw/

Essentially an online, annotated bibliography of sites relevant to the study of the American West. As the site's name implies, most of the resources and links are related to ethnicity in the West. Designed by the Washington State University American Studies program.

New Mexico Ghost Towns

http://www.vivanewmexico.com/ghosts/ghosts.html

David Pike's compendium of New Mexican ghost towns has a list of most of the depopulated urban areas in the state. His ranking system (which could also be used simply as a list of the ghost towns in New Mexico) is nicely done. Surprisingly, some of the ghost towns on the list still have residents. The individual ghost town pages contain few pictures, but provide information on the towns and short essays by Pike.

The Overland Trail

http://www.over-land.com/

A site dedicated to Ben Holladay's Overland Trail, created by Elizabeth Larson. Contains a large amount of information, including a clickable map to articles that describe the route itself, stopovers, Indian problems along the route, and other topics. Links to other sites are categorized by topic and include brief descriptions.

The Silent Westerns: Early Movie Myths of the American West

http://xroads.virginia.edu/~HYPER/HNS/Westfilm/west.html

Mary Halnon's site devoted to the portrayal of the West in silent film includes excellent essays on the early film industry and the mythologized elements in Western movies.

Vigilantes of Montana: Secret Trials and Midnight Hangings

http://montana-vigilantes.org/

This site, maintained by Louis Schmittroth, contains a wealth of information on the Montana Vigilantes. The site contains online books and articles by well-known Montana historians. The politics of the site are apparent, but the information contained within is well worth perusing.

Who Killed William Robinson?

http://web.uvic.ca/history-robinson/

A wonderful resource for teachers, this site by Ruth Sandwell and John Lutz takes the reader through a historical mystery to determine the identity of a murderer. Contains primary documents and asks pertinent questions dealing with race, politics, and settlement.

Women Artists of the American West, Past and Present

http://www.sla.purdue.edu/waaw/

Created by Susan Ressler of Purdue University and Jerrold Maddox of Penn State, this online exhibit of female artists provides essays on those artists and on particular groups of artists.

Yukon and Alaska History

http://arcticculture.miningco.com/library/blYAindex.htm

A subsite within the Mining Company, a commercial Web indexer. Contains articles on Yukon and Alaskan history and culture, covering early pioneers and mining in the region with an emphasis on the Klondike gold rush.

Chapter 18

Women's History

Tracy Penny Light

About.com: Women's History

http://womenshistory.about.com

This site includes Web links on women's history topics, original articles, an index of news stories on women's history, an index of recent book reviews, women's quotes, an online forum, and occasional chats.

African-American Women

http://scriptorium.lib.duke.edu/collections/african-american-women.html

Part of the Special Collections Library at Duke University, this site includes manuscripts and texts by African-American women, focusing on the slave experience.

African-American Women Writers of the Nineteenth Century

http://digital.nypl.org/schomburg/writers_aa19/

The New York Public Library's index of online books by and about African-American women, searchable by author, title, or category.

American Women's History: A Research Guide

http://frank.mtsu.edu/~kmiddlet/history/women.html

This rich and well-updated resource includes bibliographies of print and Internet materials, helpful information for researchers, a subject index to research sources, and links to electronic discussion lists.

Anthony, Susan B.: Anthony's Rochester Home

http://www.susanbanthonyhouse.org/

This site includes information on Susan B. Anthony's Rochester, New York, home, now a National Historic Landmark, and biographical information on one of the best-known American women.

Bible Passages on Women

gopher://dept.english.upenn.edu/11/Courses/Lynch3/Bible

This site contains Bible passages on the role and status of women, mostly from the Christian New Testament, some from Hebrew Scriptures.

Bryant, Emma Spaulding (Letters)

http://scriptorium.lib.duke.edu/bryant/

Part of the Special Collections Library at Duke University, this collection of letters written by Bryant to her husband, John Emory Bryant, in summer 1873 recounts her visit to relatives in Illinois and Ohio while her husband tended to his political affairs in Georgia. Because these letters are unusually frank for this time period, they reveal much about the relationships between husbands and wives in this era and about medical practices that were often kept private.

Celebrating Women's Achievements

http://www.nlc-bnc.ca/2/12/index-e.html

A series of portraits that highlight the achievements of women from Canada's past in sports, activism, the book trade, politics, librarianship and bibliography, society, music, and literature. Each woman's life and achievements are described, followed by a list of suggested readings. The National Library adds a new theme to this site every year to celebrate Women's History Month.

Celebration of Women Writers

http://digital.library.upenn.edu/women/

Extensive collection of links to biographies of and online books by women writers, including many international writers. Lists names and birth/death years for authors whose works and biography are not (yet?) online.

Civil War Women

http://odyssey.lib.duke.edu/collections/civil-war-women.html

Part of the Special Collections Library at Duke University, this site includes primary sources for studying the lives of women during the American Civil War.

Diotima: Materials for the Study of Women and Gender in the Ancient World

http://www.stoa.org/diotima/

One of the Web's best examples of how to make resources available online. Contains an extensive range of topics; primary sources, some in translation; secondary sources, including essays from a variety of other sites; and some graphic images. Includes Biblical studies.

Distinguished Women of Past and Present

http://www.DistinguishedWomen.com/

Danuta Bois's collection of short, basic biographies of women, most of which include a short bibliography for more information. Includes searches by name and field of endeavor.

Documents from the Women's Liberation Movement

http://scriptorium.lib.duke.edu/wlm/

Part of the Special Collections Library at Duke University, this site includes texts and scanned images and documents from the 1969–1974 U.S. women's liberation movement. Flyers, pamphlets, and booklets provide a view into that energetic period of women's history.

The Emma Goldman Papers

http://sunsite.berkeley.edu/Goldman/

Since 1980, the Emma Goldman Papers Project has collected, organized, and edited tens of thousands of documents by and about Goldman, an anarchist and feminist, from around the world. Electronic resources include a sampling of photographs and primary historical documents, biographical and bibliographical essays and finding aids, and samples from a number of publications about Emma Goldman.

Famous American Women

http://www.plgrm.com/history/women/

A helpful index to notable women—no content here, just formatted search engine links.

Feminist Collections: A Quarterly of Women's Studies Resources

http://www.library.wisc.edu/libraries/WomensStudies/fcmain.htm

Online essays often include Web site reviews and information on how to study women's issues using Web resources.

4,000 Years of Women in Science

http://www.astr.ua.edu/4000WS/4000WS.html

This site provides a brief introduction to the history of women in science. It contains a large collection of biographies, photographs, and references and can be searched alphabetically, by field, or by the time in which the scientist completed the bulk of her work.

Gage, Matilda Joslyn

http://www.pinn.net/~sunshine/gage/mjg.html

This site contains information about the life and writings of Matilda Joslyn Gage, the nineteenth-century women's rights leader (and mother-in-law of *Oz* author Frank Baum). The site also provides information and links on other women in the nineteenth century and on early feminists, a Gage newsletter, and conferences.

Gifts of Speech

http://gos.sbc.edu/

Archive of women's speeches from around the world that have influenced history or were given by famous women.

Godey's Lady's Book Online

http://www.history.rochester.edu/godeys/

Godey's Lady's Book was a popular nineteenth-century women's magazine whose articles and fashions helped shape the middle-class American woman. A good resource for fashions, lifestyle research, and the articles and poetry.

Guide to Uncovering Women's History in Archival Collections

http://www.lib.utsa.edu/Archives/links.htm

A geographical listing of libraries with archival collections relating to women's history. Heavy on the United States but also includes international collections, mostly in English-speaking countries.

Hawaii Women's Heritage

http://www.soc.hawaii.edu/hwhp/

Exhibits on the life of women in the history of Hawaii.

Hearts at Home: Southern Women in the Civil War

http://www.lib.virginia.edu/exhibits/hearts/

Images of manuscripts, letters, journals, and other documents, showing the many aspects of life for Southern women. Topics range from music, poetry, and religion to slavery, hard times, and war work.

Herstory: An Exhibition

http://library.usask.ca/herstory/

This retrospective exhibition is an attempt to capture the flavor of twenty years of work on a unique feminist project to honor the history of Canadian women. It samples the pages of *Herstory: The Canadian Women's Calendar* from 1974 to 1995 and reflects on the process and the people that created them.

History of Women's Suffrage

http://www.rochester.edu/SBA/history.html

From the University of Rochester's Susan B. Anthony Center for Women's Leadership, this site provides a brief history of women's suffrage in America, including a bibliography and links.

H-Minerva

http://www.h-net.msu.edu/~minerva/

Focused on the study of women and war and women in the military in many eras. Site hosts a moderated discussion list, archives of discussions, conference and call-for-papers announcements, and book reviews.

H-Women

http://www.h-net.msu.edu/~women/

Directed to researchers, teachers, and librarians, this site hosts a moderated discussion list, archives of women's history syllabi, book reviews, bibliographies, and discussion threads.

Images of Women in Prints from the Renaissance to the Present

http://www.lib.virginia.edu/dic/bayly/women/docs/home.html

This online exhibit from the Bayly Art Museum shows how women have been seen in history, through prints and contemporary writing.

International Alliance for Women in Music Home Page

http://music.acu.edu/www/iawm/

Resources for women in music. Includes extensive modern resources and links to resources on historical women composers.

Jewish Women's Archive

http://www.JWA.org/main.htm

The mission of the Jewish Women's Archive is to uncover, chronicle, and transmit the rich legacy of Jewish women and their contributions to our families and communities, to our people and our world. Included is the Virtual Archive database, which consists of 500 archival images and the records of over 200 women, from collections held in repositories in the United States and Canada. The archive is searchable by subject, occupation, and genre of the primary source material (i.e., oral histories, diaries, personal papers). The site also contains access to a discussion forum and a place to share stories.

Lesbian History Project

http://www-lib.usc.edu/~retter/main.html

Annotated links to print and Web resources for studying lesbian history. Many eras represented; also includes links for studying lesbians of color.

Living the Legacy: The Women's Rights Movement, 1848–1998

http://www.legacy98.org/

This site was designed for the 150th anniversary of the Women's Rights Convention at Seneca Falls, New York. The resources on this valuable site include teaching and activism ideas and an overview of 150 years of women's rights.

Madam C.J. Walker (1867–1919)

http://www.madamcjwalker.com/

Although this site mainly serves as an advertisement for the work of Walker biographer A'Lelia Bundles, this site does offer a brief biography, photos, and bibliography of Walker, an African-American millionaire, inventor, and social activist.

Matrix: Resources for the Study of Women's Religious Communities

http://matrix.bc.edu/

A scholarly resource for the study of women's religious communities from 400 to 1600 C.E., this site provides profiles of individuals and communities ("monasticon"), an image library, a glossary, an index of secondary sources, and a bibliography.

Medieval Women

http://www.georgetown.edu/labyrinth/subjects/women/women.html

Georgetown's Labyrinth project lists key links for researching medieval women, including Hildegard of Bingen, Joan of Arc, and Julian of Norwich. It also points to good bibliographies.

Medieval Women Web Sites

http://www.library.wisc.edu/libraries/WomensStudies/fc/fcwebho.htm

Cynthia Ho, Amelia Washburn, and Tim Gauthier suggest and review key Web sites for studying medieval women's history.

National First Ladies' Library

http://www.firstladies.org/

This Web site launched by Hillary Rodham Clinton on February 22, 1998, is devoted to the history and legacy of America's First Ladies. The Web site contains 40,000 selected books, manuscripts, journals, newspaper articles, and other materials.

National Women's Hall of Fame

http://www.greatwomen.org/

This Seneca Falls, New York, museum Web site honors a woman each month and includes information on visiting the museum, a history of the museum, classroom educational activities, and an online catalog of books and gifts.

National Women's History Museum

http://www.nmwh.org

This U.S. women's history project presents online exhibits while working toward a building of its own. Exhibits include Political Culture and the Imagery of American Suffrage and Motherhood, Social Service, and Political Reform: Political Culture and Imagery of American Woman Suffrage.

National Women's History Project

http://www.nwhp.org/

The organization behind Women's History Month, this site includes classroom ideas, suggested ways to honor women's history in local communities, a listing of events nationwide, membership information, links, and more. The materials are particularly aimed at the middle and high school levels. Includes an online catalog of educational and promotional materials.

New York Public Library: Women's Studies/History Research Guide

http://www.nypl.org/research/chss/grd/resguides/women/womhist.html

A list of books available at the New York Public Library (and, usually, other libraries as well) on topics in women's history.

9,000 Years of Anatolian Woman

http://www.arzu.com/turknet/ninethousand/index.html

Gunsel Renda's online illustrated exhibit of artifacts spanning 9,000 years of history tells the story of the Anatolian woman, illustrating woman's creativity, productivity, and prominence in all the civilizations that have flourished in the peninsula from ancient times to modern.

The Ninety-Nines: International Organization of Women Pilots

http://www.ninety-nines.org/index.html

Women in aviation, including astronauts who made history or are making it. The site includes the stories of women who have made a significant contribution to aviation as well as information on the history of women in aviation generally.

Notable Women Ancestors

http://www.rootsweb.com/~nwa/

Genealogical information on researching women ancestors. Site includes contributed essays on women, both famous and not.

Notable Women with Liberal Religious Connections

http://www.geocities.com/Wellesley/Garden/1101/

List of women with Unitarian, Universalist, Ethical Culture, and Free Religion connections, plus an annotated bibliography for those doing research on the topic.

The Shadow Story of the Millennium

http://www.nytimes.com/library/magazine/millennium/m2/index.html

Articles, images, audio, and forums: key issues in women's history in the last 1,000 years. Note that users must fill out a subscription form to access this site (subscription is free).

Social Studies: Women's History

http://www.socialstudies.com/c/@0/Pages/womenindex.html

Products, mostly for purchase, for teaching women's history from kindergarten through 12th grade. Some essays and some curriculum units (with reproducible master) are available without charge on the site.

Sources for Women's Studies in the Methodist Archives

http://rylibweb.man.ac.uk/data1/dg/methodist/methfem.html

A bibliographic essay on women in Methodist history and sources found at the Methodist Archives.

Suffragists Oral History Project

http://library.berkeley.edu/BANC/ROHO/ohonline/suffragists.html

Online transcripts of interviews, taped in the 1970s, with twelve leaders and participants in the U.S. suffrage movement.

University Publications of America: Women's Studies

http://www.lexisnexis.com/academic/2upa/Aws/Womens%20Studies.htm

These guides to manuscript collections and other resources detail historical information on aspects of women's history.

Victorian Women Writers Project

http://www.indiana.edu/~letrs/vwwp/vwwp-links.html

This site is a collection of links to journals, online projects on individual authors and related topics, syllabi, and information related to Victorian women writers and society.

Voice of the Shuttle: Gender Studies

http://vos.ucsb.edu/shuttle/gender.html

Extensive Webliography, including much of current as well as historical interest.

Votes for Women: Selections from the National American Woman Suffrage Association Collection, 1848–1921

http://lcweb2.loc.gov/ammem/naw/nawshome.html

From the Library of Congress, letters and other writings plus images from the collection donated by Carrie Chapman Catt.

What Did You Do In the War, Grandma?

http://www.stg.brown.edu/projects/WWII_Women/tocCS.html

High school students' oral history project, documenting women's roles in World War II. Excellent both as an information resource and as a model for a student project in women's history.

What's New in Women's History?

http://xroads.virginia.edu/g/DRBR/gordon.html

Linda Gordon, women's historian, on the history and purpose of women's history.

Witch Craze Links

http://shanmonster.lilsproutz.com/witch/links/index.html

Resources on the witch craze in seventeenth-century America and in Europe, along with a host of other sites in related genres.

Women and Social Movements in the United States, 1830–1930

http://womhist.binghamton.edu

The history of women in the United States is connected to the history of the social movements they founded and in which women developed and applied leadership skills. Student essays on a broad range of topics.

Women at MBL: The Early Years

http://hermes.mbl.edu/women_of_science/women.html

The Marine Biology Laboratory at Woods Hole, Massachusetts, was one of the earliest schools to accept female science students. A number of those students between 1850 and 1930 are profiled on this page, which includes photographs.

Women Come to the Front

http://lcweb.loc.gov/exhibits/wcf/wcf0001.html

Women journalists and photographers at the front in World War II. Primary sources include newspaper and magazine articles and photographs from the Library of Congress.

Women in America, 1820–1842

http://xroads.virginia.edu/~hyper/detoc/fem/home.htm

Selections from writings (letters, journals, books) of notable European travelers to early nineteenth-century America, excerpted to highlight their observations on women's lives.

Women in World History.com

http://www.womeninworldhistory.com/

This commercial site contains an extensive collection of curriculum materials on women in world history. Some sample lesson plans are free, and the essays and other materials will interest many researchers who are not teachers.

Women Mathematicians

http://www.agnesscott.edu/lriddle/women/women.htm

More than 100 biographies, with bibliographies of print and Web resources. Many have photographs.

Women Nobel Laureates

http://www.almaz.com/nobel/women.html

Women who have won the Nobel Prize for their contributions to science, peace, and literature.

Women's Early Music, Art, Poetry

http://music.acu.edu/www/iawm/pages/index.html

This extensive site from Abilene Christian University contains essays and links on a wide array of information related to women and the arts, including Early Spirituality; Eastern Music, Arts, and Poetry; and Women and Geometry, which focuses on quilting.

Women's History

http://www.thehistorynet.com/WomensHistory/

Every month features a different issue of *Women's History* magazine with interesting articles and photographs on all aspects of women in history.

Women's Internet Information Network (WiiN)

http://www.undelete.org/

This site by Irene Stuber, Director of (WiiN), includes more than 20,000 profiles of notable women.

Women's Legal History Biography Project

http://www.stanford.edu/group/WLHP

Biographies of more than 100 American women lawyers and judges.

Women's Studies Programs, Departments and Research Centers

http://research.umbc.edu/~korenman/wmst/programs.html

From the University of Maryland, Baltimore County, Joan Korenman, Director of the Center for Women and Information Technology, provides this extensive list of women's studies programs. About half of the programs are in the United States, and the other half are in other countries. Includes links to several other lists of such programs.

Women Veterans

http://userpages.aug.com/captbarb/

"Captain Critical" presents a large collection of online material on women in the military. Documents the role of women in American wars from the Revolution through today's news.

Chapter 19

Historiography

Guido Abbattista

Metasites and General Historical Methodology

Historiology

http://www.cannylink.com/historyhistoriology.htm

A short index of sites on historical methodology at the Cannylink Internet Guide.

History and Historiography, Carnegie Mellon University

http://eng.hss.cmu.edu/history/

A valuable collection of links to historical resources.

The History Index at the University of Kansas

http://www.ukans.edu/history/VL/

This site provides an extensive list of links to historical sites on all the relevant subdivisions of historical research.

Voice of the Shuttle

http://vos.ucsb.edu/shuttle/history.html#historiography

On the history page of this well-known metaindex, under the category Historiography, there is a choice of the best sites of historiographical interest.

Yahoo!: Index of History Resources

http://dir.yahoo.com/Arts/Humanities/History/Historiology/

This index enumerates several sites of historical interest: It is worth browsing in search of materials of a more definitely historiographical-methodological character.

Electronic Libraries and Historiographical Texts

American Hypertexts

http://xroads.virginia.edu/~HYPER/hypertex.html

A large collection of textual resources on American history, including *The Federalist Papers*, Tocqueville's *Democracy in America*, and works by Francis Parkman and Frederick Jackson Turner.

Aragonese Historiography

http://eng.hss.cmu.edu/history/aragonese-historiography.txt

An online essay on the essentials of Aragonese historiography, this resource is part of the English Server at the Carnegie Mellon University.

Fernand Braudel Center

http://fbc.binghamton.edu/

The French historian Fernand Braudel made a profound impact on how historians view and practice their discipline. He played a leading role in the articulation of social history and interdisciplinary studies. This Web site at Binghamton University, State University of New York, provides a wealth of resources relating to Braudel. Among the members of its scientific board is Immanuel Wallerstein.

CHPE: Centre d'histoire de la pensée économique: Bibliothèque virtuelle de la pensée économique

http://panoramix.univ-paris1.fr/CHPE/textes.html

Located at the Université de Paris-I, this virtual library gives access to rich materials on the history of economic thought, as well as the history of historiography and methodology in modern Europe—for example, texts by Giovanni Botero, Matthew Hale, Lord Bolingbroke, Jean-Jacques Rousseau, Adam Ferguson, Thomas Malthus, Frederic Maitland, and Benedetto Croce.

Crusade Historiography

http://www.uni-heidelberg.de/subject/hd/fak7/hist/ol/logs/mt/
t7/940901-051/

At this Web location, users concerned with historical narratives of the Crusades can read a series of mails belonging to a thread of discussion on the theme of Crusade historiography. More mails on different aspects of the history of historiography, methodology, and philosophy of history (for example, philosophies of history and contemporary historical research on the Middle Age; definitions of "medieval") can be read at the same site under the URL http://www.uni-heidelberg.de/subject/hd/fak7/hist/ol/logs/mt/t7/.

Eliohs: Electronic Library of Modern Historiography

http://www.eliohs.unifi.it/

An electronic and virtual library of texts concerning modern (mainly seventeenth- to eighteenth-century) historiography, philosophy of history, and methodology. This is the only resource born out of a project expressly devoted to the history of historiography, and it led to the creation of the electronic journal *Cromohs* (see below). Its catalog includes electronic editions of historical, methodological, and philosophico-historical works from the sixteenth to the twentieth century produced by Eliohs and includes links to texts of the same kind electronically published elsewhere on the Net.

Gallica (Bibliothèque Nationale de France)

http://gallica.bnf.fr/

The French national library offers online versions of many nineteenth-century French historians's most important works.

Historians and Philosophers

http://www.scholiast.org/history/histphil.html

This site by P. Rasmussen consists of a biographical dictionary of historians and philosophers (arranged in four sections: ancient, medieval, early modern, and modern period), in the form of original or linked biographical profiles, (sometimes) bibliography, and external links to electronic editions of main works. The biographies are very unequal in content and value. A useful reference site for history of historiography, but still heavily under construction.

The Historian Underground: Making History Relevant for Life

http://www.geocities.com/SoHo/Cafe/8579/under.htm

A voice from outside the academic world. This site is designed to provide views about the object of history that challenge the normal aims of the historian's craft. It is based on the presupposition that normal academic historical method has lost touch with the importance of history for people's lives. This site's editors, therefore, attempt to gather articles that question traditional ways of thinking and stir up a bit of controversy. These pages go deep into an examination of the relation of history, philosophy, and literature as well as evaluating education and its role.

The Hume Archives

http://www.utm.edu/research/hume/

This very important site, maintained by Jim Fieser, includes Hume's writings, commentaries, eighteenth-century reviews of Hume's works, and early biographies. Also available are some writings by the Scottish philosopher documenting his ideas on history and his historical treatment of such subjects as man's religious sentiments.

The Internet Classics Archive at the Massachusetts Institute of Technology

http://classics.mit.edu/index.html

Offers full texts of works by Greek, Jewish, Roman, Persian, and other historians, such as Herodotus, Thucydides, Strabo, Xenophon, Josephus, Plutarch, Julius Caesar, Livy, Tacitus, Firdousi, and Lao-tzu. Texts are translated into English and available for free downloading in text-only format. This site, on the Internet since 1994, is sponsored in part by the MIT Program in Writing and Humanistic Studies.

Internet Public Library Online Texts

http://readroom.ipl.org/bin/ipl/ipl.books-idx.pl?type=deweystem&q1=901

Classic texts of interest for the methodology of history and general views of the historical process are present in this remarkable electronic library at the University of Michigan. Among the collection are writings by Francis Bacon, John Milton, James Dunbar, John Millar, Constantin-François Volney, T.B. Macaulay, Charles Babbage, Edwin Seligman, Antonio Labriola, Joel Salit, and Charles Kingsley.

Labyrinth

http://www.georgetown.edu/labyrinth/

This project from Georgetown University hosts a selection of contemporary sources on Medieval history arranged on a linguistic basis. Each Labyrinth Library section (e.g., *Auctores et fontes*) does not give direct access to digital editions, but provides a small choice of external sites loosely referring to several areas of European medieval history. Among these, users may find important electronic editions of relevant sources, but may frequently be disappointed to be offered heterogeneous links not critically selected.

Liber Liber

http://www.liberliber.it/biblioteca/index.htm

An excellent, multidisciplinary, searchable collection of mainly Italian, but also foreign texts, books, articles, documents, theses, and reviews. Every text is accompanied by information about the author and a short introduction. Works by Italian early modern and modern historians can be found here: Dino Compagni, Giovanni Villani, Niccolò Machiavelli, Francesco Guicciardini, Giambattista Vico, Vincenzo Cuoco, Francesco de Sanctis, and Antonio Labriola. This site, part of Progetto Manuzio, is hosted at the University of Milan.

Philosophy of History Archive

http://www.nsu.ru/filf/pha/

This Russian site introduces itself as follows: "The International Philosophy of History Archive (PHA) administered by Prof. Nikolai S. Rozov is a Web node that indexes links and materials related to the Philosophy of History and Theoretical History (PH and TH) on the Internet. It aims to serve those whose research interests include the rational theoretical explanatory approaches to World History and Modernity, the scientific predictions of global future trends, and the application of philosophical and scientific research results to Global Praxis." The site contains a list of internal and external links to e-texts and sites related to philosophy of history and theoretical history.

The Scriptorium: Center for Biblical Antiquities

http://www.scriptorium.org/

The Scriptorium: Center for Biblical Antiquities is a nonsectarian research center working in conjunction with the Van Kampen Foundation, which serves as the repository for the Van Kampen Collection of ancient artifacts, manuscripts, and rare printed materials. The collection consists primarily of biblical texts in all representative forms and is supplemented by secondary resources and the personal library of Eberhard Nestle, a leading nineteenth-century German biblical scholar. The scriptorium sponsors various academic initiatives reflecting the faculty's commitment to public education, scholarly research, and innovative pedagogy.

Giambattista Vico Home Page

http://www.connix.com/~gapinton/

This site, maintained by Giorgio A. Pinton, offers a biography and chronology of the life of one of the most important eighteenth-century European philosophers of history, plus bibliographies relating to his major works.

Voltaire: *Oeuvres diverses*

http://perso.wanadoo.fr/dboudin/Voltind.htm

This electronic library of works by Voltaire includes some historical works.

Voltaire Page

http://www.geocities.com/Athens/7308/

A site compiled by F. DeVenuto and expressly devoted to one of the most outstanding Enlightenment historians, with links to related sites.

Voltaire Society of America: Web Sites on Voltaire

http://humanities.uchicago.edu/homes/VSA/websites.html

More sites on the great Enlightenment philosopher and historian.

World History Archives

http://www.hartford-hwp.com/archives/10/index.html

World History Archives provides a selection of materials from Hartford Web Publishing. This site hosts a collection of essays, excerpts from classics of historiography, messages, dialogues, shorter essays on interpretative aspects of world history (e.g., the peculiarity of world history, Eurocentrism, the limits and divisions of history, the world systems approach). This material has been mainly selected from the H-Net list for world history. It is an interesting collection of ideas and insights expressed through the medium of a discussion list.

Electronic Journals

Cromohs

http://www.unifi.it/riviste/cromohs/

This electronic journal, founded in 1995, is expressly devoted to the history, theory, and methodology of historiography. It publishes in yearly issues original articles, review essays, and short reviews. Among its services are a very useful current bibliography of monographs and periodical literature and a list of relevant events. It was born as both a journal and an electronic library of sources. The library, called Eliohs (q.v.), has grown so much as to acquire a distinct identity. Chief editors and initiators of both *Cromohs* and Eliohs are Guido Abbattista and Rolando Minuti.

Histos: The Electronic Journal of Ancient Historiography

http://www.dur.ac.uk/Classics/histos/about.html

This journal, founded in 1997, is published at the Durham Classics Department and contains articles, essays, reviews, notices on research projects, and conferences on all aspects of ancient historiography.

Reviews in American History

http://muse.jhu.edu/journals/reviews_in_american_history/toc/rahv026.html

An invaluable tool for an up-to-date survey of contemporary historiographical production and debates, this electronic journal covers both general theoretical and methodological topics and, in particular, American history research.

Print Journals with Web Sites

History and Theory

http://www.wesleyan.edu/histjrnl/hthome.htm

This is the site of the well-known journal of historical methodology and philosophy of history established in 1960, which represents the main reference for contemporary research and debate on these topics.

Storia della Storiografia

http://www.cisi.unito.it/stor/home.htm

Storia della Storiografia—History of Historiography—Histoire de l'Historiographie—Geschichte der Geschichtsschreibung is a journal founded in 1982 by the International Commission for the History of Historiography. It publishes in four languages articles on all relevant aspects of the history and theory of historiography and the historical profession. Its Web site provides general information on the journal's activity and complete indexes of past, current, and forthcoming issues with an archive of contributors.

Teaching History: A Journal of Methods

http://www.emporia.edu/socsci/journal/main.htm

This is the Web site of a journal whose aim is to give general information and indexes of current and past issues. Designed for history teachers at all levels who wish to read about, or contribute to, innovative methods of teaching history, it is edited by Samuel Dicks and maintained by Michael Handley at the Division of Social Sciences of Emporia State University.

Didactic Resources

Internet Modern History Sourcebook: Studying History

http://www.fordham.edu/halsall/mod/modsbook.html

http://www.fordham.edu/halsall/mod/modsbook01.html

A first-rate didactic project devoted to a full presentation of the problem of historiographical research, knowledge, and methodology and of theories of history in the modern age. The site includes excerpts from primary sources and a rich library of essays, pages of important works on the subject, and lectures, being collectively a large anthology of class materials. Many of these materials are not locally produced, but just linked on the Net.

National Standards for World History

http://www.iac.net/~pfilio/part1.html

The electronic text of one of the most controversial documents on the reform of history teaching in the United States.

Ten Commandments of Good Historical Writing

http://www.bluffton.edu/~schlabachg/courses/10commnd.htm

This site, by Theron F. Schlabach, contains a list of practical, common-sense (but at times controvertible) suggestions from a teacher to beginning or amateur historians. Schlabach's views of what a historian-to-be's work ought to be are interesting but better considered as provocative suggestions than as mandatory commandments.

Chapter 20

Historic Preservation and Conservation

Charlene Mires and Anne Rothfeld

Advisory Council on Historic Preservation

http://www.achp.gov

Created by the independent federal agency that advises the president and Congress on historic preservation issues, this site offers links to historic preservation officers throughout the United States and information about the National Historic Preservation Act of 1966.

American Institute for Conservation of Historic and Artistic Works

http://aic.stanford.edu/

This organization of professional conservators shares its expertise on how to care for prized possessions from paintings and photographs to home videotapes. The site also offers advice on how to locate and select a professional conservator.

Built in America: Historic American Buildings Survey/ Historic American Engineering Record, 1933–Present

http://memory.loc.gov/ammem/hhhtml/hhhome.html

As part of its American Memory project, the Library of Congress has begun digitizing the vast documentation of American architecture, engineering, and design collected by the Historic American Buildings Survey and the Historic American Engineering Record. As the records go online, they can be searched by keyword, subject, and geographic area.

CoOL: Conservation Online

http://palimpsest.stanford.edu

From Stanford University Libraries, information on a wide range of conservation topics of interest to libraries and their users, including digital imaging and the conservation and use of electronic records.

Council on Library and Information Resources

http://www.clir.org/home.html

Offers online publications related to current issues in the preservation of library materials.

Heritage Conservation and Historic Preservation

http://home.vicnet.net.au/~conserv/hp-hc.htm

The State Library of Victoria in Australia has assembled this online library about conservation issues. International in scope, the many topics addressed by articles and accompanying Web links include information about caring for cultural objects such as books and paper, film and photography, and sound and magnetic materials.

Keeping Our Word: Preserving Information Across the Ages

http://www.lib.uiowa.edu/ref/exhibit

This virtual version of an exhibit by the University of Iowa Libraries addresses the issues of preserving materials from cave paintings and clay tablets to electronic media. The exhibit includes links for doing further research on preservation issues.

National Archives and Records Administration: Archives and Preservation Resources

http://www.nara.gov/nara/preserva

From the experts at the National Archives, information about preserving documents and photographs.

National Center for Preservation Technology and Training

http://www.ncptt.nps.gov

This project within the National Park Service includes an extensive, annotated database of online resources in archaeology, history, historic architecture and landscapes, and conservation of materials and objects. The database includes links for subscribing to listservs related to preservation and conservation.

Links to the Past: National Park Service Cultural Resources

http://www.cr.nps.gov

A site of great scope and depth, this project of the National Park Service is the place to start for information about visiting historic sites throughout the national parks system, teaching with historic places, and volunteering at historic sites. Online exhibits cover topics such as the life of Frederick Douglass and camp life at Gettysburg, and virtual tours take Web visitors to historic places in Detroit, Seattle, and other regions of the country. The site also serves as the gateway to programs such as Tools for Teaching (http://www.cr.nps.gov/toolsfor.htm), the Historic American Buildings Survey/Historic American Engineering Record (http://www.cr.nps.gov/habshaer) and the National Register of Historic Places (http://www.cr.nps.gov/nr).

National Preservation Institute

http://www.npi.org

This organization offers online registration for its numerous training seminars in historic preservation and cultural resources management.

National Trust for Historic Preservation

http://www.nthp.org

This private, nonprofit organization dedicated to saving historic buildings, neighborhoods, and landscapes offers a site with information about the group's mission and many projects, including its annual list of the nation's most endangered places. A link to its *Preservation* magazine offers tables of contents, book reviews, and excerpts. A link to the National Trust's Main Street Center (http: //www.mainst.org), which works to revitalize historic and traditional commercial areas, provides information about the history and preservation of Main Street communities and advice for organizing a Main Street revitalization project.

Northern States Conservation Center

http://www.collectioncare.org

Northern States Conservation Center of Saint Paul, Minnesota, here offers numerous articles about the management and preservation of museum collections, including advice about museums' use of the World Wide Web.

PreserveNet

http://www.preservenet.cornell.edu

Incorporating the PreserveNet Information Service and the PreserveNet Law Service, this site at Cornell University includes extensive links to preservation organizations, education programs, conferences and events, and job and internship opportunities. The Law Service offers texts of major state and federal preservation legislation and models for preservation ordinances. This is also the host site for the Guide to the African-American Heritage Preservation Foundation, Inc. (http://www.preservenet.cornell.edu/aahpf/homepage.htm).

RLG DigiNews

http://www.rlg.org/preserv/diginews

Online newsletter by the Research Libraries Group in cooperation with the Cornell University Library Department of Preservation and Conservation, focusing on preservation through digital imaging.

The Society of Architectural Historians

http://www.sah.org

This organization's collection of Internet resources includes links to collections of images of historic buildings.

State Historic Preservation Legislation Database

http://www.ncsl.org/programs/arts/statehist_intro.htm

The National Conference of State Legislatures offers this database of state legislation and constitution articles governing historic sites, archaeological sites and materials, and significant unmarked burial sites.

World Heritage

http://www.unesco.org/whc/nwhc/pages/home/pages/homepage.htm

Home page for the UNESCO project that encourages the preservation of cultural and natural heritage sites around the world. This site includes information about more than 500 World Heritage sites, including those considered endangered.

World Monuments Fund

http://www.worldmonuments.org

The site of this private, nonprofit organization working to safeguard works of art and architecture includes information about the fund's international list of 100 most endangered sites.

Chapter 21

Living History and Historic Reenactment

Bambi L. Dingman

Metasites

Histreenact: The Historical Reenactment Web Site

http://www.montacute.net/histrenact/welcome.htm

Links to general suppliers and craftsmen, historical information, online reenactment information, and societies that re-create different time periods.

Living History Online

http://www.LivingHistoryOnline.com/

An online magazine that serves as a reference source for all historical periods. This site contains excellent articles, an events calendar, bibliographies, and a search capability.

Reenactor's WebMall

http://rampages.onramp.net/~lawsonda/mall/

A comprehensive source for reenacting information, including a sutlers list, arranged by time period.

U.S. Regular Army Reenacting Unit Directory

http://www.halcyon.com/strandjr/Regs/

A huge index of reenacting units, sorted by time period. Some organizations have links to their Web pages, while others have e-mail contact information.

General Sites

The Alliance of Early American Interpreters

http://members.xoom.com/AEAI/index.html

The Alliance of Early American Interpreters is dedicated to re-creating the lives of civilian colonists in America in the period 1750 to 1790. Its Web site has membership information, an events calendar, recipes, and related sites.

American Longrifle Association

http://www.liming.org/alra/

A period trekking group and umbrella organization spanning the years 1750 to 1850. A calendar of events can be found online, as well as photographs and a bibliography.

Angelcynn

http://www.angelcynn.org.uk/

All content is related to Anglo-Saxon living history representing the period 400 to 900 C.E.: clothing and appearance of the early Christian Anglo-Saxons, weapons and armor, history, and related links.

Association for Living History, Farm and Agricultural Museums (ALHFAM)

http://www.alhfam.org/

Home of the Association for Living History, Farm and Agricultural Museums. The association's Web page has conference information, employment classifieds for living history specialists, planning tips for living history sites, and extensive links to living history organizations throughout the world.

Buckskins and Black Powder

http://www.geocities.com/Yosemite/Gorge/7186/index.htm

This excellent site has links to a variety of black powder and buckskinning sites on the Web. Also includes information about black powder clubs, the fur trade era, and re-creating history.

Butler's Rangers

http://iaw.on.ca/~awoolley/brang/brang.html

This corps of rangers served in the American Revolution and is re-created at living history events today. Information about the rangers, both past and present, can be found on this site, as well as historical source material and other information.

C & D Jarnagin Company

http://www.jarnaginco.com/

A provider of fine wares for the period 1750 through 1865, with a full complement of uniforms and equipment for American troops.

Camp Chase Gazette

http://www.campchase.com/

A well-known publication devoted to American Civil War re-creation. The online edition contains informative articles, a virtual roster of Civil War reenactors, upcoming events, and other relevant information.

Camp Life

http://www.cr.nps.gov/csd/gettex/

Gettysburg National Park holds the largest Civil War collection in the National Park System, with more than 40,000 cataloged items. A unique aspect of the collection is that many of the pieces are common, everyday items that allow us a glimpse into the lives of the soldiers who owned them. Now a portion of the collection can be viewed online in this virtual museum of photographs and artifacts devoted to everyday camp life.

Castle Keep Ltd.

http://www.reenact.com

Living history information and supplies for reenactors, categorized by period of interest, from medieval times to the twentieth century.

The Civil War Artillery Page

http://www.cwartillery.org/artillery.html

Information about organization and drill, weapons, ammunition, equipment, history, and reenactment of field and foot artillery units of the American Civil War.

Clothing of the Ancient Celts

http://www47.pair.com/lindo/Textiles_Page.htm

The primary focus of this Web page is prehistoric and classical Celtic culture and costuming, with a wealth of information about hair, jewelry, dyes, and textiles and links to other Celtic sites.

Compagnie Franche de la Marine du Detroit

http://www.richnet.net/~kamoore/

A volunteer living history interpretation organization devoted to all Detroit impressions, including marine, militia, Native American and civilian, c. 1754–1760. The company Web page has original and current unit history.

Company of Saint George

http://www.chronique.com/george.htm

Fostering the spirit of chivalry by portraying a tournament company of the fourteenth and fifteenth century, this site offers ceremony information, upcoming events, and a discussion about the role of historic interpreters.

Coon 'n Crockett Muzzleloaders

http://www.coon-n-crockett.org/

This page is loaded with information about the club, the muzzleloading hobby, photos, upcoming events, and more.

The Costume Page

http://members.aol.com/nebula5/tcpsupp.html

This is the definitive source for costuming information on the Web, conveniently sorted by period of interest. Links to costume suppliers, accessories, and patterns for every time period.

Digital History Ltd.

http://digitalhistory.org

A comprehensive site for everything related to the French and Indian War, including well-written accounts of the battles, forts, and participants, as well as links to groups that are currently re-creating colonial North American history.

Elizabethan Fencing and the Art of Defence

http://jan.ucc.nau.edu/~wew/fencing.html

An interesting page related to the art of fencing and swordplay. Topics include period masters, terminology, types of blades, and links to other fencing sites on the Web.

Elizabethan Period Costumes

http://www.resort.com/~banshee/Faire/Costume/index.html

A complete source of information on Elizabethan clothing, patterns, and footwear.

Fall Creek Sutlery

http://fcsutler.com/

Supplies for Civil War reenactors and Victorian era enthusiasts.

Flintlock FAQ

http://www.aye.net/~bspen/flintlockfaq.html

A beginner's guide to flintlock shooting with a concise history of flintlock weapons and answers to questions about flintlock performance.

French and Indian War Magazine Online

http://members.aol.com/fiwar/home.html

An electronic magazine that will interest French and Indian War reenactors. This informative site has a great listing of reenactment groups and other topics related to the war, such as British and French forts, music, and clothing.

GI Journal

http://www.militaria.com

Articles of interest to World War I and World War II reenactors and links to division Web pages, reproduction uniforms, and military history magazines.

The Gunfighter Zone

http://www.gunfighter.com

A Web site for reenactors of the Old West and Cowboy Action Shooting groups, with links to discussion boards, suppliers, books, magazines, and informative articles.

The Historical Maritime Society

http://www.hms.org.uk/

Re-creates British Navy life from 1793 to 1815 (Napoleonic War period).

Historical Reenactors

http://novaroma.org/via_romana/reenactments/index.html

Costuming information, reenactment guidelines, and a listing of reenactment groups portraying military and civilian life during the Roman era, compiled and presented by Nova Roma, an organization dedicated to the study and restoration of ancient Roman culture.

Historic Arms and Armour

http://www.historicenterprises.com/

Specializes in highly accurate handmade replicas of museum pieces. Although this is a commercial site, it includes a great deal of historical information and interesting photos of the company's work.

Hudson's Bay Company Digital Collection

http://collections.ic.gc.ca/

A digital collection of artifacts from the fur trade era, presented by the Manitoba Museum of Man and Nature.

19th Indiana Volunteer Infantry, Company A

http://www.19thindiana.com/

Civil War reenactors and nineteenth-century civilian impressionists. The Web page has an event schedule, company newsletter, and historical information.

Jas. Townsend & Son

http://www.jastown.com/

A mail order company specializing in historic clothing, camp gear, tents, books, music, knives, tomahawks, oak kegs, and other assorted items for the period 1750 to 1840.

1st Kansas Volunteer Infantry and Kansas Women's Relief Corps

http://www.cs.twsu.edu/~crgrier/1stks.html

A great company Web page.

King's Arms Press and Bindery

http://www.kingspress.com/

Specialized reprints of eighteenth-century books and pamphlets, including drill books and regulations, as well as military treatises.

Knighthood, Chivalry and Tournaments Resource Library

http://www.chronique.com/

Information on books, battle accounts, codes of conduct, armoring techniques, and more. Also includes a lengthy index of sites related to chivalry, armor, and reenactment groups.

Le Poulet Gauche

http://www.lepg.org/

A compendium of information on the history, daily life, and culture of sixteenth-century France. This site re-creates Le Poulet Gauche, a sixteenth-century alehouse, and offers information on food, drink, gaming, clothing, fencing, tradesmen, and suppliers.

Links to the Past

http://www.cr.nps.gov/colherit.htm

An amazing Web page from the National Park Service with online archives for many historic sites, as well as battle summaries, battlefield information, national landmarks, online exhibits, and much more.

Longshot's Rendezvous

http://members.aol.com/lodgepole/longshot.html

A source of rendezvous information for mountain men, buckskinners, and muzzleloaders of Missouri and Illinois. Also includes a guide to getting started in rendezvous and links to other sources.

28th Massachusetts Volunteer Infantry, Company A, C, and H

http://www.28thmass.org/

A well-designed Web page with information for historical research and reenacting.

Medieval/Renaissance Food Homepage

http://www.pbm.com/~lindahl/food.html

A comprehensive site containing recipes, primary sources, clip art, medieval cooking articles, and food publications.

Milieux: The Costume Site

http://www.milieux.com/costume/

A comprehensive list of links to costuming sites with diversified themes, such as medieval costuming, armor, Civil War uniforms, colonial garb, and modern accessories.

Morningside Books

http://www.morningsidebooks.com

Noted for its Civil War collection and as a recognized dealer of Don Troiani artwork.

Mountain Men and the Fur Trade

http://www.xmission.com/~drudy/amm.html

An online research center devoted to the history and traditions of trappers, explorers, and traders, with a digital collection, a bibliography, an archive of trade records, and links to Web sites related to the fur trade era.

National Renaissance Faire Directory

http://Renaissance-Faire.com/Locations.htm

A listing of Renaissance Faires around the country, with links to Web pages and event information.

NetSerf

http://www.netserf.org/

A huge index arranged by subject matter with links to all things medieval—religion, culture, art, and literature, etc.

47th New York State Volunteers: "Washington Grays"

http://www.awod.com/gallery/probono/cwchas/47ny.html

A federal reenacting unit. Its Web page has an extensive unit history and reenactment information.

5th New York Volunteer Infantry, Company A: Duryée's Zouaves

http://www.zouave.org/

An excellent company Web page with a detailed history, roster, and extensive photo gallery.

North/South Alliance

http://www.nsalliance.org/

Information on the First Confederate and First Federal Divisions in the American Civil War and an event listing.

The Northwest Territory Alliance

http://www.nwta.com/

This group strives to re-create the lifestyle, culture, and arts of the Revolutionary War era with an accurate representation of uniforms, weaponry and battlefield tactics. This Web site offers forms and documents useful to reenactors, an event schedule, a chronology of events in the War for Independence, pattern lists, publications, and more.

Oakhill Enterprises

http://www.frontiernet.net./~oakhill

Guns, clothing, and accessories for the period 1640 to 1840.

The Patriots of Fort McHenry

http://www.bcpl.lib.md.us/~etowner/patriots.html

This organization hopes to preserve the historical legacy of the patriots who defended Baltimore in 1814. Fort McHenry is best known as the scene of the battle which Francis Scott Key witnessed and wrote about in the "Star Spangled Banner."

Plimoth Plantation

http://www.plimoth.org/

Plimoth Plantation's Pilgrim Village brings to life the Plymouth of 1627. This Web site provides information about the village and also includes educational information for reenactors.

Pre-1840's Buckskinning

http://www.geocities.com/Yosemite/2839/index.html

Contains a lengthy list of rendezvous groups around the United States, publications, trader events, and buckskinning classifieds.

Proper Elizabethan Accents

http://www.resort.com/~banshee/Faire/Language/index.html

Pronunciation guide, drills, and vocabulary to perfect your accent for the Faire.

Rationed Fashion

http://www.geocities.com/SoHo/coffeehouse/6727/rationed_fashion.html

American fashion during World War II with style descriptions, designers, images, and sources.

Reenacting.com

http://www.dstylus.com/victorianlady/index.html

An online guide to civilian impressions of the Civil War, with helpful tips for creating interesting female impressions for both the Union and Confederacy.

Reenactor Net

http://www.reenactor.net/

A list of links to reenactor Web sites, categorized by time period.

Reenactors Page

http://www2.tsixroads.com/~rodbond/reenacting.html

This Web site offers photos, history, trivia, event reviews, and related links for reenactors and Civil War enthusiasts.

Regia Anglorum

http://www.regia.org/

A society with a vast number of resources available for portraying the British people as they were 100 years before the Norman conquest. The Web site has membership and contact information.

64th Regiment of Foot

http://freenet.vcu.edu/sigs/reg64/

Members of the 64th Regiment portray British infantry soldiers from the time of the Revolutionary War. Their Web page has information on the British army, regimental colors, the Brown Bess, women and the army, and plenty of primary reference material.

Renaissance Faire Overview

http://www.resort.com/~banshee/Faire/General/faire.html

An introduction to attending Faires and a description of what to expect.

Renaissance Magazine

http://www.renaissancemagazine.com

Well-known to reenactors as an informative print magazine, the online version is packed with useful information as well. Includes past features on books, music, movies, and products, with links to related Web sites.

The Rolls Ethereal

http://www.waks.org/rolls/

This is an online directory of members of the Society for Creative Anachronism, with hundreds of searchable listings.

Roman Life

http://www.dl.ket.org/latin1/things/romanlife/

This site contains historical information on Roman life and directions for making your own Roman-style costumes.

Roman Orgy

http://www.diax.ch/users/julien.courtois/orgy/

An excellent site with information about the art of Roman cooking, recipes, historical documents, and links to related sites.

The 42nd Royal Highland Regiment: "The Black Watch"

http://www.42ndrhr.org/index.php

This well-designed site is a terrific source of information on period music, dancing, uniforms, and everything related to the Black Watch of the late 1700s in North America.

SCA (Society for Creative Anachronism) Music and Dance Homepage

http://www.pbm.com/~lindahl/music_and_dance.html

Links to primary sources, articles, and sound files related to Renaissance music and dance.

SCRIBE's History Archives

http://www.faire.net/SCRIBE/archives/History.Htm

These pages contain hundreds of text files related to the history of the Renaissance and the Middle Ages, including listings of Renaissance Faire participants, guilds, groups, song lyrics, and events around the country. Images and articles related to period crafts, such as Celtic knotwork, heraldic crests, brewing, cooking, blacksmithing, and textiles can also be found at this site.

Second Panzer Division

http://www.panzerdivision.org

The largest and best-equipped German reenacting unit in North America. Its Web site has information about equipment and tactics, a bibliography, and links to World War II reenactors.

Shadows of the Past

http://www.sptddog.com/sotp.html

This organization's guide to reenacting the Old West contains articles, historical resources, photographs, literature, and links to related sites.

Society for Creative Anachronism (SCA)

http://www.sca.org/

This site, dedicated to researching and re-creating pre-seventeenth-century European history, has a huge amount of information on topics related to medieval history, such as the art of combat, including official documents, events, and more.

1st South Carolina Artillery, C.S.A.

http://www.awod.com/gallery/probono/cwchas/1scart.html

Reenacts the history of the men who manned the artillery of the Confederate defenses of the South Carolina coast during the American Civil War. This Web site has history, photos, and a bibliography.

A Stitch Out of Time

http://home.flash.net/~wymarc/

Medieval embroidery techniques from the ninth through sixteenth centuries.

Trans-Mississippi Rifles Infantry

http://members.aol.com/rlhtmr

This Web site has membership information, an events listing, and extensive links to Civil War reenacting groups for both Union and Confederate soldiers.

Trev's Rendezvous Down Under

http://www.geocities.com/Yosemite/Trails/1878/

This site has contact information for many groups who have only e-mail, as well as for organizations that are already on the Internet.

U.S. Civil War Center

http://www.cwc.lsu.edu/cwc/civlink.htm

The Civil War Center is an attempt to index all the Civil War sites on the Web, including national parks, battlefields, roundtables, reenacting groups, and events. This should be one of the first stops for users interested in re-creating the American Civil War.

4th U.S. Infantry Regiment, Company C

http://www.halcyon.com/strandjr/4thUS_Inf/

Information about Civil War arms and equipment, regimental insignia, and the Army of the Potomac.

The Viking Home Page

http://www.control.chalmers.se/vikings/indexframe.html

Reenactors and organizations interested in Viking culture will want to bookmark this page, which has information about sagas, eddas, runes, Viking ships, culture, exhibitions, and links to groups that are interpreting this time period.

42nd Virginia Volunteer Infantry

http://www.erols.com/va42nd/present.html

A helpful introduction to reenacting, an authenticity code, reference room, and related information.

Welcome to Fort Erie and the War of 1812

http://www.iaw.on.ca/~jsek/

Great information about the Fort Erie siege and the War of 1812 reenactment units.

White Oak Society, Inc.

http://www.whiteoak.org/

This Web site has a wealth of information about rendezvous and the fur trade era, from interpreters who portray authentic characters of the eighteenth century.

World War I Trenches on the Web

http://www.worldwar1.com/index.html

A compendium of information for the World War I reenactor. This history of the Great War has a reference library, World War I poster reproductions, interesting articles, and reenactor photographs.

Chapter 22

Genealogy

Samuel E. Dicks

Genealogists have created many Internet sites, publications, and other research tools that are also of use to biographers, social historians, military historians, and others. Probate, military, census, immigration, and land records are among the many kinds of materials most familiar to genealogists. Many sources can be accessed only by visiting a location or arranging for a local researcher, but the Internet makes it easy to find out the kinds of materials available before a trip is planned, make contact with others working on the same family lines, discover sources more easily, and, in some cases, obtain detailed genealogical information by the Internet or by mail. Religious and fraternal organizations, and many other groups, often have materials of value; some of these can be located in Cyndi's List and RootsWeb (see below) or by using search engines and published reference works. The single most useful reference work is *The Source: A Guidebook of American Genealogy*, published by Ancestry.com (see below) and available at most public libraries.

Most Useful Sites

American Family Immigration History Center (Ellis Island Records)

http://www.ellisislandrecords.org/

More than 22 million people entered the United States through Ellis Island from 1892 to 1924. The ships' manifest records ordinarily include the immigrants' given name and surname, ethnicity, last place of residence, name of ship and departure port, arrival date, age, gender, and marital status, along with the location of their name on the manifest. Numerous other Web sites provide background on the Ellis Island experience, including Ancestry.com and RootsWeb.com. This is a new Web site that plans to add additional information in the future. Interest has been high—try again later if you are unable to access it or try this alternative site—http://sites.netscape.net/stephenpmorse/ellis.html. If you are searching for passenger records before 1892, try the Immigrant Ships Transcribers Guild, which is compiling a list of earlier ship passengers (http://istg.rootsweb.com/).

Ancestry.com

http://ancestry.com/

Ancestry.com, a publisher of genealogy books, is also a highly popular, low-cost subscription library of genealogical databases. Most newly added databases are free for ten days, and many sites are permanently free. Free sites include several noted columnists, genealogy lessons, and the SSDI or Social Security Death Index, which lists millions of deceased people and provides instructions on gaining additional information. Thousands of other invaluable sites are available to subscribers, including on-screen original pages of most federal censuses and the genealogy periodical index of the Allen County Public Library of Fort Wayne, Indiana, which includes over a million articles. Ancestry has a free daily newsletter that notes new sites, links, and other useful information and also publishers several basic books and magazines for genealogists.

Cyndi's List of Genealogy Sites on the Internet

http://www.cyndislist.com/

Cyndi Howells's Web site is the best-known and most comprehensive genealogy site, with 100,000 links to states, counties, provinces, nations, military sites, ethnic sites, and other sites too numerous to note. The United States site is at http://www.cyndislist.com/genusa.htm. Browse through Cyndi's List slowly over several days. There is a great deal here worth exploring. The site is also available in book form.

Family History Library (LDS Church, Salt Lake City)

http://familysearch.org/

The Church of Jesus Christ of Latter-Day Saints maintains the world largest family history library; information from these holdings continues to be added to this Web site. The International Genealogical Index (IGI) is one of the most commonly used sites. Local Family History Centers, commonly operated by volunteers in many Mormon churches, can provide additional information and arrange for the borrowing of microfilm. Church records from overseas and local government records are among the many holdings that may accessed online or, in some cases, only by visiting a local center. As with all sites, information provided should be verified by other sources. Personal Ancestral File (PAF), a widely used free genealogy software program, may be downloaded free; numerous databases on CD-ROM are also available at minimal cost. Freedmen's Bank Records, a major African-American database, is among the more important low-cost sources available on CD-ROM. This unique Web site has numerous avenues which should be explored over many days.

The Genealogy Page: National Archives and Records Administration

http://www.nara.gov/genealogy/genindex.html

The National Archives is one of the most user-friendly sites provided by the federal government. Census schedules, immigration and naturalization records, ship passenger records, military and military pension records, and Native American records are among the sources most commonly used by genealogists. Many of the microfilmed materials, including the census schedules and military pension indexes, are also in the thirteen regional branches of NARA, which may also be accessed from this site. This site provides information on the holdings in each regional branch and how one may receive copies of materials or additional information. Among the useful links from this site are Clues in Census Records, 1850–1920 (http://www.nara.gov/genealogy/cenclues.html) and The Soundex Machine (http://www.nara.gov/genealogy/soundex/soundex.html). Soundex is a system originally developed in the 1930s for Social Security applicants who were born before birth certificates were common and who needed to prove their date of birth. It provides a code that takes into account different spellings and acts as an index to most census schedules since 1880. Another Soundex converter that allows you to list several soundex numbers at once is http://www.bradandkathy.com/genealogy/yasc.html.

RootsWeb

http://www.rootsweb.com/

Rootsweb is the oldest and largest genealogy site. One of its best-known features is the Rootsweb Surname List (RSL) which is a sort of international bulletin board where one can connect with others pursuing the same surnames (http://rsl.rootsweb.com/). The site also includes a list of resources for each state (http://www.rootsweb.com/roots-l/usa.html#Statelist). Rootsweb deserves several hours or days of exploring, and a good place for beginners to start is at http://www.rootsweb.com/~rwguide/. Rootsweb also has free e-mail newsletters that provide information on new sites and on problems or experiences encountered by others.

State Historical Societies and Archives

http://www.ohiohistory.org/links/arch_hs.html

Most states have a state historical society and a state archive. The historical society will probably include microfilm copies of newspapers and census records, private papers donated to the society, early state and local histories, and other publications relating to the region. A state archive is ordinarily the custodian of official state government papers, such as those of the governor or adjutant general. In some states the state archive and state historical society are a single institution, usually in the state capital. Elsewhere they are separate organizations and may even be in different cities. Newspapers or other materials may also be in a state library or a state historical library. The Ohio Historical Society provides links to most state historical societies and archives; other state societies, archives, and libraries can be located at the Cyndi's List or RootsWeb sites (see above). State archives may also be found at http://aagsnc.org/library/archives.html or at http://ils.unc.edu/archives/archive7.html.

USGenWeb

http://www.usgenweb.org/

The USGenWeb Project, manned by volunteers, is one of the most useful sites for quickly accessing states and counties. The site provides a map which one can click to access states and counties (http://www.usgenweb.org/statelinks.html), plus other projects and links.

Additional Sites

African-American Genealogy: Christine's Genealogy Website

http://ccharity.com/

This provides information and links to most other sites that deal with African-American genealogy. Also see the African-American page on Cyndi's List (http://www.CyndisList.com/african.htm).

British Information for Genealogists

http://www.pro.gov.uk/readers/genealogists/default.htm

The British Public Record Office provides information and links for those researching families from the British Isles. Users can go to Resources for Genealogists to access numerous other links. Cyndi's List, above, provides additional links for the United Kingdom and for other parts of the world.

Center for Life Stories Preservation

http://www.storypreservation.com/home.html

This unusual site provides many memoirs and life stories of slaves, veterans, pioneers, and others. It includes information for students and teachers who wish to use oral history and other techniques to understand and preserve early family experiences.

The Civil War Soldiers and Sailors System

http://www.itd.nps.gov/cwss/

The National Park Service, in conjunction with the National Archives and Records Administration, the Genealogical Society of Utah (LDS Church), the Federation of Genealogical Societies, the United Daughters of the Confederacy, and numerous other military and genealogy organizations, is developing a computerized database of all soldiers and sailors of the Civil War, both Union and Confederate. The Web site is also available at numerous military cemeteries. Individuals not yet listed here may be located at state or local Web sites—users can check county historical and genealogical sites, state archives, and historical societies. Also, indexes to pension files are available through the National Archives branches and other locations with the use of Soundex. These may also be located at Ancestry.com (fee based).

The Commonwealth War Graves Commission

http://www.cwgc.org/

Personal and service details of the 1.7 million soldiers of the British Commonwealth who died in World War I or World War II. Also includes civilian casualties and other information.

Family Tree Maker Online

http://www.familytreemaker.com/

Broderbund's Family Tree Maker has one of the largest software programs for genealogists. It also provides much free information on its Web site.

Federation of East European Family History Societies (FEEFHS)

http://feefhs.org/

A basic Web site for Central and Eastern European countries, including Switzerland and Germany. Indexes connect with related Web sites from all parts of the world.

The Genealogical Database

http://www.gentree.com/gentree.html

This site contains links to all known databases on the Web. Family sites are included only if a database is available for searching. An index lists most, but not all, of the databases on the site.

Helm's Genealogy Toolbox

http://genealogy.tbox.com/

Matthew L. Helm's site is one of the oldest and best-known sites for a wide variety of information and links. There is information on genealogy software and other topics.

International Black Sheep Society of Genealogists

http://homepages.rootsweb.com/~blksheep/

An organization for those with horse thieves or other scoundrels among their ancestors; the site has many interesting stories and useful links.

JewishGen

http://www.jewishgen.org/

JewishGen is the primary Internet source for those engaged in Jewish genealogy. It connects with numerous databases, including JewishGen Family Finder, which connects people searching the same ancestral towns and surnames. For locating Holocaust survivors, see Missing Identity (http://www.jewishgen.org/missing-identity/).

Korean War and Vietnam War Casualties

http://www.nara.gov/nara/electronic/kcashr.html
http://www.nara.gov/nara/electronic/vcasal.html

These sites contain the National Archives' lists, by state, of the casualties of the Korean War and of the Vietnam War.

Native American Genealogy: The Cherokee Genealogy Page

http://www.allthingscherokee.com

Users can scroll down past the Cherokee sites to other Native American genealogy sites and to other sites useful to historians. Also see Cyndi's List (http://
www.CyndisList.com/native.htm).

Public Libraries

http://www.publiclibraries.com/

Local public libraries often have genealogical holdings for their communities;
large metropolitan libraries usually have extensive holdings. Public libraries or
local historical and genealogical societies generally have basic reference works,
as well as such local resources as community histories, church records, obituar-
ies, city directories, and compilations of area cemetery, birth, marriage, and
death records. If a public library cannot be found here, use a search engine,
such as www.dogpile.com, to find local communities and libraries. For state
libraries, go to http://www.publiclibraries.com/state_library.htm.

The 10,000 Year Calendar

http://calendarhome.com/tyc/

This is a site of great practical use to historians and genealogists. It provides a
calendar for any month of any year desired, information on calendar changes,
Mayan and Chinese calendars, and other information. For a simpler calendar of
any month and year, go to http://alabanza.com/kabacoff/Inter-Links/cgi/cal.cgi.

USGS National Mapping Information Query Form

http://geonames.usgs.gov/pls/gnis/web_query.gnis_web_query_form

For those doing genealogical research, this U.S. Geological Survey Query Form
is useful for locating obscure places, cemeteries, and other sites in the United
States. In most cases, one is able to gain the coordinates and also maps indicating the locations. Many Canadian sites may be located at http://
geonames.nrcan.gc.ca/english/cgndb.html and at http://atlas.gc.ca/english/
index.html. Maps for other places in the world are available at http://
uk2.multimap.com/. For British locations, see http://www.geog.port.ac.uk/
gbhgis/ and http://www.streetmap.co.uk/.

U.S. Immigration and Naturalization Service

http://www.ins.usdoj.gov/graphics/aboutins/history/index.htm

This site, titled "INS, Genealogy, and Education," contains considerable information on immigration history and laws, much of it designed for classroom use. For INS forms and fees, go to http://www.ins.usdoj.gov/graphics/formsfee/index.htm.

U.S. Surname Distribution

http://www.hamrick.com/names/index.html

The 1850, 1880, and 1920 U.S. Census and 1990s phone books are used to show the distribution of surnames by states at these four different times. Use the arrow next to the "Display" button and go to "All Periods" for quick comparisons. Hamrick software also has programs to facilitate the use of photographs in compiling a genealogy.

U.S. Vital Records Information

http://vitalrec.com/index.html

Modern state and territory sites for finding birth, marriage, divorce, and death records are available here. Some earlier records are available at local, rather than centralized state offices; some of the earlier records are available online. Go to "Related Links" provided for each state and territory for many additional useful sites.

Chapter 23

State Historical Societies

Leo E. Landis, Scott A. Merriman, and Dennis A. Trinkle

Metasite

National Council on Public History (NCPH) Page of Historical Societies
http://www.iupui.edu/~ncph/societies.html

Canada

Canada's National History Society
http://www.historysociety.ca/

United States

Alabama Department of Archives and History
http://www.archives.state.al.us/

Alaska Historical Society
http://www.alaska.net/~ahs/ahsinfo.htm

Arizona Historical Society

http://www.tempe.gov/ahs/ (Central Division)

http://www.infomagic.net/~ahsnad/index.html (Northern Division)

http://w3.arizona.edu/~azhist/rio.htm (Rio Colorado Division)

http://w3.arizona.edu/~azhist/index.html (Southern Division)

California Historical Society, San Francisco

http://www.calhist.org/

Colorado Historical Society

http://coloradohistory.org/home.htm

Connecticut Historical Society

http://www.chs.org/

The Historical Society of Delaware

http://www.hsd.org/

Florida Historical Society

http://florida-historical-soc.org/

Georgia Historical Society

http://www.georgiahistory.com/

Historical/Genealogical Societies in Georgia

http://widow.mindspring.com/~bevr/bevrgen.html

The Hawaiian Historical Society

http://www.hawaiianhistory.org/index.html

Idaho State Historical Society
http://www2.state.id.us/ishs/index.html

Illinois State Historical Society
http://www.prairienet.org/ishs/

Indiana Historical Society
http://www.indianahistory.org/

State Historical Society of Iowa
http://www.iowahistory.org/

The Kansas State Historical Society
http://www.kshs.org/

Kentucky Historical Society
http://www.des.state.ky.us/agencies/khs/

Louisiana Historical Society
http://www.louisianahistoricalsociety.org

Louisiana State Museum
http://lsm.crt.state.la.us/

The Center for Maine History
http://www.mainehistory.org/

Maryland Historical Society
http://www.mdhs.org/

Maryland Historical Trust

http://www.marylandhistoricaltrust.net

The Massachusetts Historical Society

http://www.masshist.org/

Michigan Historical Center

http://www.sos.state.mi.us/history/history.html

Minnesota Historical Society

http://www.mnhs.org/

Mississippi Historical Society

http://mshistory.k12.ms.us/mshistsociety.html (magazine)
http://www.mdah.state.ms.us/admin/mhistsoc.html (membership)

Missouri Historical Society

http://www.mohistory.org

The Montana Historical Society

http://his.state.mt.us/index.html

Nebraska State Historical Society

http://www.nebraskahistory.org/

Nevada Historical Society

http://dmla.clan.lib.nv.us/docs/museums/reno/his-soc.htm

New Hampshire Historical Society

http://www.nhhistory.org/index.html

New Jersey Historical Commission
http://www.state.nj.us/state/history/hisidx.html

New Jersey Historical Society
http://www.eventworksnj.com/njhist/njhistorical.html

New Mexico State Records Center and Archives
http://www.state.nm.us/cpr/

New York Historical Society
http://www.nyhistory.org/

New York State Historical Association
http://www.nysha.org

North Carolina Division of Archives and History
http://www.ah.dcr.state.nc.us/

State Library of North Carolina
http://prioris.dcr.state.nc.us/ncslhome.htm

The State Historical Society of North Dakota
http://www.state.nd.us/hist/

The Ohio Historical Society
http://www.ohiohistory.org/

Oklahoma Historical Society
http://www.ok-history.mus.ok.us/

Oregon Historical Society

http://www.ohs.org/

The Historical Society of Pennsylvania

http://www.hsp.org/

The Rhode Island Historical Society

http://www.rihs.org

South Carolina Historical Society

http://www.schistory.org/

South Dakota State Historical Society/Office of History

http://www.sdhistory.org/

East Tennessee Historical Society

http://www.east-tennessee-history.org/

West Tennessee Historical Society

http://www.wths.tn.org/

Texas Historical Commission

http://www.tsl.state.tx.us/

Texas State Historical Association

http://www.tsha.utexas.edu/

The Utah State Historical Society

http://www.dced.state.ut.us/history/

Vermont Historical Society

http://www.state.vt.us/vhs/

Virginia Historical Society

http://www.vahistorical.org/index.htm

Washington State Historical Society

http://www.wshs.org/

West Virginia Division of Culture and History

http://www.wvculture.org/

West Virginia State Archives

http://www.wvculture.org/history/

State Historical Society of Wisconsin, Archives Division

http://www.shsw.wisc.edu/index.html

Wyoming State Historical Society

http://wyshs.org/

Chapter 24

History Books on the Internet

Susanna Betzel

Book Search Networks

The Internet has brought about one of the greatest changes—and advances—in the out-of-print/rare book trade in decades. With the advent of Internet search networks, which can search the inventories of thousands of dealers worldwide in seconds, it has suddenly become far easier to hunt down that elusive out-of-print (or, for that matter, in-print) book and to compare prices among dealers offering it. The following networks are leaders in the field:

Advanced Book Exchange

http://www.abebooks.com
Used, out-of-print, and rare books. Especially recommended.

Alibris

http://www.alibris.com/home.cfm
Used, out-of-print, and rare books.

Amazon.com

http://www.amazon.com

New books. Also does searches for rare books.

Antiqbook

http://www.antiqbook.com/

Includes a larger percentage of rare/antiquarian book dealers, especially European.

Barnes and Noble

http://www.barnesandnoble.com/

New books. Also does searches for rare books.

Bibliofind

http://www.bibliofind.com

Used, out-of-print, and rare books. Especially recommended; the fastest and most efficient of the networks.

Bookfinder

http://www.bookfinder.com

Simultaneously searches most of the above networks and displays the results on a single page. Bookfinder also searches the in-print databases at Amazon.com (see above) and Powell's Books (see below).

Books and Book Collecting

http://www.trussel.com/f_books.htm

This is a fabulously useful site for all facets of out-of-print book buying and collecting. It includes SetMaker, a free search/sell forum for odd volumes from multivolume sets; BookSeek, links to the online catalogs of many dealers who are not members of the large networks; and direct links to major library catalogs, the search networks, and many large individual book dealers worldwide who have their own searchable sites.

Individual Book Dealers

The following is just a sampling of book dealers and bookstores worldwide who specialize in history books (new, remaindered, and/or out-of-print) or who have strong history sections, and who have a presence on the Internet, either as members of one of the networks or with their own Web sites and online catalogs. Owner or proprietor is listed at the beginning of each description.

Note: Credit cards: AE = American Express; D = Discover; MC = MasterCard; V = Visa.

Alden Books, Inc.

Email: aldenbks@cdt.infi.net

Web site: http://www.aldenbooks.com

Karen and Steve Deutsch and Maria and Charles Melchioris. Specialty: General history, scholarly. Number of history books: 2,500. Credit cards: AE MC V. Location: USA.

Antiquariat Hohmann

Email: antiquariat-hohmann@t-online.de

Wilhelm Hohmann. Specialty: Economic and business history. Number of history books: 5,000; fifty percent of total stock is history books. Credit cards: No; foreign checks accepted. Location: Germany.

Archer's Used and Rare Books, Inc.

Email: archers@megsinet.net

Paul Bauer. Specialty: General history, Americana. Number of history books: 1,000. Founded 1986. Credit cards: MC V. Location: USA.

The Avid Reader Used and Rare Books, Inc.

Email: avid@avidreader.com

Web site: http://www.avidreader.com

Barry Jones. Specialty: General, American, scholarly, American regional, Southern, genealogy. Number of history books: 15,000; fifty percent of total stock is history books. Credit cards: D MC V. Location: USA.

Beulahland Books

Email: beulahland@coslink.net

William Tompkins. Specialty: General history. Number of history books: 4,000. Founded 1980. Credit cards: D MC V. Location: USA.

Book CloseOuts, Inc.

Email: als@bookcloseouts.com

Web site: http://www.bookcloseouts.com

Al Siebring, Customer Service. Specialty: General history. Number of history books: 3,000. Founded 1982. Credit cards: MC V. Location: USA.

Book House in Dinkytown

Email: bookhous@pro-ns.net

Kristen Eide-Tollefson. Specialty: General history. Number of history books: "40 cases." Founded 1976. Credit cards: AE D MC V; foreign checks accepted. Location: USA.

Books Unlimited

Email: otierney@booksunlimited.com

Web site: http://www.booksunlimited.com

Joseph, Barbara, and Owen Tierney. Specialty: General history, American. Number of history books: 10,000. Founded 1988. Credit cards: D MC V. Location: USA.

Calhoun Book Store

Email: calhounbk@aol.com

Virginia Lou Seay. Specialty: General history, university press. Number of history books: 6,000. Founded 1961. Credit cards: No; foreign checks accepted with surcharge. Location: USA.

Chameleon

Email: afrank@uswest.net

Web site: http://www.abebooks.com/home/chameleon/

Alan D. Frank. Specialty: General history, Native and Western American, African, African-American, history of medicine, art history. Number of history books: 8,000. Credit cards: MC V. Location: USA.

Clifton Books

Email: jhodgk9942@aol.com

Web site: http://www.bibliofind.com/cliftonbooks.html

John Hodgkins. Specialty: General history, British history since 1600. Number of history books: 4,500 listed on the Web; 25,000 in stock; all of the stock is history books. Founded 1969. Credit cards: AE MC V Access; U.S. dollars and checks accepted. Location: UK.

Comenius-Antiquariat

Email: shess@access.ch

Web site: http://www.comenius-antiquariat.com

Samuel Hess and Joerg Zoller. Specialty: General history, Swiss, social history, anarchism. Number of history books: 6,000. Credit cards: MC V; foreign checks accepted with surcharge. Location: Switzerland.

Ed Conroy, Bookseller

Email: edconroy@wizvax.net

Edward Conroy. Specialty: Russian, military, political/social science, university press. Number of history books: 36,000; 90 percent of total stock is history books. Founded 1987. Credit cards: MC V; U.S. and British checks accepted. Location: USA.

D.K. Publishers Distributors Ltd.

Email: dkpd@del3.vsnl.net.in

Web site: http://www.dkpdindia.com

Parmil Mittal. Specialty: Asian. Number of history books: 7,000. Founded 1974. Credit cards: No; foreign checks accepted. Location: India.

Editions

Email: nleditions@aol.com

Web site: http://www.nleditions.com

Norman and Joan Levine. Specialty: General history. Number of history books: 20,000. Founded 1948. Credit cards: D MC V. Location: USA.

Expatriate Bookshop of Denmark

Email: expatbks@post11.tele.dk

John Jackson. Specialty: General history, South Asia. Number of history books: 2,000. Credit cards: No; foreign checks accepted. Location: Denmark.

Franklin's Old Book Shop

Email: oldbooks@usit.net

Web Site: http://www.auldbooks.com/biblio/clients/franklin (under construction)

Ed Franklin. Specialty: General history. Number of history books: 4,000. Credit cards: yes. Location: USA.

Great Northwest Bookstore

Email: gnw@greatnorthwestbooks.com

Web site: http://www.greatnorthwestbooks.com

Phil Wikelun, John Henley, and Grace Pastine. Specialty: General, American West, prehistory. Number of history books: 85,000; fifty percent of total stock is history books. Founded 1977. Credit cards: AE D MC V; foreign checks accepted. Location: USA.

Greenfield Books

Email: greenfld@escape.ca

Web site: http://www.greenfieldbooks.com/

Specialty: General history, military, nautical, Canadian, polar exploration. Number of history books: 8,000. Credit cards: AE MC V; U.S. and Canadian checks accepted. Location: Canada.

Ground Zero Books, Ltd.

Email: gzbooksltd@aol.com

R. Alan Lewis. Specialty: Military history, world wars, Vietnam, American Civil War. Number of history books: 50,000; entire stock is military history books. Founded 1978 and operated by trained historians. Credit cards: AE D MC V. Location: USA.

Gutenberg Holdings

Email: gutenbrg@ziplink.net

Web site: http://gutenbergholdings.com

Rhett Moran. Specialty: General history, American. Number of history books: 13,000. Credit cards: AE D MC V. Location: USA.

Peter J. Hadley: Bookseller

Email: books@hadley.co.uk

Web site: http://www.hadley.co.uk

Peter J. Hadley. Specialty: General history, English history. Number of history books: 1,200; fifty percent of total stock is history books. Founded 1984. Credit cards: MC V Switch; checks in U.S. dollars accepted. Location: UK.

Caroline Hartley Books

Email: Hartleybk@clara.net

Caroline Hartley. Specialty: General history, British. Number of history books: 3,500. Founded 1983. Credit cards: MC V. Location: UK.

History to Go

Email: old_stuff@bigfoot.com

Lance Sprung. Specialty: Historic documents, letters, autographs, signed books, newspapers, broadsides, manuscripts, diaries, from the Middle Ages to the present. Number of documents: about 3,500. Not a book dealer per se, but certainly of interest to historians; entire stock is historical items. Plans to issue catalogs. Credit cards: MC V (in shop only). Location: USA.

R.R. Knott Bookseller

Email: rrknott@cyberus.ca

Web site: http://www.cyberus.ca/~rrknott

R.R. Knott. Specialty: Medieval, Canadian, military, ancient. Number of history books: 6,000; fifty percent of total stock is history books. Founded 1980. Credit cards: MC V; foreign checks accepted. Location: Canada.

Labyrinth Books

Email: books@labyrinthbooks.com

Web site: http://www.labyrinthbooks.com/

Specialty: General history, scholarly/university press. Number of history books: Thousands—new and remaindered. Credit cards: AE MC V. Location: USA.

David M. Lesser, Fine Antiquarian Books LLC

Email: dmlesser@lesserbooks.com

Web site: http://www.lesserbooks.com

David Lesser. Specialty: Americana. Number of history books: 10,000; ninety-five percent of total stock is history books. Credit cards: MC V. Location: USA.

McDermott Books

Email: mcdermottbooks@gdinet.com

Patrick McDermott. Specialty: General history. Number of history books: 10,000. Credit cards: D MC V. Location: USA.

O and I Books

Email: oibooks@sprint.ca

Web site: http://www.oibooks.com

Juan M. Ormaechea. Specialty: General history, Hispanic. Number of history books: 1,000. Credit cards: V; checks accepted in all major currencies. Location: Canada.

The Old Bookroom

Email: books@OldBookroom.com

Web site: http://www.OldBookroom.com

Sally and Barbara Burdon. Specialty: Asia, Africa, Middle East, Australia. Number of history books: 15,000. Founded 1969. Credit cards: AE MC V Diners. Location: Australia.

The Owl at the Bridge

Email: owlbridge@home.com

Samuel and Penelope Hough. Specialty: General history, medieval, Italian Renaissance. Number of history books: 4,000. Founded 1981. Credit cards: MC V; foreign checks accepted with surcharge. Location: USA.

Parmer Books

Email: parmerbook@aol.com

Web site: http://www.stairway.org/parmer/index.html

Jean Marie Parmer. Specialty: Voyages, exploration, discovery, Western Americana. Number of history books: 3,000; ninety-five percent of total stock is history books. Founded 1983. Credit cards: yes; foreign checks accepted with surcharge. Location: USA.

The Personal Navigator

Email: persnav@shore.net

Web site: http://www1.shore.net/~persnav/books1.htm

Samuel W. Coulbourn. Specialty: American, nineteenth-century diaries, journals, and autograph books. Number of history books: 500. Credit cards: MC V. Location: USA.

Mark Post, Bookseller

Email: markpost@att.net

Mark Post. Specialty: American, European, medieval, colonial Africa, historical fiction. Number of history books: 1,200. Credit cards: MC V. Location: USA.

Powell's Books

Email: powellschicago@MSN.com

Web site: http://www.powells.com/

Specialty: General scholarly. Number of history books: Probably in the tens of thousands; Powell's is a vast warehouse dealer of remaindered and out-of-print university press books. Credit cards: yes. Location: USA.

Prairie Reader Bookstore

Email: praireader@ctos.com

Hans Knoop. Specialty: General history, western U.S., U.S. presidents, Colorado history. Number of history books: 15,000; fifty percent of total stock is history books. Credit cards: AE D MC V. Location: USA.

Priceless Books

Email: priceless@net66.com

Web site: http://www.abebooks.com/home/priceless

William Thornhill, Michael Vaillancourt, and Leslie Troutman. Specialty: General history. Number of history books: 3,000. Credit cards: D MC V. Location: USA.

John William Pye Rare Books

Email: pyebooks@tiac.net

John William Pye. Specialty: Ancient, ancient Egypt, Egyptology. Number of history books: 3,000; ninety percent of total stock is history books. Credit cards: MC V. Location: USA.

Gaston Renard Fine and Rare Books (Books Australasia)

Email: booksaus@ozemail.com.au

Web site: http://bibliocity.com/dealers/renard

Julien Renard. Specialty: General, Australian, Pacific Rim, exploration/discovery/voyages. Number of history books: 10,000. Founded 1945. Credit cards: AE MC V Bankcard; checks accepted in Australian dollars, U.S. dollars, British sterling. Location: Australia.

Richard Owen Roberts Booksellers and Publishers

Email: roberts@safeplace.net

Web site: http://www.abebooks.com/home/RORoberts/

Richard Owen Roberts. Specialty: General history, Church history. Number of history books: 15,000. Founded 1961. Credit cards: MC V. Location: USA.

Serendipity Books

Email: serendip@merriweb.com.au

Web site: http://members.iinet.net.au/~serendip/

Ilonka and David McGill. Specialty: Australia, the Pacific, Southeast Asia, university press/academic books. Number of history books: 11,000; fifty percent of total stock is history books. Founded 1974. Credit cards: AE MC V Bankcard; U.S. and British checks accepted with surcharge for conversion. Location: Australia.

Neil Shillington: Bookseller

Email: neilsbks@bellsouth.net

Neil Shillington. Specialty: European, American, historical biography, Jewish, history related to theology. Number of history books: 3,000. Founded 1980. Credit cards: pending; foreign checks accepted. Location: USA.

Strand Book Store, Inc.

Email: strand@strandbooks.com

Specialty: General history. Number of history books: 30,000. No searchable Web site or online catalog, and not a member of a network, but as the largest used bookstore in New York City, the Strand cannot be ignored. Credit cards: AE MC V. Location: USA.

Naomi Symes Books

Email: naomi@symes.demon.co.uk

Web site: http://www.naomisymes.com/

Naomi Symes. Specialty: Social history, women's history, British, Victorian, eighteenth century. Number of history books: 1,200. Credit cards: MC V; foreign checks accepted with surcharge for conversion. Location: UK.

Time and Again Books

Email: mcurtis@inetport.com

Web site: http://www.abebooks.com/home/mcurtis

Michael S. Curtis. Specialty: American. Number of history books: 2,000. Credit cards: yes. Location: USA.

Tomes of Glory Books

Email: ppodolick@aol.com

Web site: http://www.abebooks.com/home/TMSFGLRY/

Phillip A. Podolick. Specialty: Military, American, American Civil War. Number of history books: 7,500; ninety percent of total stock is history books. Credit cards: AE MC V. Location: USA.

Tricolor Books

Email: tricolor@mhonline.net

Web site: http://www.angelfire.com/ny/tricolorbks

Susanna Betzel. Specialty: French history, eighteenth/nineteenth-century British and European history, French Revolution. Number of history books: 3,000; entire stock is history books. Credit cards: No; foreign checks accepted with a three-dollar surcharge for conversion. Location: USA.

Triple A Books

Email: tripleabks@aol.com

Web site: http://www.abebooks.com/home/aaaalways

David A. Katz. Specialty: American, Russian, American presidential biography. Number of history books: 8,000; seventy-five percent of total stock is history books. Credit cards: MC V. Location: USA.

Valley Books

Email: orders@valleybooks.com

Web site: http://www.valleybooks.com

Lawrence and Charmagne Pruner. Specialty: General history, New England. Number of history books: 4,000. Founded 1975. Credit cards: AE MC V. Location: USA.

Vintage Books

Email: vintageb@teleport.com

B. Milner. Specialty: General history, regional (Washington state), history of crime, transportation history, sports history. Number of history books: 10,000. Founded 1975. Credit cards: AE D MC V. Location: USA.

Volk and Iiams, Booksellers

Email: christ@vibooks.com

Web site: http://www.abebooks.com/home/vibooks/

Christine Volk and Shep Iiams. Specialty: African-American, women's. Number of history books: 3,000. Credit cards: MC V. Location: USA.

Webster's Bookstore Cafe

Email: usedbook@vicon.net

Web site: http://www.abebooks.com/home/zeppelin

Elaine Meder and Fred Ramsey. Specialty: General history, British, British Commonwealth, American presidential, Russian/Soviet. Number of history books: 10,000. Founded 1974. Credit cards: AE D MC V. Location: USA.

Winghale Books

Email: winghale@enterprise.net

Web site: http://www.abebooks.com/home/JOHNSTON/

Irwin and Hilary Johnston. Specialty: European, American, British, classical, medieval (all scholarly). Number of history books: 10,000; self-described as the leading dealer in academic history books in the U.K. Founded 1985. Issues snailmail catalogs. Credit cards: AE MC V; U.S. checks accepted with surcharge. Location: UK.

Wolf's Head Books

Email: wolfhead@aug.com

Web site: http://wolfsheadbooks.com

Harvey Wolf and Barbara Nailler. Specialty: Americana, military, Florida, American Civil War, World War I and II. Number of history books: 10,000. Founded 1980. Credit cards: AE D MC V. Location: USA.

Woodland Park Bookstore

Email: woodbook@lex.infi.net

Diana Turnbull. Specialty: General history. Number of history books: 12,000; fifty percent of total stock is history books. Founded 1985. Credit cards: yes; foreign checks accepted. Location: USA.

Xerxes Fine and Rare Books and Documents

Email: catra@xerxesbooks.com

Web site: http://xerxesbooks.com

Carol Travis. Specialty: General history. Number of history books: 2,500. Founded 1980. Credit cards: AE MC V. Location: USA.

Chapter 25

Maps and Images

Martin V. Minner

Maps

Metasites

Cartography: Calendar of Exhibitions

http://users.supernet.com/pages/jdocktor/exhibit.htm

A worldwide compendium of exhibits on the history of cartography.

Mercator's World

http://www.mercatormag.com/links.html

The online version of *Mercator's World: The Magazine of Maps, Exploration and Discovery* provides a useful set of links divided by subject area. The most helpful for historians are in the areas of cartography, history, libraries and collections, and museums. A section on education provides handy links for teachers.

Odden's Bookmarks

http://oddens.geog.uu.nl/index.html

An extensive site at Utrecht University providing a searchable list of more than 13,000 links to cartographic sites, map collections, and other map resources.

Perry-Castañeda Map Collection: Historical Map Web Sites

http://www.lib.utexas.edu/Libs/PCL/Map_collection/map_sites/
hist_sites.html

Compiled by the Perry-Castañeda Library at the University of Texas, this site offers an extensive list of links to historical map Web sites. Useful for world history as well as United States and European history.

Exhibits and Collections

Color Landform Atlas of the United States

http://fermi.jhuapl.edu/states/

Provides a variety of maps for each of the fifty states, including shaded topographical maps, satellite images, county maps, and scans from an 1895 Rand McNally atlas.

Cultural Maps

http://xroads.virginia.edu/~MAP/map_hp.html

An American Studies project at the University of Virginia, this site seeks to create an American historical atlas examining the physical landscape as well as mapmakers' mental and cultural terrain. At present the site includes U.S. territorial maps from 1775 to 1920, excerpts from an essay on the South by John Shelton Reed, and links to a number of useful exhibits and collections.

The Earth and the Heavens: The Art of the Mapmaker

http://www.bl.uk/exhibitions/maps/

This is the online version of a British Library exhibition that explored attempts to represent the earth and the cosmos. Online images range from a world map by Ptolemy to a world geological map from 1849.

1895 U.S. Atlas

http://www.livgenmi.com/1895.htm

Created by genealogist Pam Rietsch, this site provides scans of U.S. state maps from an 1895 atlas. The site also offers detailed scans at the county level.

Exploring the West from Monticello

http://www.lib.virginia.edu/exhibits/lewis_clark/home.html

Based on an exhibit at the University of Virginia's Alderman Library, this site examines the planning of the Lewis and Clark expedition and the history of North American cartography from Columbus to Jefferson.

Greenwood's Map of London 1827

http://www.bathspa.ac.uk/greenwood/home.html

This site is based entirely on a detailed 1827 map of the city of London and allows visitors to zoom in on a selected portion of the city. The site provides links to present-day maps and aerial photographs to permit comparison with the city of 1827.

University of Georgia Rare Map Collection

http://scarlett.libs.uga.edu/darchive/hargrett/maps/maps.html

The University of Georgia's Hargrett Rare Book and Manuscript Library provides online images of many historical maps from its collection, with an emphasis on maps of Georgia.

Library of Congress Geography and Maps: An Illustrated Guide

http://www.loc.gov/rr/geogmap/guide/

This site, an introduction to the Library of Congress's cartographic collections, features selected images in a variety of subject areas.

Map Collections: 1500–1999

http://lcweb2.loc.gov/ammem/gmdhtml/gmdhome.html

Part of the Library of Congress's American Memory project, this site provides online images in the following subject areas: cities and towns, conservation and the environment, discovery and exploration, cultural landscapes, military battles and campaigns, transportation, and general maps.

MapHist

http://www.maphist.nl/

The MapHist e-mail discussion group for map historians maintains an online archive of maps that have been discussed on the list.

Maps of the Pimería: Early Cartography of the Southwest

http://www.library.arizona.edu/pimeria/welcome.html

Based on maps from the University of Arizona Library Map Collection, this exhibit examines the cartographic history of the region of New Spain formerly known as Pimería, encompassing what is now southern Arizona and northern Sonora. Online images cover the period from 1556 to 1854.

National Geographic: Maps

http://www.nationalgeographic.com/maps/

The online version of *National Geographic* provides a variety of map resources including MapMachine, an easy-to-use feature that lets users point-and-click to zoom in on the map of their choice. The Historical Maps section includes panoramic maps, railroads, explorations, battles, and general maps.

The Newberry Library: Maps and History of Cartography Collections

http://www.newberry.org/nl/collections/L3cover.html

The Newberry Library's site includes bibliographic material on the library's Maps and History of Cartography Collections. A link to the Hermon Dunlap Smith Center for the History of Cartography leads to information about teaching with historical maps.

Osher Map Library

http://www.usm.maine.edu/~maps/

This site provides online versions of exhibits that have appeared at the Osher Map Library and Smith Center for Cartographic Education at the University of Southern Maine. Among the exhibits available online are Road Maps: The American Way, Charting Neptune's Realm: From Classical Mythology to Satellite Imagery, and The "Percy Map": The Cartographic Image of New England and Strategic Planning During the American Revolution.

The U.S. Civil War Center

http://www.cwc.lsu.edu/links/links3.htm#Maps

The U.S. Civil War Center, a division of Louisiana State University Libraries Special Collections, has compiled an extensive list of links to Civil War maps.

Images

Metasites

Australian National University

http://rubens.anu.edu.au/

The Australian National University's ArtServe site provides links to worldwide art and architecture sites, primarily emphasizing the Mediterranean Basin.

The Daguerreian Society: Links

http://daguerre.org/resource/links.html

The Daguerreian Society maintains an excellent list of links to sites that feature daguerreotype images. The site also provides links to sites on photographic history in general.

Massachusetts Institute of Technology: Rotch Visual Collections

http://libraries.mit.edu/rvc/imgcolls/imgcol1.html

The Rotch Visual Collections at Massachusetts offer an excellent page of links to image collections on the Web organized by subject area, such as anthropology and archaeology, art, photography, and urban design.

Mother of All Art History Links Pages

http://www.umich.edu/~hartspc/histart/mother/

An extensive annotated collection of links to visual resources, image collections, online exhibitions, and museums. Sections on Africa, Asia, and Islam, as well as on Europe and the Americas, make this metasite a valuable resource for world history.

NM's Creative Impulse: The Artist's View of World History and Western Civilization

http://history.evansville.net/

Compiled by Nancy B. Mautz, a teacher in Evansville, Indiana, this award-winning metasite provides a rich collection of links organized around a two-semester high school course on world history. Emphasizing art as a way to study world history, the site offers links to many images of use to teachers.

Exhibits and Collections

American Memory

http://memory.loc.gov/ammem/amtitle.html

The American Memory site, produced by the National Digital Library Project of the Library of Congress, provides access to more than 7 million digitized primary source items on U.S. history and culture. Collections available online include advertising, baseball cards, maps, motion pictures, music, photographs, and posters.

American Museum of Photography

http://www.photographymuseum.com

A virtual museum drawing from the private collection of William B. Becker. Several current galleries of historical interest deal with slavery, spirit photography, and daguerreotypes made by the firm of Southworth & Hawes.

The Center for Creative Photography

http://www.library.arizona.edu/branches/ccp/ccphome.html

Offers an index of the center's collection of more than 60,000 photographs as well as selected online images. The center maintains more than 100 collections of papers, manuscripts, and artifacts pertaining to photographers and photographic organizations and provides an archive list and finding aid in PDF format.

The Center for Documentary Studies

http://cds.aas.duke.edu/index.html

The Center for Documentary Studies promotes documentary work encompassing photography, filmmaking, oral history, folklore, and writing. Recent online exhibits featuring photography are Behind the Veil: Documenting African American Life in the Jim Crow South and Indivisible: Stories of American Community.

City-Gallery.com

http://www.city-gallery.com/

A genealogy site emphasizing photographic research and preservation. Members can upload family photos to an online album, contribute to message boards, or create a digital family album. The site provides access to PhotoGen, an e-mail discussion list on family photography and genealogy.

Collected Visions

http://cvisions.nyu.edu/mantle/index

Although not historical, the Collected Visions project offers a provocative perspective on how photographic images shape personal memory. The site invites visitors to submit photographs and to create photo essays from their own photographs or from other visitors' submissions.

The Daguerreian Society

http://www.daguerre.org/home.html

The Daguerreian Society's excellent site features a selection of digitized daguerreotype images and informative explanatory text. Galleries deal with the American vision in the daguerreotype era, images of California gold mining, and scenic daguerreotypes. The site's resource page offers a history of the daguerreotype, nineteenth- and twentieth-century published sources, a bibliography, and information on the daguerreotype process. One very helpful feature is the Tips for Best Viewing page.

Denver Public Library Photography Collection

http://gowest.coalliance.org/

This site features exhibits based on the photography collection in the Denver Public Library's Western History/Genealogy Department. Galleries cover the history of flight, Native American women, urban beautification, Fourth of July celebrations, and an elite World War II Army division that trained in the Rockies.

Digitizing Medieval Manuscripts: Creating a Scholarly Resource

http://medieval.mse.jhu.edu/

Created in conjunction with a Johns Hopkins University colloquium on digitizing medieval manuscripts, this site provides links to several noteworthy digitization projects.

George Eastman House International Museum of Photography and Film

http://www.eastman.org/home.htm

The George Eastman House, an important resource for research in the history of photography, does not provide online access to its collections but offers selected images in four areas: daguerreotypes, nineteenth-century British and French photography on paper, American nineteenth-century holdings, and important photography from the late nineteenth and early twentieth centuries. A downloadable video clip shows photographs taken with banquet and panoramic cameras.

Images from the History of Medicine

http://wwwihm.nlm.nih.gov/

Provides online access to more than 60,000 images in the prints and photographs collection of the History of Medicine Division of the U.S. National Library of Medicine. Offers keyword searching and a browsing function. This valuable collection includes portraits, caricatures, drawings, and a variety of other media.

Images of African-Americans from the 19th Century

http://digital.nypl.org/schomburg/images_aa19/

A valuable selection of images from the Schomburg Center for Research in Black Culture of the New York Public Library. The archive can be searched by keyword or subject area.

I.N. Phelps Stokes Collection of American Historical Prints

http://www.nypl.org/research/chss/spe/art/print/stokes/stokes.htm

Provides selected images from the New York Public Library's I.N. Phelps Stokes Collection of American Historical Prints. The collection consists largely of town views, historical scenes, and some maps.

John H. White: Photographing Black Chicago

http://www.nara.gov/exhall/americanimage/chicago/white1.html

A collection of photographs of Chicago's African-American community taken in 1973–74 by John H. White, then a photographer for the *Chicago Daily News*, for a federal documentary project.

Lester S. Levy Sheet Music Collection

http://levysheetmusic.mse.jhu.edu

Part of the special collections at the Milton S. Eisenhower Library at Johns Hopkins University, this collection contains more than 29,000 pieces of music and focuses on American popular music from 1780 to 1960. All are indexed on the site and many, including illustrated covers, are available online.

LIFE Online

http://www.lifemag.com/Life/features/index.html

All *LIFE* front covers from 1936 to 1972, the period when the magazine was published weekly, can be browsed online or searched by keyword or date. The site's Features section offers exhibits of archival photos in areas such as war, space, civil rights, and politics. A section on *LIFE* master photographers features Larry Burrows's Vietnam coverage, W. Eugene Smith's 1946 photo essay "Country Doctor," and a fifty-year retrospective on Alfred Eisenstaedt.

Living Landscapes

http://royal.okanagan.bc.ca/histphoto/index.html

A searchable archive of photographs from the Thompson/Okanagan region of British Columbia, Canada. Sponsored by the Royal British Columbia Museum and Okanagan University College.

Motion Picture and Television Reading Room

http://lcweb.loc.gov/rr/mopic/

The Library of Congress offers many early motion pictures online in QuickTime, MPG, and Real Media formats. Subject areas and periods range from popular entertainment in the 1870s to the consumer economy of the 1920s. The site also provides access to sound recordings in Real Player, MP3, and WAV formats.

Museum of the City of New York: Prints and Photographs Collection

http://www.mcny.org

The museum's exhibitions on New York history make excellent use of images. One noteworthy project, New York Before the War, provides access to photographs taken under the auspices of the Works Projects Administration's Federal Arts Project. Other valuable photographic exhibitions of historical interest are

Looking North: Upper Manhattan in Photographs, 1896–1939; Gotham Comes of Age: New York Through the Lens of the Byron Company, 1892–1942, and Berenice Abbott: Changing New York.

NASA Multimedia Gallery

http://www.nasa.gov/gallery/index.html

The National Aeronautics and Space Administration's multimedia gallery features a searchable archive of hundreds of thousands of still images. The gallery also provides access to NASA-related audio, video, and works of art.

National Archives Online Exhibit Hall

http://www.nara.gov/exhall/exhibits.html

The showpieces of the National Archives and Records Administration's site are online images of the Declaration of Independence, Constitution, Bill of Rights, and many other important historical documents. The site also features several excellent exhibitions of historical images: Picturing the Century, a photographic retrospective of the twentieth century; Powers of Persuasion, a collection of thirty-three World War II propaganda posters; and Portrait of Black Chicago, an exhibition of photographs of 1970s Chicago.

National Museum of Photography, Film and Television

http://www.nmpft.org.uk/home.asp

Provides an introduction to the museum's collections and selected images.

New York Public Library

http://www.nypl.org/research/chss/spe/art/photo/photo.html#online

The New York Public Library's Photography Collection provides online access to its exhibition Berenice Abbott: Changing New York, 1935–1938 and to two projects on Lewis Hine: Work Portraits, 1920–1939 and Construction of the Empire State Building, 1930–1931. The library's exhibition Small Town America: Stereoscopic Views from the Robert Dennis Collection presents digitized versions of 12,000 stereographic images from New York, New Jersey, and Connecticut from the 1850s to the 1910s.

Panoramic Photographs

http://www.nara.gov/exhall/americanimage/panorama/panoram1.html

An excellent selection of high-resolution panoramic photographs from the National Archives and Records Administration's Still Picture Branch. The photographs date from approximately 1864 to 1921 and include the wreck of the U.S.S. *Maine*, the San Francisco earthquake, World War I images, and many other subjects.

Princeton University: Seeley G. Mudd Manuscript Library

http://www.princeton.edu/~mudd/

Features recent exhibits from the Mudd Library including photographs and audiovisual items. Among recent exhibits are A Voice of Conscience: The Legacy of Adlai Stevenson, which includes video clips of interviews, speeches, and campaign commercials.

Royal Photographic Society

http://www.rps.org/index.html

The Royal Photographic Society's site offers an archive of recent exhibitions held at the society's Octagon Galleries in Bath. Of particular interest is Faces of the Century, an exhibition of 100 prints representing the last 100 years of British history.

The Samuel Putnam Avery Collection

http://www.nypl.org/research/chss/spe/art/print/collections/avery/avery.htm.bak

Provides a selection of images from the collection formed by New York art dealer Samuel Putnam Avery and donated to the New York Public Library in 1900. The collection is made up of more than 17,000 etchings and lithographs from the late nineteenth century.

The Siege and Commune of Paris, 1870–1871

http://www.library.northwestern.edu/spec/siege/

The Charles Deering McCormick Library of Special Collections at Northwestern University has digitized more than 1,200 photographs and images from the Siege and Commune of Paris. Visitors can browse through categorized lists of images or use the site's online search feature.

Small Towns, Black Lives

http://www.blacktowns.org

Created by Wendel White, professor of art at Richard Stockton State College of New Jersey, this project presents documentary images of historically African-

American communities in southern New Jersey. The project includes contemporary and historical photographs, historical documents, and QuickTime video clips. White also uses panoramic images to give visitors a 360–degree view of selected communities and historic sites.

Smithsonian Institution

http://photo2.si.edu/

Offers numerous online exhibitions and a searchable database of images in the Smithsonian collections. A few of the projects of historical interest are: The Presidential Inaugural, Magic Lanterns, Magic Mirrors: A Centennial Salute to Cinema, and Reflections on the Wall: The Vietnam Veterans Memorial.

Temple of Liberty: Building the Capitol for a New Nation

http://lcweb.loc.gov/exhibits/us.capitol/s0.html

A Library of Congress exhibit on the history and meaning of the U.S. Capitol, including many maps, prints, architectural drawings, and photographs from the eighteenth to the twentieth century. Of particular interest is the discussion of visual symbols of the nation.

They Still Draw Pictures

http://orpheus-1.ucsd.edu/speccoll/tsdp/

An impressive collection of more than 600 drawings made during the Spanish Civil War by schoolchildren in Spain and in French refugee centers. Each drawing is accompanied by a caption identifying the artist by name, age, and location, as well as notes found on the front and back of the artwork. The images are from the Southworth Spanish Civil War Collection at the University of California, San Diego.

UCR/California Museum of Photography

http://www.cmp.ucr.edu/

An excellent site based on the museum's collection of historical and contemporary images. One of the site's strengths is a project drawn from the hundreds of thousands of stereographic images in the museum's Keystone Mast Collection. By using three-dimensional red/blue glasses, visitors to the site can see the images in a format that simulates the effect of a stereographic viewer. The site also features a searchable database of Ansel Adams photographs and galleries on a variety of photographic topics.

United Nations Photo

http://www.un.org/av/photo/

The United Nations Photo site provides a selection of some of the approximately 200,000 images in the United Nations Photo Library. The site's U.N. Pictorial History section includes a timeline of images from the League of Nations to the present.

The U.S. Civil War Center

http://www.cwc.lsu.edu/cwc/links/links3.htm#Images

This site provides links to many Civil War images including photographs, prints, paintings, and cartoons. The project is the work of the U.S. Civil War Center, a division of the Louisiana State University Libraries Special Collections.

Virtual Greenbelt

http://www.otal.umd.edu/~vg/

Created by the Department of American Studies at the University of Maryland, Virtual Greenbelt provides images, oral history interviews, and other sources pertaining to the New Deal-era planned suburban community of Greenbelt. Images range from planning and construction under the Roosevelt administration to recent community life.

Women Come to the Front

http://lcweb.loc.gov/exhibits/wcf/wcf0001.html

An excellent Library of Congress exhibit that focuses on women who served as journalists, photographers, and broadcasters in World War II. Includes photographs, posters, newspaper clippings, and introductory essays.

Frank Lloyd Wright: Designs for an American Landscape, 1922–1932

http://lcweb.loc.gov/exhibits/flw/flw.html

The online version of a 1996–1997 exhibit at the Library of Congress, this site integrates many of Wright's drawings into a helpful essay on his work from 1922 to 1932. David G. DeLong, professor of architecture at the University of Pennsylvania, served as guest curator. The project includes images of five hypothetical study models created for the exhibit on the basis of Wright's drawings.

Chapter 26

Libraries

Laura Winninghoff and Jessie Bishop Powell

Library of Congress

Library of Congress

http://www.loc.gov

Arguably one of this country's premier collections, the Library of Congress collects in all areas *except* medicine and technical agriculture. Items are in many formats (books, periodicals, maps, music, prints, photographs, recorded sound, and videos), and most items are available through interlibrary loan. On the Web site, one can search the library's holdings, including some links to digitized materials, but the catalog is available only during limited hours:

> Monday–Friday: 4:40 a.m.–9:30 p.m.
> Saturday: 8:00 a.m.–5:00 p.m.
> Sunday: 11:35 a.m.–5:00 p.m.
> (Eastern Time)

There are two search options: a word search or browse. Browsing is a much more general search, and most records used in this type of search are available at any time Monday through Friday; they give an indication of the library's holdings in a certain area, but not call numbers for specific works. A word search is more specific and available only during the hours stated above, and the types of materials one can search are also limited (e.g., most pre-1975 *cataloged* items are not available). Note: all inquiries by author or title and Boolean searches for subject, name, series, notes, and so on are considered "word" searches.

The library also makes available its *experimental* search system, which has only 10 percent of the library's holdings entered. Two major improvements over the current catalog are the possibility of browsing a shelf (or section) without being in the library and performing a search for "related" materials. This latter improvement is a very good way to determine the correct Library of Congress Subject Heading (LCSH) once you have narrowed your topic. These Subject Headings, the basis of entry in most library catalogs, are not always intuitive terms or phrases.

Other Libraries and Collections

American Memory: Historical Collections of the National Digital Library

http://memory.loc.gov/ammem/ammemhome.html

American Memory is the collective term for those items deemed by the Library of Congress important to the cultural history of the United States. The level of cataloging varies with the collection and depends partly on the format, its age, and its acquisition date. Most collections are searchable and many have finding aids such as subject and author lists.

The Bancroft Library (UC, Berkeley)

http://sunsite2.berkeley.edu/oac/

Access to the Bancroft Library's collections, via the Online Archive of California, including access to UC, Berkeley Finding Aids and the California Heritage Digital Image Access Database.

The Beinecke Library

http://www.library.yale.edu/orbis/

Yale's library of rare books and manuscripts is searchable through ORBIS, Yale's online catalog.

Bibliothèque Nationale de France

http://www.bnf.fr/web-bnf/catalog/index.htm

Catalog of the French National Library, in French, with an English gateway under construction. The above link is to the summary page for all four catalogs, including GALLICA, an effort to chronicle nineteenth-century France through digitized images and sound.

British Library Public Catalog

http://opac97.bl.uk/

British Library Public Catalog provides access to the major catalogs of the British Library in London and Boston Spa. Presently, individual collections have separate catalogs but all can be searched using the form given on the Web page. The collections include humanities, social science, hard science, technology, and business collections cataloged from 1975 to the present, all music cataloged from 1980 to the present, and all reference materials cataloged before 1975 (including the archives and materials of the former India Office and colonial Africa). In the older reference materials, please note that the "D-" before items means that the original was destroyed during World War II and has since been replaced. Finally, all serials from 1700 to the present are included in the catalog.

Hours of operation: Monday–Saturday: 4 a.m.–midnight (GMT)

The Center for Research Libraries

http://wwwcrl.uchicago.edu OR Telnet://crlcatalog.uchicago.edu (login as "guest" at prompt)

The Center for Research Libraries is a consortium of college and university libraries from all over the United States. The center holds materials deemed by many libraries important but too obscure to take up valuable shelf space in their own institution. Through membership in the CRL, libraries take advantage of these materials and their patrons have fairly quick access to them. Currently, 98 percent of the nearly 5 million entries in the CRL's catalog are available online, including books, newspapers, serials, microforms, archival collections, and other research materials. There is a handbook on the Web page describing the holdings in certain areas; a name authority file is also available.

EuroDocs: Primary Historical Documents from Western Europe

http://www.lib.byu.edu/~rdh/eurodocs/

Compiled by Richard Hacken, a librarian at Brigham Young University, this list of links connects to Western European (mainly primary) historical documents that are transcribed, reproduced, and, in some cases, translated.

The Getty Research Institute for the History of Art and the Humanities

http://opac.pub.getty.edu

Collections include Western art, archaeology, and architecture from the Bronze Age to the present, with a special strength in French, German, Russian, Italian, and American avant-garde materials. There are also extensive collections on the conservation of cultural heritage and historic preservation and an unparalleled auction catalog collection with more than 110,000 volumes of materials from the late seventeenth century to the present. Included in the Special Collections are artists' journals and sketchbooks, albums, architectural drawings, early guidebooks, emblem books, prints, and drawings. The Getty collection's strengths are in Futurism, Dada, Surrealism, the Bauhaus, Russian Constructivism, and Fluxus. Many items from the research library are available for interlibrary loan.

The Hagley Library

http://www.hagley.lib.de.us/library.htm

The Hagley Museum and Library's focus is American Business and Technological History. As of this writing, the catalog is under construction.

The Kinsey Institute for Research in Sex, Gender and Reproduction

http://www.indiana.edu/~kinsey/

Collections at the Kinsey Institute are searchable via KICAT, at Telnet:// infogate.ucs.indiana.edu. Login as "guest" and when prompted to choose a catalog, type KICAT. The catalog is also available at http://www.iucat.iu.edu/uhtbin/cgisirsi/tn31OJYmdl/28779029/60/69.

KICAT does not contain records for all items in the library, nor does it contain records for the Institute's art and archival collections. Records are continually being added to the online catalog as part of the library's retrospective conversion project. Information on other materials is available only through onsite finding aids and published book catalogs (citations available on the Web site).

For help in using the library's holdings of sex-related magazines, films and videos, newspapers and tabloids, pulp fiction, and books still cataloged in Dr. Kinsey's system of categories, users must consult with library staff.

Records for these materials will be entered into the online catalog as quickly as legal restrictions and resources permit. Until then, access is limited to information available through in-house files, lists, and databases. E-mail libknsy@indiana.edu or call (812) 855-3058 for more information about the library.

Labriola National American Indian Data Center at Arizona State University

http://www.asu.edu/lib/archives/labriola.htm

The Labriola National American Indian Data Center, part of the ASU Libraries, brings together current and historic information on government, culture, religion and worldview, social life and customs, tribal history, individuals from the United States, Canada, and Sonora and Chihuahua, Mexico. All materials held by the center are searchable via ASU's online catalog (http://catalog.lib.asu.edu/).

The Lilly Library

http://www.indiana.edu/%7eliblilly/

At present, the Lilly Library's online resources include searchable indexes of the manuscript collections, chapbook collection, and French Revolution documents. The library's holdings are searchable via Indiana University's catalog, IUCAT (Telnet://infogate.ucs.indiana.edu. Login as "guest," and when prompted enter IUCAT). This is a command-driven catalog. Users can also reach the IU catalog on the Web at http://iucat.iu.edu/index_main.html.

The National Library of China

http://www.nlc.gov.cn/etext.htm

Non-Chinese-speaking visitors to this site submit questions to librarians who then search for the information, so this site is most useful if researchers have a specific question or request. The catalog is searchable by those whose computers register Chinese characters.

The Newberry Library

http://www.newberry.org/nl/collections/virtua.html

The Newberry is slowly adding to its Web-based catalog, but currently only 15 percent of collections are searchable. Where available, OCLC has the complete holdings of the Newberry already as part of its database. Bibliographic guides are available on the Web site for beginning researchers.

The New York Public Library

http://catnyp.nypl.org/

CATNYP is the online catalog of The Research Libraries of The New York Public Library. This catalog includes materials added to the collections after 1971, as well as some materials acquired before 1971. At this time, however, the best place to search the libraries' holdings is the 800–volume *Dictionary Catalog of The Research Libraries*, published by G.K. Hall. Copies of this catalog are available at many research institutions and all NYPL Research Libraries. There is a link on the Web page to a global list of libraries that own a copy of the *Catalog*.

OhioLink

http://www.ohiolink.edu

This is the communal catalog for all libraries (public, private, college, and university) in Ohio.

OLIS (Oxford University Libraries' Online Catalog): Oxford's Bodleian Library, University of Oxford

telnet://library.ox.ac.uk

Without a password from Oxford you may not search any other Oxford library (although all are listed). This is a command-driven search, and most materials are available for interlibrary loan.

Oriental Institute Research Archives

http://www-oi.uchicago.edu/OI/DEPT/RA/ABZU/ABZU.HTML

This is a guide to resources for the study of the ancient Near East consisting of primary and secondary indexes of information, available on the Internet. The guide is compiled and updated by Charles E. Jones, research archivist at the Oriental Institute Research Archives at the University of Chicago.

The Library Company of Philadelphia

http://www.librarycompany.org/

Founded in 1731 by Benjamin Franklin, the Library Company of Philadelphia has over half a million items covering American history and culture from the seventeenth to the nineteenth century. The online catalog, WolfPAC, currently includes about 20 percent of the collection, with more added daily. However, this online catalog also includes records from the Union catalog of the Philadelphia Area Consortium of Special Collections Libraries (PACSCL): the Academy of Natural Sciences, the Balch Institute for Ethnic Studies, Saint Charles Borromeo Seminary, and the Philadelphia Museum of Art. Joining in the near future are the Rosenbach Museum and Library, the Presbyterian Historical Society, the Athenaeum, and the Historical Society of Pennsylvania. Several other PACSCL member libraries have, or will soon have, catalogs available through the PACSCL Web site, or through their individual institution's Web site. These include the American Philosophical Society, the Free Library of Philadelphia, the University of Pennsylvania, Winterthur, The Hagley Museum and Library, Temple University, the College of Physicians of Philadelphia, the Wagner Free Institute of Science, Bryn Mawr, Haverford, and Swarthmore.

Public Records Office–UK

http://www.pro.gov.uk/finding/catalogue/default.htm

At present, the catalog of the PRO (United Kingdom) contains references only to selected policy records of twentieth-century British government departments.

The Schlesinger Library

http://www.radcliffe.edu/schles/

(Searchable via Harvard's online catalog at Telnet://hollis.harvard.edu)

The Schlesinger Library at Radcliffe College is the foremost library on the history of women in America. Its holdings of audiovisual materials, books, ephemera, manuscripts, oral histories, periodicals, and photographs document the social history of women in the United States, primarily during the nineteenth and twentieth centuries.

Schomburg Center for Research in Black Culture

http://www.nypl.org/research/sc/sc.html

(Holdings searchable via CATNYP, the New York Public Library catalog, http://catnyp.nypl.org)

The Schomburg Center for Research in Black Culture is a national research library devoted to collecting, preserving, and providing access to resources documenting the experiences of peoples of African descent throughout the world. The center provides access to, and professional reference assistance in, the use of its collections to the scholarly community and the general public through five research divisions. The center's collections include art objects, audio and videotapes, books, manuscripts, motion picture films, newspapers, periodicals, photographs, prints, recorded music discs, and sheet music.

University of Oklahoma Western History Collections

http://libraries.ou.edu/depts/westhistory/

This collections' aim is to provide opportunities for research into the development of the Trans-Mississippi West and Native American cultures. Catalog information for many of the materials within the Western History Collections may be accessed through the University of Oklahoma Libraries online catalog, OLIN. Catalog information for Western History Collections material is divided as follows: choose "OU Catalog" from the Libraries menu to search for books held by the Western History Collections, or choose "Archives" from the Libraries menu to search for manuscript and photo collections of the Western History Collections.

Top Ten Research Libraries in the United States*

---

1. Harvard University

http://hollisweb.harvard.edu/

telnet://hollis.harvard.edu

Excellent instructions on searching strategies for HOLLIS (Harvard Online Library Information System) and other command-driven search systems are available at http://www.radcliffe.edu/schles/libcolls/search/index.htm.

2. Yale University

http://www.library.yale.edu/orbis/

ORBIS is available in a Web-based or Telnet platform, with links to both appearing on this page.

---

*Digest of Education Statistics, U.S. Department of Education, National Center for Education Statistics, 1997, page 464, table 417.

3. University of Illinois at Urbana-Champaign

http://www.library.uiuc.edu/

This gateway provides access to search systems for library materials and serials. The catalog is, as of this writing, Telnet accessible, with an experimental Web catalog available for users as well.

4. University of Texas at Austin

http://dpweb1.dp.utexas.edu/lib/utnetcat/

5. University of Michigan

http://www.lib.umich.edu/libhome/mirlyn/mirlynpage.html

6. University of California at Berkeley

http://www.lib.berkeley.edu/Catalogs/guide.html

UC Berkeley provides multiple options in searching its collections, and this page lists all of them, along with a chart indicating which system to use for specific searches. Pathfinder is the Berkeley-specific catalog, MELVYL (Web or Telnet) contains the holdings of all nine campus libraries of the University of California, and GLADIS is the technical services catalog.

7. Columbia University

http://www.columbia.edu/cu/libraries/indexes/resource_type_10.html

CLIO (Columbia Libraries Information Online) and all other New York City area libraries have links on this page. Each library at Columbia has its own catalog (e.g., Law School, Medical School, Teacher's College), necessitating many searches to get a complete picture of the holdings on most subjects.

8. Stanford University

http://www-sul.stanford.edu/search/socii/

Socrates II, the Web-based catalog for Stanford, is only available to those with a Stanford ID. The general public can, however, access the older, Telnet-based and command-driven Socrates from this page.

9. University of California at Los Angeles
http://www.library.ucla.edu/

10. The University of Chicago
http://webpac.lib.uchicago.edu/webpac-bin/wgbroker?new+-access+top

Chapter 27

Archives and Manuscript Collections

Susan Ferentinos

Information for Researchers

Primary historical research can be intimidating for the beginner. The following sites provide background for new researchers that will make the structure of archives seem less daunting.

Introduction to Archives

http://www.umich.edu/~bhl/bhl/refhome/refintro.htm

This essay, part of the Web site of the Bentley Historical Library of the University of Michigan, details the ways in which archives differ from libraries in their collecting focus and their organization.

Library Research Using Primary Sources

http://www.lib.berkeley.edu/TeachingLib/Guides/PrimarySources.html

The library at the University of California, Berkeley, offers this step-by-step guide to primary research. It elaborates the difference between primary and secondary resources and suggests multiple avenues for tracking down primary material.

Primary Sources Research Colloquium

http://www.library.yale.edu/ref/err/primsrcs.htm

Designed to complement a Yale University course in primary research, this site supplies introductory information on using primary documents in historical research. It discusses various types of sources and provides definitions of words such as *records*, *finding aids*, and *manuscripts*. Although some parts of the site deal specifically with Yale University resources, overall it contains valuable resources for beginning researchers.

Using Archives: A Practical Guide for Researchers

http://www.archives.ca/04/0416_e.html

Maintained by the National Archives of Canada, this online essay is geared toward first-time users of archives. It discusses research strategies, what to expect from an archive, and how to locate desired material.

Information for Archivists

For those interested in learning more about the profession of collecting, organizing, and preserving historical documents, the following sites are good starting points.

Archives of the Archivist Listserv

http://listserv.muohio.edu/archives/archives.html

This page offers information on the major archivist listserv. Through links, visitors can join the list, review past postings, and search the listserv's archives for specific topics or authors.

Archives Resource Center

http://www.coshrc.org/arc/index.htm

A cooperative effort of the Council of State Historical Records Coordinators, the American Association of State and Local History, and the Society of American Archivists, the Archives Resource Center strives to be a gateway to Web-based information for archivists. The site includes links to professional organizations, lists of professional development opportunities, and descriptions of professional standards.

Conservation OnLine (CoOL)

http://palimpsest.stanford.edu/

Maintained by Stanford University Libraries, Conservation OnLine is a clearinghouse of information on the conservation of manuscript material. Visitors can access online articles on a wide range of conservation topics, such as pest management or digital imaging. Lists of conservation professionals and organizations throughout the world (though mostly in English-speaking countries) are also provided, and the entire site is searchable.

Encoded Archival Description (EAD) Official Web Site

http://lcweb.loc.gov/ead/

Encoded Archival Description promises to make collection finding aids widely available on the Web. The Library of Congress maintains the EAD Official Web Site, which contains an introduction to the format, relevant links, and application guidelines.

Society of American Archivists (SAA)

http://www.archivists.org/

The Society of American Archivists is the major American professional organization for archivists. Its Web site provides information about the organization, position papers, job postings, professional development opportunities, and a list of SAA publications.

Archives, Manuscripts, and Special Collections

With such a wealth of historic documents available, it can be difficult to know where to begin. The following list includes information on locating sources, along with the Web sites of repositories particularly well known in their area of specialty. Most repositories affiliated with larger institutions (such as universities or national governments) enable the user to search catalogs through their Web sites; however, a significant portion of collections have not been electronically cataloged. Researchers should contact the reference staff of the repository to ensure that they have not missed valuable sources.

The institutions in North America and Western Europe generally maintain more sophisticated Web sites than those in other regions. In an effort to include multiple historical fields, I have included sites from throughout the world that are distinctive within their region, though they may appear somewhat basic to North American eyes. All sites are in English unless otherwise noted.

Metasites

(Lists for a specific country or genre are located under the appropriate subheading.)

Gabriel: National Libraries of Europe

http://www.konbib.nl/gabriel/en/countries.html

This site provides address, phone number, e-mail address, major collections, operating hours, and mission for the national libraries of over thirty-five nations in Eastern and Western Europe. It also provides links to the individual servers of each library.

Guide to the Archives of Intergovernmental Organizations

http://www.unesco.org/archives/guide/uk/index.html

A joint project between the United Nations Educational, Scientific, and Cultural Organization (UNESCO) and the International Council on Archives, Section of Archivists of International Organizations (ICS/SIO), this guide provides the general history of approximately eighty intergovernmental organizations, along with information on accessing the archives of each group.

Ready, 'Net, Go! Archival Internet Resources ✓

http://www.tulane.edu/~lmiller/ArchivesResources.html

Describing itself as an "archival meta-index," this site has compiled lists of major archival resources around the globe. Master lists of archives and archival search engines allow researchers to quickly access clearinghouses of information, such as multirepository catalogs. The site's Professional Resources and Tools for Archivists sections point users to resources of particular interest to archivists.

Repositories of Primary Sources ✓

http://www.uidaho.edu/special_collections/Other.Repositories.html

The University of Idaho maintains this international listing of over *4,600* repositories. It is as close to a comprehensive list as is available, and using the links on this site is one of the quickest ways to locate a specific library. The list is arranged by region and also includes a section of links to additional lists.

UNESCO Archives Portal ✓

http://www.unesco.org/webworld/portal_archives/Archives/

This site includes links to archival repositories around the world, online primary sources, and professional information for archivists. Searchable lists of archives are arranged by both topic and country.

Africa

Africa Research Central: A Clearinghouse of African Primary Sources

http://www.africa_research.org/

Africa Research Central provides information on manuscript repositories with holdings of Africana. African, European, and North American libraries are included. For African repositories, users can search a database to find institutions in specific countries or with particular types of holdings (such as business records or government archives). The database lists contact information, use restrictions, Web address, and published inventories for each institution, though some of the data is incomplete. For European and North American repositories, the site provides direct links to home pages. The clearinghouse also offers information on the preservation crisis facing manuscripts in Africa.

Africa South of the Sahara: Libraries and Archives

http://garamond.stanford.edu/depts/ssrg/africa/libs.html

Stanford University's list of resources in African studies includes links to Africana collections around the world, bibliographies, and digitization projects.

Archives in South Africa

http://www.archives.org.za/archivesa.html

Compiled by the South African Society of Archivists, this page provides links to archival repositories in South Africa.

Electronic Journal of Africana Bibliography

http://sdrc.lib.uiowa.edu/ejab/1/

This issue of *Africana Bibliography* carries the subtitle *Guides, Collections and Ancillary Materials to African Archival Resources in the United States*. It provides a bibliography of archival resources on the history of Africa that are available in the United States through print or microfilm. Selections are grouped by country, region, and language. The site is similar to a print resource in that it provides few hypertext links.

Repositories of Primary Sources: Africa and the Near East

http://www.uidaho.edu/special-collections/africa.html

Part of the comprehensive University of Idaho list of primary source repositories, this page links to manuscript collections throughout Africa and the Near East. The sources are divided by country and include sites in a variety of languages.

African-Americans

African-American Archives, Manuscripts and Special Collections: A Guide to Resources

http://www2.lib.udel.edu/subj/blks/internet/afamarc.htm

The University of Delaware library has compiled this guide to resources in African-American history. The list of links is divided into repositories, subject guides, and the finding aids of particular collections housed throughout the United States.

Amistad Research Center

http://www.tulane.edu/~amistad/

The Amistad Research Center, an independent library housed at Tulane University, holds one of the preeminent groupings of manuscript material pertaining to African-American history. The center's mission is to enable "the study of ethnic history and culture and race relations in the United States"; about 90 percent of its materials pertain to African-Americans. Its Web site contains lists of manuscript collections, arranged both alphabetically and by major subject, and a growing collection of digitized images from its collections. The site devotes an entire section to the *Amistad* slave ship uprising, including historical essays and descriptions of the center's resources on this topic.

Moorland-Spingarn Research Center, Howard University

http://www.founders.howard.edu/moorland_spingarn/

The Moorland-Spingarn is a research center devoted to the study of people of African descent in Africa and the Americas, with a particular emphasis on black "families, organizations, institutions, social and religious consciousness, and the continuing struggle for civil rights and human justice." Its manuscripts department reflects this mission with its offering of oral history projects, personal and organizational papers, a special music collection, and prints. The center's Web site provides brief biographies of interviewees in the Black Military History and Civil Rights Documentation oral history projects, digital samples of historic photographs, descriptions of manuscript holdings, and a special bibliography of library resources in African-American women's history.

Schomburg Center for Research in Black Culture

http://www.nypl.org/research/sc/sc.html

The Web site of the Schomburg, a research branch of the New York Public Library, carries many of the features of its parent organization's site: multiple digital resources, clear logistical information, and extensive description of its holdings. The center is devoted to the study of the African diaspora, and its strength lies in twentieth-century history, literature, and the performing arts. Its site provides access to online exhibits, a "multimedia sampler" (utilizing video and sound technology), and digitized examples of its holdings.

Asia and the Pacific

Directory of Archives in Australia

http://www.asap.unimelb.edu.au/asa/directory/

Maintained by the Australian Society of Archivists, this site offers contact information, hours, collecting focus, and Web links to the major repositories of Australia. Visitors can search the site by subject.

National Archives of Japan

http://www8.cao.go.jp/koubunsho/index_e.html

The English language pages of the Japanese National Archives offer descriptions of major holdings, a guide for users, and a list containing the contact information of the archives of Japanese prefectures and some Japanese cities.

National Archives of Singapore

http://www.museum.org.sg/NAS/nas.shtml

Singapore's National Archives has a wide collection of materials documenting the country's heritage, including oral histories, photographs, and public records. The site contains information on the holdings, as well as samples of material held in the collections.

Register of Australian Archives and Manuscripts (RAAM)

http://www.nla.gov.au/raam/

This searchable catalog of manuscript collections held in Australia contains more than 37,000 documents.

Repositories of Primary Sources: Asia and the Pacific

http://www.uidaho.edu/special-collections/asia.html

Part of the comprehensive University of Idaho list of primary source repositories, this page links to manuscript collections throughout Asia and the Pacific. The sources are divided by country.

Canada

Canadian Archival Resources on the Internet

http://www.usask.ca/archives/menu.html

Indexed by name, location, and repository type, this online guide provides links to the home pages of Canadian archives.

National Archives of Canada

http://www.archives.ca/08/08_e.html

The National Archives of Canada Web site offers a variety of paths into the Canadian past. Visitors can click on particular topics to access a variety of digitized collections; a genealogy page describes the archive's many family history resources; and ArchiviaNet, the archive's online research tool, serves as a portal into various catalogs and finding aids.

National Library of Canada

http://www.nlc_bnc.ca/index_e.html

The mission of the National Library of Canada is to collect and preserve Canada's published heritage. Available from this site are the Canada National Library catalog, digital collections, and research guides on specific aspects of Canadian history.

Europe—Eastern

Levéltárak (Archives): Hungary

http://www.lib.uni_miskolc.hu/lib/archive/kapcsolat/ukanIndex/h4levtar.htm

This site provides a list of archives in Hungary; however, this page and most of the archival sites it links to are in Hungarian, with no translation available.

PIASA Archival Information Center

http://www.piasa.org/archives.html

The Polish Institute of Arts and Sciences of America (PIASA) provides this electronic guide to archival collections concerning Poland and the Polish-American community. Resources are divided into those in Poland and those in North America.

Slavic and East European Collections at UC, Berkeley

http://www.lib.berkeley.edu/Collections/Slavic/collect.html

The University of California, Berkeley, collects widely in materials on Slavic and East European countries, including the former Soviet Union. Included in the Special Collections department is an array of modern (post-1989) in-dependent Russian periodicals, an extensive arrangement of materials from the Czech Republic, and information pertaining to writers and literature in this region.

Slovene Archives

http://www.pokarh_mb.si/today.html

This site provides a listing of archives in the Republic of Slovenia. For each institution that does not have its own Web site, the Slovene Archives site gives contact information along with a preliminary description of its collections. The site supplies links to those repositories that maintain their own Web pages. While the Slovene Archives page is in English, some of the links connect to pages in Slovene.

State Archives in Poland

http://www.archiwa.gov.pl/index.eng.html

This site not only details the holdings of the Polish State Archives, it also answers FAQs about Polish archives in general and provides links to other Polish repositories. While the major pages of the site have been translated into English, some links from the main page lead to information available only in Polish.

Europe—Western

ARCHIESPA: Índice de páginas Web sobre archivos de España: Spain

http://rayuela.uc3m.es/~pirio/archiespa/

ARCHIESPA is a metasite providing links to hundreds of resources on archives in Spain. Links are available to various archives, Spanish archival organizations, online articles about Spain's repositories, digital manuscripts, directories to other libraries in Europe, and links to additional lists of resources. Users should be aware that this site does lack some currency, so some links are no longer accurate. The site is in Spanish.

Archives Hub: United Kingdom

http://www.archiveshub.ac.uk/

This gateway catalog allows users to search for archival collections held in colleges and universities in the United Kingdom. Searches by repository, subject, document type, and personal name are possible, and the advanced search form enables full-text searching. Search results include a description of the collection's contents.

Archives in Germany

http://www.bawue.de/~hanacek/info/earchive.htm

The bulk of this site is in German; however, the initial page is in English and provides a glossary of German words frequently used on the subsequent pages (as well as on other German archival sites). The home page lists German archives divided by type (church, state, private, etc.). Following the link on a particular repository leads to a page (in German) providing introductory information on the institution.

Archivos Estatales: Spain

http://www.mcu.es/lab/archivos/index.html

Spain's Ministry of Education and Culture maintains this site, which provides an overview of state libraries and archives. Users can search a bibliography of Spanish archives, access information on specific repositories, and read a general description on the organization and policies of the libraries within this system. The site is in Spanish.

ARCHON: Archives Online: United Kingdom

http://www.hmc.gov.uk/archon/archon.htm

ARCHON is a clearinghouse of information for users of British archives and manuscripts. It offers a list, with links, of all repositories in the United Kingdom, along with information on British history and resources for those in both the history and archival professions. The site also contains a register of ongoing, planned, or completed archival projects.

Bodleian Library, University of Oxford: United Kingdom

http://www.rsl.ox.ac.uk/

One of the most famous libraries in the world, the Bodleian houses an extensive array of Western manuscripts, reaching back into ancient times. The library's Web site allows access to multiple catalogs of holdings, some online finding aids, and general library information. In addition, numerous digital library projects, such as an online collection of medieval manuscripts, are available for viewing.

Bundesarchiv Online: Germany

http://www.bundesarchiv.de/index.html

Visitors to the National Archives of Germany Web site can access a timeline of the library's history, descriptions and indexes of its major holdings, and a list of the library's publications. The site is entirely in German.

Les Centres de Ressources Documentaires: France

http://mistral.culture.fr/culture/sedocum/ceresdoc.htm

This list, maintained by the French Ministry of Culture, provides access to the major repositories of France, grouped by subject area. Users can access data regarding address, hours of operation, major holdings, and library history. The site is completely in French.

Latin America

Benson Latin American Collection, University of Texas at Austin

http://www.lib.utexas.edu/benson/index.html

The Benson Collection contains over 2 million pages of manuscripts on Mexico, Central America, the Caribbean, South America, and the American Southwest during the period it was part of Mexico and the Spanish Empire. In addition, it houses one of the largest collections of secondary material on this region. Archival collection descriptions, bibliographies, online exhibits, and information about visiting the library are available through the library's home page.

Biblioteca Nacional de México

http://biblional.bibliog.unam.mx/bib01.html

This site gives visitors information on Mexico's National Library and its holdings. The repository owns over 2 million items, including rare books and manuscripts, all of which pertain to Mexican history. Currently, this site is available only in Spanish.

Biblioteca Nacional del Perú

http://www.binape.gob.pe/

Peru's National Library has created multiple avenues of exploration on its Web site. Visitors can search library catalogs, view online historical photographs, peruse a listing of the library's publications, and access information on other branches of Peru's national library system. The site is entirely in Spanish.

H-LatAm Archives

http://www2.h_net.msu.edu/~latam/archives/

The H-Net listserv for Latin American history maintains this resource of information on archives in Latin America. Researchers who have physically visited a repository complete a questionnaire, which is then posted to this site. Details include contact information, access requirements, information on collections, descriptions of the facilities, and tips for visiting the repository, such as nearby hotels, restaurants, and public transportation. Users of the site should be aware, however, that descriptions are up to five years old and so might be outdated.

Latin American Library: Tulane University

http://www.tulane.edu/~latinlib/lalhome.html

Tulane's Latin American Library is comprised of both secondary and primary sources, as well as an extensive collection of Latin American rare books. Primary sources include historical newspapers, photographs, and manuscripts. This site contains information on the library's holdings, summaries of recent Latin American exhibits, a bibliography of dissertation research, and links to related sites. Also included are digital representations of Mayan rubbings and other "treasures of the collection."

Military History and Peace Collections

Hoover Institution: Library and Archives

http://www_hoover.stanford.edu/homepage/library.html

The Hoover Institution on War, Revolution, and Peace at Stanford University boasts collections from throughout the world. The library has particularly strong holdings on the Chinese Revolution, the Russian Revolution, the Nazis, and Italian fascism. At its Web site, visitors can find information about the Hoover Institution, descriptions of its holdings, historical essays on the collections, bibliographies, and links to related sites.

Swarthmore College Peace Collection

http://www.swarthmore.edu/Library/peace/

This research archive collects and maintains materials pertaining to nongovernmental efforts toward peace. Its holdings include manuscripts, periodicals, and extensive ephemera (such as posters, flyers, and buttons). This site provides collection descriptions, subject guides, online exhibits, and resources for the further study of peace movements.

U.S. Army Military History Institute

http://carlisle_www.army.mil/usamhi/index.html

The U.S. Army Military History Institute collects and organizes resources on American military history, including oral histories, manuscript material, photographs, and maps. Its manuscript collections include the personal papers of individuals connected to the U.S. army, as well as curriculum materials from the U.S. Army War College, dating back to the school's inception in 1901. The Web site contains collection finding aids, a large digital collection, and transcripts of dozens of oral history interviews with veterans of various twentieth-century military actions.

Virginia Military Institute Archives

http://web.vmi.edu/archives/~archtml/index.html

The Virginia Military Institute (VMI) has extensive holdings on United States military history in the nineteenth and twentieth centuries. The Web site provides genealogy information on VMI alumni, detailed information on the archives' Civil War collections, textual transcriptions of some of the Civil War material, and selections from the library's photograph collection.

Russia and the Former Soviet Union

ArcheoBiblioBase: Archives in Russia

http://www.iisg.nl/~abb/index.html

This English language resource provides information on Russian archives. The material is divided into three sections: federal archives (administered by the Rosarkhiv), major federal agencies that maintain their own records, and local state archives in Moscow and St. Petersburg. Under each category are lists of archives with contact information, previous names, major holdings, access restrictions, and the titles of any recently published guides. This resource is now searchable, though the limited information given about each repository demands that search terms remain general.

Estonian Historical Archives

http://www.eha.ee/

Previously the Estonian State Central Archives, the Estonian Historical Archives houses documents from Estonia's history, including the eras of Swedish rule, Soviet affiliation, and independent statehood. Its home page offers an essay on the history of the archives, information for researchers planning to visit the repository, and descriptions of its holdings. An English language version of the site is available.

National Library of Russia

http://www.nlr.ru:8101/eng/

This repository owns copies of every publication produced in Russia. In addition, it houses collections of Greek writings from the early Christian era, European codices (handwritten books) and manuscripts, and Eastern texts illustrating the development of writing in that region. The National Library site's English-language offerings are considerable, providing access to online exhibits and databases (although the databases themselves are in Russian).

State Archives of Latvia

http://www.arhivi.lv/engl/en-lvas-frame.htm

Collecting the documentary heritage of Latvia since 1919, the State Archives of Latvia is today a joint system of numerous collection agencies. Its Web site details major holdings and supplies information on visiting each of its branches.

Sexuality

Archiv für Sexualwissenschaft/Archive for Sexology

http://www2.hu-berlin.de/sexology/

This institute contains numerous resources for the study of sexuality and the history of sexology, most pertaining to Europe and the United States. Its Web site includes articles on the history of sexology, samples from the collection, syllabi for graduate and undergraduate courses, and descriptions of the institute's holdings.

Human Sexuality Collection, Cornell University

http://rmc.library.cornell.edu/HSC/

Cornell University's Sexuality Collection seeks to document historical shifts in attitudes toward sexuality. It has particular strengths in gay, lesbian, bisexual, and transgender history and in the politics of pornography. Its Web site describes its holdings, includes bibliographies of published sources, and features an informative guide with advice on how to research the history of sexuality.

Kinsey Institute for Research in Sex, Gender, and Reproduction

http://www.indiana.edu/~kinsey/

Dr. Alfred C. Kinsey gained worldwide attention in the 1940s with the publication of his controversial book *Sexual Behavior in the Human Male*. The Kinsey Institute, which he founded, continues his work by facilitating the study of human sexuality. The library houses materials in numerous formats (including manuscripts, periodicals, photographs, and artifacts) from throughout the world, ranging in date from 3200 B.C.E. to the present. The institute is not open to the general public, and researchers must gain approval to access the materials; the necessary steps for doing this are described on the Web site. The site also offers essays describing the life of Dr. Kinsey, the often colorful history of the institute, and the library's holdings; information on exhibits (with links to some online exhibition catalogs); a catalog of publications; a photographic history; and a list of grant opportunities. The institute's annotated list of other repositories collecting in the history of sexuality is particularly useful and can be accessed directly at http://www.indiana.edu/~kinsey/centers.html#Speclib.

Lavender Legacies: Guide to Sources in North America

http://www.archivists.org/saagroups/lagar/home.htm

Compiled by the Lesbian and Gay Archives Roundtable of the Society of American Archivists, Lavender Legacies lists manuscript repositories with significant holdings in gay and lesbian history. While the list is not searchable by keyword, it is indexed by both repository name and location.

United States

Congressional Collections at Archival Repositories

http://www.lib.udel.edu/ud/spec/c_clctns.html

While the National Archives holds the collections of many members of Congress, other collections are scattered throughout the United States in various repositories. The University of Delaware has compiled this list of the locations of congressional collections to aid researchers in finding the material they require. Many names on the list contain links to biographical essays or collection descriptions maintained by the holding institution.

The Library of Congress

http://www.loc.gov/

The Library of Congress, the largest library in the world, adds about 10,000 items to its collections each day. Its Web site is designed to assist the public in accessing this mind-boggling array of information. From its home page, users can find out more about the library's collections, search its catalog, or read answers to FAQs. America's Library, a special section for children, introduces young people to the nation's heritage; the THOMAS clearinghouse supplies information on current and past congressional bills; and the Copyright Office, affiliated with the library, provides answers to an array of copyright questions. The library's online exhibit gallery contains dozens of offerings, and the American Memory collection (discussed in more detail in the Digital Collections section below) acts as a portal into the National Digital Library Program, devoted to digitizing major collections of "historical Americana."

National Archives and Records Administration (NARA)

http://www.nara.gov/

This extensive site contains something for every historian interested in U.S. history. An online exhibit hall provides access to digital exhibitions that include a photographic journey through the twentieth century and images of the Declaration of Independence and Constitution; the Digital Classroom supplies lesson plans and teaching strategies for a variety of age levels; a genealogy page (http://www.nara.gov/genealogy/) discusses the family history resources available both at the National Archives and elsewhere on the Web. Online versions of Federal Register publications are available, and the Archives and Preservation section offers information to archivists and records managers. Of course, the site also provides a searchable catalog and collection descriptions. For more information on NARA's online documents, see the Digital Collections section below.

NUCMC Home Page (National Union Catalog of Manuscripts Collections) ✓

http://lcweb.loc.gov/coll/nucmc/nucmc.html

This online version of the National Union Catalog of Manuscripts Collections allows users to search for manuscript material located throughout the

United States. Users enter a subject or keyword, and NUCMC returns a list of relevant collections and their locations. This database is a useful starting point for archival research.

Presidential Libraries

http://www.nara.gov/nara/president/address.html

At this site, the National Archives and Records Administration provides contact information and Web links to all of the U.S. presidential libraries, along with an overview of the presidential library system.

State Archives and Historical Societies

http://www.ohiohistory.org/textonly/links/arch_hs.html

In the United States, state archives provide access to the records of each state's government, and state historical societies normally contain collections of historical manuscripts pertaining to state history. This page, part of the Ohio Historical Society Web site, provides links to state archives and historical societies in the United States.

United States Immigration History

California Ethnic and Multicultural Archives (CEMA)

http://www.library.ucsb.edu/speccoll/cema.html

The University of California, Santa Barbara, administers this repository devoted to documenting the history of African-Americans, Latinos, Asian-Americans and Native Americans in California. CEMA's Web site houses lists of collections, along with explanatory essays detailing the historical significance of each major manuscript group. The archive's collecting policy is also accessible, so researchers can quickly ascertain the relevance of the library's holdings to their work.

Chicano Research Collection, Arizona State University

http://info.lib.asu.edu/lib/archives/chicano.htm

Arizona State University owns an extensive Chicano Research Collection, which documents the experience of Mexican-Americans through books, newspapers, periodicals, photographs, manuscripts, and ephemera. The collection's Web site offers information on these holdings, access to an online exhibit of Chicano history, and links to related sites.

Immigration History Research Center

http://www1.umn.edu/ihrc/

The Immigration History Research Center (IHRC) of the University of Minnesota maintains this Web site, which provides information on its holdings and mission. The collection focus is on American immigration and ethnic history, particularly as it pertains to groups from Eastern, Central, and Southern Europe and the Near East—those most involved in the immigration wave of the late nineteenth and early twentieth centuries. The site provides advice to genealogical researchers, collection descriptions, and an online catalog of publications distributed by the IHRC.

Women

Sallie Bingham Center for Women's History and Culture, Duke University

http://scriptorium.lib.duke.edu/women/

The Bingham Center at Duke University has a broad collecting focus that includes political activities, labor, Southern writers, religion, and education. The bulk of the materials pertains to women in the United States, though other countries are represented. The archive's Web site is part of Duke's award-winning Scriptorium site. Through it, researchers can access online versions of many holdings and more than fifteen Web-based bibliographies on topics pertaining to women's history. A list of links to other resources on women's history is also available (http://scriptorium.lib.duke.edu/women/article.html), as are numerous digital collections. For more information on Duke's digital collections, see the Digital Collections section of this book.

Guide to Uncovering Women's History in Archival Collections

http://www.lib.utsa.edu/Archives/links.htm

The Archives for Research on Women and Gender at the University of Texas,

San Antonio, has compiled a state-by-state listing of repositories with online descriptions of their women's history collections. The list is annotated and provides a hyperlink to each institution's home page.

Schlesinger Library, Radcliffe Institute for Advanced Study at Harvard

http://www.radcliffe.edu/schles/

The Arthur and Elizabeth Schlesinger Library on the History of Women in America is one of the most respected libraries on its topic in the world—and an excellent starting point for researchers. Examples of the manuscript collections include the personal papers of Charlotte Perkins Gilman, Betty Friedan, and Harriet Beecher Stowe. Visitors to its Web site will find descriptions of the Schlesinger's collections along with eighteen bibliographies on various aspects of women's history, from women in science to culinary resources.

Sophia Smith Collection of Women's History Manuscripts, Smith College

http://www.smith.edu/libraries/ssc/

With documentary strengths in women's political activism, women working abroad, and women in the arts and professions, the Sophia Smith Collection at Smith College houses substantial primary evidence of women's historical experience. Its Web site provides logistical information, thematic subject guides, and a list of collections. The permanent online exhibit, Agents of Social Change: New Resources on Twentieth-Century Women's Activism, chronicles women's role in the major reform movements of the century, including labor, civil rights, and welfare reform.

Chapter 28

Special Collections

Anne Rothfeld and Susan Tschabrun

Metasites

Archives Around the World: UNESCO Archives Portal

http://www.unesco.org/webworld/portal-archives

Not nearly as complete as Terry Abraham's Repositories of Primary Sources (below), this UNESCO site is worth knowing about for the important role UNESCO plays in helping archives around the world. This listing of over 4,000 links covers archives in Europe, North America, Latin America, Asia, and the Pacific as well as international archival organizations, professional associations, archival training, international cooperation, and Internet resources.

ARCHON: Archives Online

http://www.hmc.gov.uk/archon/archon.htm

The main gateway to repositories with manuscript material for British history, ARCHON is a key British resource for both archivists and researchers. The Royal Commission on Historical Manuscripts maintains the site. Researchers will be most interested in the British National Register of Archives (NRA) at http://www.hmc.gov.uk/nra/nra.html. The NRA leads researchers to a wide variety of manuscript collections, including papers of individuals of note, estates, local authorities, and societies, located both inside and outside the United Kingdom. Users may search the indexes by name of individual or corporate body, type of corporate body, and place name.

Repositories of Primary Sources

http://www.uidaho.edu/special-collections/Other.Repositories.html

With over 4,600 links, this Web site is by far the most complete listing of Web sites for actual (not virtual) archives and special collections departments. Updated frequently by Terry Abraham of the University of Idaho, the site arranges its links by geographical region (continent, country, state, and province). Additional Lists is a good jumping-off point for other archive and special collections metasites.

RLIN AMC Search Form

http://lcweb.loc.gov/z3950/

This important search gateway will lead the researcher to descriptions of holdings for a large number of manuscript and archival repositories, predominately, but not exclusively, in the United States. Select from one of three straightforward, fill-in-the-blank search forms. This electronic catalog derives from the print source, the National Union Catalog of Manuscript Collections, a project of the Library of Congress. Check the List of RLIN Library Identifiers on the search forms to see a list of the participating institutions.

www.archivesinfo.net

http://www.archivesinfo.net

Originating out of a University of London master's project by Simon Wilson, this site—mainly targeted at archivists—provides two important listings of archival links useful to researchers: UK Archival Repositories on the Internet and Overseas Archival Repositories on the Internet. One of the best features of these lists is the annotations prepared by the site's author that briefly indicate each site's contents.

General Sites

Africa Research Central: A Clearinghouse of African Primary Sources

http://www.africa-research.org

A collaboration between a history professor and an academic librarian at California State University, San Bernardino, this site assists researchers to locate often scarce information about archives, libraries, and museums with primary source collections related to Africa. The site focuses on repositories in Africa, but also provides information for those in Europe and North America. An im-

portant mission of the site is to alert researchers to the preservation crisis under
way in many countries in Africa and to indicate ways to help.

American Memory: Historical Collections for the National Digital Library

http://lcweb2.loc.gov/ammem/

The forty-two multimedia collections of over 7 million digitized documents,
photographs, recorded sound, moving pictures, and text selected from the Library of Congress's vast Americana holdings cover topics as diverse as twentieth-century architectural design and ballroom dancing. The collections may be
searched by keyword or browsed by titles, topics, or collection type. A fun
spin-off is Today in History, which presents people, facts, and events associated with the current day's date. Educators are particularly targeted in the Learning Page with activities, lesson ideas, and other information to help teachers
use the primary source material at American Memory in their classrooms.

Annuaire des archives et des bibliothèque nationales, des bibliothèque parlementaires et des centres nationaux d'information scientifique et technique de la Francophonie

http://www.acctbief.org/publica/anuinfsc.htm

This directory, originally published in print form in 1996, has been converted
into a searchable Web database by the publishers, Canadian-based BIEF (Banque
internationale d'information sur les États francophones). The directory includes
basic contact information for the national archives and libraries of forty-seven
francophone countries. Further descriptive information about the listed institutions can often be found in a BIEF companion Web site, titled *Profis géo-documentaires des états et gouvernements membres des sommets francophones*.
Together, these databases are an important source of scarce information about
archives for many smaller, non-Western countries.

Archives and Knowledge Management: Scholarly Online Resource Evidence and Records

http://www.dcn.davis.ca.us/~vctinney/archives.htm

Created and maintained by V. Chris and Thomas M. Tinney Sr., retired genealogical specialists, this Web site includes links to resources of particular interest
to genealogists, including a link to the Genealogy on the Web site and the Salt
Lake City LDS Family History Center. The Tinney Family organizes their links

to archives, libraries, and many other types of resources in a variety of categories, from Business, Community and Geography, and Religion to Surnames.

Archives in Deutschland

http://www.uni-marburg.de/archivschule/deuarch.html

This list of archival resources, maintained by Karsten Uhde of the Archivschule Marburg in Germany, brings together links of interest to both archivists and researchers. Historians and genealogists will find the following pages particularly useful: Archives in Germany, listing German archives by type (state, city, church, etc.); Archives in Europe; non-European Archives; and Genealogy.

Archives of American Art

http://artarchives.si.edu/start/htm

The Smithsonian maintains the Archives of American Art (AAA) and its Web site to provide researchers with access to "the largest collection of documents on the history of the visual arts in the United States"—13 million items, including the papers of artists, dealers, critics, art historians, museums, and art-related organizations of all kinds. The letters, sketchbooks, diaries, and other paper archives are supplemented with a large oral history interview collection and a sizable photograph collection. General collection descriptions of AAA treasures can be found in the Smithsonian online catalog (SIRIS) as well as RLIN, and the Smithsonian is beginning to make more detailed finding aids available as well.

Archives of Traditional Music at Indiana University

http://www.indiana.edu/~libarchm/

This Web site provides information about an important and unusual archive of ethnographic sound materials housed at Indiana University. The largest such university-based archive in the United States, the Archives of Traditional Music preserves commercial and field recordings of vocal and instrumental music, folktales, interviews, and oral history from the state of Indiana, the United States, and the diverse cultures of the world. Holdings can be searched using the IUCAT online catalog.

ArchivesUSA

http://archives.chadwyck.com/

Chadwyck-Healey, Inc., has developed a product that is an important tool for researchers interested in locating archival material in the United States. Although ArchivesUSA is a subscription service and therefore not available for free over the Web, it is an important resource that some libraries and archives make available to the public. ArchivesUSA integrates the entire print edition of the National Union Catalog of Manuscript Collections with other sources of information to create a more complete record for a greater number of repositories than is available through RLIN AMC (see above).

The Avalon Project at the Yale Law School: Documents in Law, History and Government

http://www.yale.edu/lawweb/avalon/avalon.htm

Directed by William C. Fray and Lisa A. Spar, the Avalon Project is a major source of digital primary source documents in the fields of law, history, economics, politics, diplomacy, and government. Access to the documents is by time period (mainly century), author/title, and subject. Major collections include the Nuremberg Trials Collection and the Native American Treaty Collection. A recent addition to the digital repository is a section on the Cuban Missile Crisis and its aftermath with over 250 documents (including editorial notes), prefatory essay, and lists of persons and abbreviations—a good example of the project's aim not simply to mount static text, but to add value.

Black Film Center/Archive

http://www.indiana.edu/~bfca/

By and about African-Americans, the historic 700 films housed at the Black Film Center/Archives at Indiana University consist of both Hollywood and independent efforts. Supplementing the films and videotapes are interviews, photographs, and other archival material. The Web site gives access to descriptions of the repository's holdings, the Frame by Frame database, and related Internet sites.

Canadian Archival Resources on the Internet

http://www.usask.ca/archives/menu.html

A comprehensive list of links to Canadian archives and associated resources on the Internet, this guide is the work of two Canadian archivists: Cheryl Avery, University of Saskatchewan Archives, and Steve Billinton, Archives of Ontario. Researchers can locate archives by name, type (provincial, university, municipal, religious, and medical), and Canadian region and find links to archival educational resources, associations, listservs, and multirepository databases.

Directory of Archives in Australia

http://www.asap.unimelb.edu.au/asa/directory/asa_dir.htm

The updated Web version of a directory originally printed in 1992, this directory of Australian archives allows researchers to browse archives alphabetically and by Australian states and to search them by keyword. There are also handy lists of links to Australian archives and finding aids on the Web.

Directory of Corporate Archives in the United States and Canada

http://www.hunterinformation.com/corporat.htm

The fifth edition of this important print directory, put out by the Society of American Archivists, Business Archives Section, has recently moved to the Web. From Amgen to Walt Disney Corporation, each corporate archive entry supplies contact information, type of business, hours of service, conditions of access, and holding information. "Corporate" is interpreted broadly, including professional associations ranging from the American Psychiatric Association to the International Longshoremen's Union. The directory may be searched by name of corporation, name of archivist, or by geographical location.

DPLS Online Data Archive

http://dpls.dacc.wisc.edu/archive.html

The Data and Program Library Service at the University of Wisconsin is creating access to a large selection of archival machine-readable datasets (raw data and documentation files) that can be downloaded for use by social science researchers. The datasets, listed in reverse chronological order or alphabetically by title, cover raw data from an extremely diverse range of historical and current topics, such as French Old Regime Bureaucrats (1661–1790), Vegetation Change in the Bahamas (1972), and the effects of the Learnfare Program (1993–1996).

EuroDocs: Primary Historical Documents from Western Europe: Selected Transcriptions, Facsimiles and Translations

http://library.byu.edu/~rdh/eurodocs/

Aiming to provide digitized documents that shed light on "key historical happenings" in political, economic, social, and cultural history, EuroDocs links to a wealth of digitized resources organized under twenty-three Western European countries from Andorra to Vatican City. Documents are also accessible from pages devoted to Medieval and Renaissance Europe and to Europe as a Supranational Region. EuroDocs is a project of Richard Hacken, the European Studies Bibliographer at the Harold B. Lee Library, Brigham Young University in Provo, Utah.

Guía preliminar de fuentes documentales etnográficas para el estudio de los pueblos indígenas de Iberoamérica

http://www.lanic.utexas.edu/project/tavera/

An important guide in the Spanish language, made available on the Web, the Guía describes the holdings related to indigenous peoples at hundreds of libraries and archives throughout Latin America, the United States, and Europe. A project of *La Fundacién Histérica Tavera* in Spain, the *Guía* is organized by country and type of archive (civil or ecclesiastical), providing contact information and holdings descriptions for all of the institutions listed.

A Guide to Uncovering Women's History in Archival Collections

http://www.lib.utsa.edu/Archives/links.htm

This guide to the archives, libraries, and other repositories on the Web with archival materials by or about women is maintained by the Archives for Research on Women and Gender Project at the University of Texas at San Antonio. Arranged by states in the United States (plus a link devoted to institutions outside of the United States), each listing includes annotations indicating which materials in a given collection may be of interest to researchers in women's history.

Historical Maps: The Perry-Castañeda Library Map Collection

http://www.lib.utexas.edu/maps

A wonderful collection of digitized historical maps from all regions of the world offered by the Libraries at the University of Texas at Austin. Maps are organized by continent (including the polar regions and oceans), and each map listing gives both publication information and file size. Although most maps are in JPEG format in the 200–300K range, some map files are much larger, so expect some slow load times. The site also includes links to other historical map collections.

International Institute of Social History

http://www.iisg.nl

Founded in 1935 in the Netherlands, IISH is one of the world's largest archival and research institutions in the field of social history, particularly labor history. Its 2,000 archival collections cover a range of topics not always well represented in traditional archives, like anarchism, revolutionary populism in nineteenth-century Eastern Europe, the French revolution and Utopian socialism, and World War II resistance movements. Collections may be identified using an online catalog, a list of archival collections, or other finding aids. Other IISH resources include the William Morris Archive on the Web; Occassio, a collection of digital social history documents; and numerous electronic publications. The institute's image collections are highlighted by virtual exhibitions such as The Chairman Smiles and Art to the People.

National Archives and Records Administration

http://www.nara.gov

NARA's Web site is a rich source of information for historians, genealogists, teachers, and students. For historians, the Research Room organizes information about historical archival records by branch of government and type of material. For genealogists, the Genealogy Page publishes practical information about using NARA's facilities nationwide, and a growing list of "quick guides" on census, military, immigration, and other types of records. Teachers and students will appreciate the Digital Classroom: Primary Sources, Activities, and Training for Educators and Students, with reproducible documents and teaching activities. The Online Exhibit Hall is a showcase for NARA treasures. Finally, NARA's searchable database, the Archival Information Locator (NAIL), contains more than 386,500 descriptions of selected NARA holdings in Washington, D.C., the regional archives, and Presidential libraries, including 106,215 digital copies of selected textual documents, photographs, maps, and sound recordings.

New York Public Library for the Performing Arts

http://www.nypl.org/research/lpa/lpa.html

"The world's most extensive combination of circulating, reference, and rare archival collections" in the performing arts, this Web site describes the library's important collections of recordings, videotapes, autograph manuscripts, correspondence, sheet music, stage designs, press clippings, programs, posters, and photographs in the areas of dance, music, and theater.

Online Archive of California

http://sunsite2.Berkeley.edu/oac

The Online Archive of California is an umbrella site bringing together information on a steadily increasing number of archival institutions in California. Its most important resource is a centralized database of 120 searchable electronic finding aids, which allows a level of precision searching for archival materials not available in more traditional online library catalogs, like RLIN AMC (above).

Portuguese Libraries, Archives and Documentation Services on the Internet

http://www.sdum.uminho.pt/bad/bibpte.htm

This simple, but useful Web site provides links to the thirty-three libraries, archives, and documentation centers in Portugal with an Internet presence. Maintained by the Working Group on Information Technologies of the *Associação Portuguesa de Bibliotecários, Arquivistas e Documentalistas*.

Social Science Data Archives: Europe

http://www.nsd.uib.no/cessda/europe.html

A map of Europe organizes links to fourteen important European social science data archives, with separate links to similar non-European institutions. Maintained by the CESSDA (Council of European Social Science Data Archives), this Web site also allows researchers to search the holdings of eleven electronic data repositories through its Integrated Data Catalogue.

Television News Archive

http://tvnews.vaderbilt.edu

Vanderbilt University holds "the world's most extensive and complete archive of television news," including 30,000 evening news broadcasts and 9,000 hours of special news-related programming. These news broadcasts have been consistently recorded and preserved by the archive since 1968. The Web site makes several searchable indexes available, including Network Television Evening News Abstracts, Special Reports and Periodic News Broadcasts, and Specialized News Collections (containing descriptive summaries of news material for major events like the Persian Gulf War of 1991). The archive is willing to loan videotapes to researchers worldwide.

United States Holocaust Memorial Museum

http://www.ushmm.org/research/collections

The Archive of the Holocaust Memorial Museum in Washington, D.C., has gathered together 13 million pages of microfilmed documents, 50,000 photo images, 200 hours of historical motion picture footage, 250 documentary or feature films, and 2,900 oral interviews related to the Holocaust, its origins, and its aftermath. The document and photographic archives may be searched individually or together using the USHMM Information Access query form available at the Web site.

USIA Declassified Historical Information

http://fbcdrom.fb10.uni-bremen.de/cd/infousa/usiaweb/usis/index.html

Pursuant to Executive Order 12958, the USIA (United States Information Agency) Declassification Unit prepares a listing of declassified documents in order to alert the general public, especially academic researchers, to information no longer classified. Researchers may do keyword searching of this listing or browse by broad topic, from Africa to Youth, to find the titles of more than 5,300 classified and unclassified one-cubic-foot boxes of records coming from the National Archives and many other document-holding federal agencies.

Chapter 29

Online Reference Desk

Anne Rothfeld

Metasites

Argus Clearinghouse

http://www.clearinghouse.net

"Provides a central access point for value-added topical guides which identify, describe, and evaluate Internet based information resources."

Avalon Project at Yale Law School

http://www.yale.edu/lawweb/avalon/avalon.html

Documents in law, history, and diplomacy from the pre-eighteenth, eighteenth, nineteenth, and twentieth centuries. "The Avalon Project will mount digital documents relevant to the fields of Law, History, Economics, Politics, Diplomacy and Government. We do not intend to mount only static text but rather to add value to the text by linking to supporting documents expressly referred to in the body of the text. The Avalon Project will no doubt contain controversial documents. Their inclusion does not indicate endorsement of their contents nor sympathy with the ideology, doctrines, or means employed by their authors. They are included for balance and because in some cases they are by our definition a supporting document."

Center for History and New Media

http://chnm.gmu.edu

"The Center produces historical works in new media, tests the effectiveness of these products in the classroom, and reflects critically on the promises and pitfalls of new media in historical practice." In addition, the center's Web pages provide electronic access to extensive directories, journals, sources, and professional discussions related to historical issues. The center's resources are designed to benefit professional historians, high school teachers, and students of history.

History Cooperative

http://www.historycooperative.org

"A project of the American Historical Association (AHA), the Organization of American Historians (OAH), the University of Illinois Press, and the National Academy Press, this site currently offers free, full-text access to recent issues of the *American Historical Review* and the *Journal of American History.* In the near future, access will be restricted to members of the AHA and OAH, and to institutions that subscribe to the print versions."

History Departments Around the World

http://chnm.gmu.edu

Sponsored by the Center for History and New Media at George Mason University. "We hope that this list will help you find ideas for creating departmental web pages, let you look in on or locate colleagues, conduct historical research, or help out with a graduate or undergraduate application."

History Resources

http://blair.library.rhodes.edu/histhtmls/histnet.html

Covering a wide range of areas and regions: general compilations; general WWW servers; electronic texts, documents, exhibits, and collections; Asian, Middle Eastern, and African history; electronic journals and listservs; North American, European, and Western history; and maps. Many links are annotated. Sponsored by Rhodes University.

H-Net Humanities and Social Sciences Online

http://www2.h-net.msu.edu

"H-Net is an international interdisciplinary organization of scholars and teachers dedicated to developing the enormous educational potential of the Internet and the World Wide Web. Our edited lists and Web sites publish peer reviewed essays, multimedia materials, and discussion for colleagues and the interested public. The computing heart of H-Net resides at MATRIX: The Center for Humane Arts,

Letters, and Social Sciences OnLine, Michigan State University, but H-Net officers, editors and subscribers come from all over the globe. H-Net's hundreds of volunteer editors foster online communities in the humanities and social sciences by monitoring email-based discussion lists and associated web sites."

INFOMINE

http://infomine.ucr.edu

"INFOMINE is intended for the introduction and use of Internet/Web resources of relevance to faculty, students, and research staff at the university level. It is being offered as a comprehensive showcase, virtual library and reference tool containing highly useful Internet/Web resources including databases, electronic journals, electronic books, bulletin boards, listservs, online library card catalogs, articles and directories of researchers, among many other types of information. INFOMINE is librarian built. Over thirty University of California and other university and college librarians have contributed to building INFOMINE."

Internet Public Library (IPL), Reference Center

http://www.ipl.org/ref

Provides links to general ready reference information and to specific subject areas. Links to additional subject-related sites are subdivided and annotated. IPL is also creating subject pathfinders. Maintained by the University of Michigan School of Information.

Research-It! Your One-Stop Reference Desk

http://www.iTools.com

A metasearch site for information including dictionaries, translations, biographical, and "quotation resources, maps, and stock quotes." Each area has its own search screen. Hosted by iTools!

Scout Report for Social Sciences and Humanities

http://scout.cs.wisc.edu/report/socsci/current/index.htm

A Publication of the Internet Scout Project, Computer Sciences Department, University of Wisconsin, Madison. "The target audience of the Scout Report for Social Sciences and Humanities is faculty, students, staff, and librarians in the social sciences and humanities. Each biweekly issue offers a selective collection of Internet resources covering topics in the field that have been chosen by librarians and content specialists in the given area of study. The Scout Report for Social Sciences and Humanities is also provided via e-mail once every two weeks. Subscription information is included at the bottom of each issue."

Reference Works

Almanacs

CIA World Factbook 2001

http://www.cia.gov/cia/publications/factbook

Complete resource of statistics, maps, and facts for over 250 countries and other entities. The *Factbook* is in the public domain. Other excellent resources are linked, including Chiefs of State and Cabinet Members of Foreign Governments and selected task force reports. Prepared by the CIA with information provided by numerous federal agencies including the Bureau of the Census, Bureau of Labor Statistics, Department of State, Defense Intelligence Agency, and U.S. Board on Geographic Names.

Information Please

http://www.infoplease.com

Information Please LLC has been publishing almanacs for over fifty years. Features a daily dictionary, encyclopedia, almanac, interactive almanac, learning networks, and theme-based almanacs covering the subject areas of the world, United States, history/government, biography, sports, entertainment, and weather/climate.

PoliSci.com Headquarters

http://www.polisci.com

Some portions of this Web site are fee-based and require a password. The site covers U.S. political information: U.S. government; state and local government; political science; economics; and political history. Includes the political reference desk (fee-based); links to news centers, newspapers, and magazines; book reviews and book listings; and the political reference almanac. Maintained by Keynote Publishing Co.

Archives

ArchivesUSA: Integrated Collection and Repository Information

http://archives.chadwyck.com

Fee-based service providing information and access to primary source holdings of 5,400 repositories, indexes to 118,000 special collections, and links to over 900 online finding aids. ArchivesUSA includes three major references: Directory of Archives and Manuscript Repositories in the United States (DAMRUS); National Union Catalogue of Manuscript Collections (NUCMC); and National Inventory of Documentary Sources in the United States (NIDS). ArchivesUSA on the Web is updated quarterly.

Historical Text Archive

http://www.historicaltextarchive.com

This site is divided into two sections: articles, books, documents, and photographs, and Web links to other sites. Organized by geographical and topical subject headings, sites focus on the studying and teaching of history.

Manuscripts Catalogue

http://molcat.bl.uk/

"This site is designed to serve as a single access point to information on the catalogs of the British Library's Department of Manuscripts, which cover accessions from 1753 to the present day. Visitors may search the catalogs index (a list of those available online can be found in the About section) by name, language, year, and other modifiers."

Repositories of Primary Sources

http://www.uidaho.edu/special-collections/Other.Repositories.html

This site lists over 4,500 Web and Gopher sites describing special collections holdings in the United States, including manuscripts and photographs. Repositories are divided geographically and subdivided by states. Additional links include other history-related Web sites with an international scope and subject specialty. Comprehensive and updated monthly. Maintained at the University of Idaho Library Special Collections and Archives.

Biographies

Biographical Dictionary

http://www.s9.com/biography

A database including over 28,000 notable men and women from ancient times to the present day, searchable by name, birth year, death year, and other keywords. The site contains links to biography-related sites, arranged by subject, and tips for students and teachers on how to use this resource in the classroom. Hosted by S9 Technologies.

Biography.com

http://www.biography.com

Searchable database with over 25,000 biographical entries and 2,500 video clips. Features discussions and materials for the classroom. Site is produced by A&E.

Dictionaries and Thesauri

The Alternative Dictionaries

http://www.notam.uio.no/~hcholm/altlang

Contains over 3,100 words and phrases in 120 different languages that would not be found in a standard dictionary. Readers and users can add words to the site.

Merriam-Webster Dictionary

http://www.m-w.com/dictionary.htm

Sponsored by Merriam-Webster, Inc. Full definitions with an online thesaurus available. Features new words recently added, word of the day, and language InfoZone, a portal to additional online resources.

Oxford English Dictionary Online

http://www.oed.com/

Fee-based service. Second edition now available, updated quarterly.

Roget's Thesaurus

http://www.thesaurus.com

Print version now online.

Wordsmyth English Dictionary-Thesaurus

http://www.wordsmyth.net

Users can search for exact words or words in phrases. Search returns definition and pronunciation guides. The site provides access to additional dictionaries and words of the week. Produced by Robert Parks and the ARTFL Project at the University of Chicago.

YourDictionary.com

http://www.yourdictionary.com

A metasite linking over 1,800 multilingual dictionaries, thesauri, and other sites relating to words and phrases. Grammar guides in selected languages are also available. Its predecessor, the Web of Online Dictionaries, was launched in 1995 at Bucknell Unviersity as a linguistic tool. YourDictionary.com also includes the Endangered Language Repository (ELR) to preserve almost extinct languages.

Dissertations and Theses

Electronic Theses and Dissertations in the Humanities

http://etext.lib.virginia.edu/ETD/ETD.html

Created in 1996, Electronic Theses and Dissertations is a directory and listing of those theses and dissertations currently in progress. Contains initiatives and a bibliography documenting arguments of electronic theses and dissertations.

Networked Digital Library of Theses and Dissertations

http://www.ndltd.org

A portal for dissemination of theses and dissertations. The site's goals include "to improve graduate education," "to increase the availability of student research," and "to empower universities."

UMIs Online Dissertation Services

http://www.umi.com:8080/hp/Support/DServices

Links to published and archived dissertations and theses and those available for purchase. Maintains a comprehensive bibliography for over 1.4 million doctoral dissertations and master's theses. Listing of best-selling dissertations is also available.

Encyclopedias

Encyclopedia Britannica Online

http://www.eb.com

This is a fee-based resource. Content is taken from the print edition. The site also includes Britannica Books of the Year, Nations of the World, Merriam-Webster's *Collegiate Dictionary*, 13,000 graphics and illustrations, and links to related Web sites.

Encyclopedia.com

http://www.encyclopedia.com

Free encyclopedia featuring more than 50,000 articles from *The Concise Columbia Electronic Encyclopedia*, third edition.

Symbols.com: Encyclopedia of Western Signs and Ideograms

http://www.symbols.com

Site contains over 2,500 Western signs with discussions of histories, uses, and meanings. Users can search using the graphic index or the word index. Online version of *Thought Signs* by Carl G. Liungman.

FAQs (Frequently Asked Questions)

Encyclopedia Smithsonian

http://www.si.edu/resource/faq

Encyclopedia Smithsonian features answers to the Smithsonian's FAQs with links to available Smithsonian resources. Topics are filed alphabetically.

FAQ Search Engine

http://www.cs.ruu.nl/cgi-bin/faqwais

This search engine allows users to search FAQs and other informative articles from a large database of newsgroups. Alphabetically indexed. From the Institute of Information and Computing Services at the University of Utrecht.

Geographic Names and Maps

Getty Thesaurus of Geographic Names

http://www.getty.edu/research/tools/vocabulary

Sponsored by the Getty Research Institute, this site currently has information for the Art and Architecture Thesaurus (AAT), the Union List of Artist Names (ULAN), and the Getty Thesaurus of Geographic Names (TGN). The TGN currently has over a million geographic names and places. Users can search by using geographic hierarchy displays, definition/description of term, other known names, and sources. AAT contains over 125,000 terms and notes for describing fine art, archival materials, and material culture. ULAN contains over 220,000 names and biographical information about artists and architects.

Perry-Castañeda Library Map Collection: Historical Map Web Sites

http://www.lib.utexas.edu/maps/Map_sites/hist_sites.html

Links to historical maps at other Web sites. Scope of site includes historical maps from Africa, Asia, the Pacific, North and South America, Europe, and the Middle East; also includes astronomical maps.

USGS (United States Geological Survey) Mapping Information: Geographic Names Information System (GNIS)

http://geonames.usgs.gov/

Contains over 2 million physical and cultural geographic features in the United States supplied by the Geographic Names Information System (GNIS) and U.S. Board on Geographic Names (BGN). Includes a search engine and links to online geographic resources.

Government and State Resources

FedStats

http://www.fedstats.gov

Statistical information gateway for over 100 federal government agencies and departments. FedStats is searchable by topics, such as demography, education, and labor. Each site provides annotated links. Includes the Statistical Abstract of the United States.

Social Statistics Briefing Room

http://www.whitehouse.gov/fsbr/ssbr.html

Access to current federal social statistics on crime, demographics, education, and health. Links are produced and provided by numerous federal agencies. Graphics are available.

THOMAS: U.S. Congress on the Internet

http://thomas.loc.gov/

Users can search for congressional bills, the Congressional Record, committee bills, and historical documents. FAQs regarding THOMAS are available. Links to other government agencies.

Indexes

Librarians' Index to the Internet

http://lii.org

Annotated directory to 7,900 Web resources arranged by subject, including over 200 history-related sites. Using the available search engine can focus a search. Produced by the Berkeley Public Library and Berkeley SunSITE.

The WWW-Virtual Library History Index

http://www.ukans.edu/history/VL

A portal to over 3,500 electronic resources arranged by different topics of history. Links also include research methods and materials, eras and epochs, and countries and regions. Users can recommend sites.

Internet Tutorials

Evaluating Internet Resources

http://library.albany.edu/internet/evaluate.html

Discusses what elements should be included in a reliable Web site and why—for example, the intended audience, the source of the content, accuracy and comprehensiveness of the content, and the style and functionality of the page.

Searching the Internet: Recommended Sites and Search Techniques

http://library.albany.edu/internet/search.html

Searching hints and tips for successful usage of subject directories and search engines within Web pages.

Libraries

The Library of Congress

http://www.loc.gov/

"The nation's oldest federal cultural institution. The Library preserves a collection of nearly 121 million items, more than two-thirds of which are in media other than books. These include the largest map, film and television collections in the world. In addition to its primary mission of serving the research needs of the U.S. Congress, the Library serves all Americans through its popular Web site and in its 22 reading rooms on Capitol Hill."

The National Agricultural Library

http://www.nal.usda.gov/

"As the Nation's primary source for agricultural information, the National Agricultural Library (NAL) has a mission to increase the availability and utilization of agricultural information for researchers, educators, policymakers, consumers of agricultural products, and the public. The Library is one of the world's largest and most accessible agricultural research libraries and plays a vital role in supporting research, education, and applied agriculture."

The National Library of Education

http://www.ed.gov/NLE/

NLE is the federal government's main resource for education information.

U.S. National Library of Medicine

http://www.nlm.nih.gov/

The World's largest biomedical library explores the uses of computer and communication technologies to improve the organization and use of biomedical information, supports a national network of local and regional medical libraries, and educates users about available sources of information.

Listservs

H-Net

http://www2.h-net.msu.edu

For historians, librarians, and archivists, H-Net hosts over 100 different topical listservs, a call for papers page, conference announcements, and employment information.

Tile.Net: The Comprehensive Internet Reference

http://tile.net

Search for discussion lists, newsgroups (Usenet), and FTP sites by entering a subject search. All of the results are linked to a page describing the listing and how to subscribe.

Quotations

Bartlett's Familiar Quotations (1901)

http://www.columbia.edu/acis/bartleby/bartlett

Sponsored by Columbia University's Bartleby Library Archive. The tenth edition, published in 1919, is available online, whereas the sixteenth edition is available in print. Includes English and French writers and wisdom from the ancients. Browse by author or search by keyword. Indexes are available to browse by author, both alphabetical and chronological.

Quotations Home Page

http://www.geocities.com/~spanoudi/quote.html

Use this home page to find quotations from twentieth-century authors and orators, arranged by topic. Provides specialized databases of quotations including Alternative Definitions, Serious Sarcasm, Childsong, Film, and Good Starts. This site contains 24,000 quotations in over thirty collections.

The Quotations Page

http://www.quotationpage.com

Users can read quotes of the day and motivational quotes of the day. This site, which can be searched, contains links to other quotation sites.

Statistics

Historical U.S. Census Data Browser

http://fisher.lib.virginia.edu/census

Descriptions of the people and the economy of the United States for each state and county from 1790 to 1970.

Statistical Abstract of the United States

http://www.census.gov/statab/www

Excellent resource for statistical information: demographics, employment, industrial production statistics, and government financial information. Online information covers data from 1995 to 2000.

Statistical Resources on the Web

http://www.l.b.umich.edu/libhome/Documents.center/stats.html

A metasite of statistical information. Searchable using the indexes, including business, demographics, labor, education, and sociology. Includes annotated links to government resources on the Web. Maintained by University of Michigan Documents Center.

U.S. Census Bureau: U.S. Gazetteer

http://tiger.census.gov/cgi-bin/gazetteer

Census data on all incorporated municipalities in the United States. Maps provided.

Student and School Information

American Universities

http://www.clas.ufl.edu/CLAS/american-universities.html

A metasite listing universities and colleges in the United States.

CollegeNet

http://www.collegenet.com

A search engine allows students to find the ideal college by using such categories as region, sports, major, and tuition. The site also covers scholarships and financial aid, college Web applications, and college recruiting. Virtual tours allow users to see campuses from their desktop, with links to the schools' Web sites.

History Departments Around the World

http://chnm.gmu.edu/history/depts

Alphabetical listing of links to history departments' home pages. Maintained by the Center for History and New Media at George Mason University.

Peterson's College Search

http://www.petersons.com/ugrad/ugsector.html

Users can search for their ideal college by major, region, and size of student population. The search results provide a link to an institution's profile, not its Web site.

Peterson's Guide: Colleges, Career Information, Test Prep, and More

http://www.petersons.com

Education resource with links to colleges and universities, graduate programs, and international programs. Users can search the database by keywords and subject specialty.

U.S. News and World Report Online: Graduate School Ranking

http://www.usnews.com/usnews/edu/beyond/bcrank.htm

Users can find a graduate program meeting their requirements. Includes methodology of rankings.

U.S. News and World Report Online: Undergraduate School Ranking

http://www.usnews.com/usnews/edu/college/corank.htm

This site allows users to locate a school by using categories, from the most expensive school to one with the best marching band! Includes methodology of rankings.

Style Manuals and Usage

Citing Electronic and Print Resources

http://www.lib.ucdavis.edu/citing/

Citation information for Modern Language Association (MLA), American Psychological Association (APA), Turabian style, *Chicago Manual of Style*, Council of Biology Editors, National Library of Medicine, and government information. Includes thorough discussions and examples.

MLA Online

http://www.mla.org/

Explanations of *MLA Handbook for Writers of Research Papers* and *MLA Style Manual* and *Guide to Scholarly Publications* are available online, including information about citing electronic resources. Official site for the Modern Language Association (MLA).

Strunk's Elements of Style

http://www.columbia.edu/acis/bartleby/strunk

The 1918 print edition is now available online.

Virtual Libraries

CARRIE: A Full-Text Electronic Library and Documents Room

http://www.ukans.edu/carrie/docs_main.html

Besides an electronic reference desk, this site contains selected full-text documents on these topics: the Catholic Church, United Nations, U.S. history, world constitutions, and World War I. Sponsored by University of Kansas.

THOR: The Virtual Reference Desk

http://thorplus.lib.purdue.edu/reference

Lists dictionaries, thesauruses, zip code directories, and other useful reference sources. Sponsored by Purdue University Libraries.

Virtual Library

http://library.albany.edu/subject/history.htm

The Virtual Library includes "sites in the news," which are hot topic sites; a reference section, which is subdivided into subject areas; subject and library catalogs, which include Internet resources and research databases; electronic publications; and fee-based services. All sites are linked, some with descriptions.

Specific Topics

Acronym Finder

http://www.acronymfinder.com

This site includes 196,000 common acronyms and abbreviations with definitions, including technology, telecommunications, computer science, and military acronyms. Updated weekly, the site contains search hints and links to other acronym sites. Sponsored by Mountain Data Systems.

The Best Information on the Net (BIOTN): The Librarians' Guide to Internet Information Sources

http://www.sau.edu/internet/

A portal to resources on the Internet. Links include hot paper topics, national and international newspapers, search engines, and a job-hunting guide. Geared for librarians and useful for historians. Site is sponsored by the librarians at O'Keefe Library, St. Ambrose University.

C-Net's Shareware

http://www.sharewarenet.com

Search engine listing over 190,000 shareware computer programs and links to sites where they can be downloaded.

Corporations

http://www.internet-propsector.org/company.html

Annotated links to corporate giving, company information, corporate directories, and stock quotes and securities. Includes links to Companies Online, CorpTech, and manufacturers' profiles. Maintained by Internet Prospector, Inc.

FinAid! The Smart Student Guide to Financial Aid

http://www.finaid.org/

"One of the most comprehensive annotated collections of information about student financial aid on the web." Includes links to loans, scholarships, and military aid; information on other types of aid; and tips for applying for aid.

Find-A-Grave

http://www.findagrave.com/index.html

Locate the graves of famous and nonfamous people. Database is organized by last name and geographic location; photos of some graves are included. Searchable by name, location, claim to fame, and date. Database currently contains over 2.5 million names in over 28,000 cemeteries.

Flags of the World

http://www.fotw.ca/flags

View more than 9,800 pages about flags and over 18,000 images. Flags can be searched by country, title, maps, and keywords. Site contains news and reports posted to the site's mailing list, a glossary, and a bibliography.

The Foundation Center: Your Gateway to Philanthropy on the WWW

http://fdncenter.org

The Foundation Center site provides grant information, funding trends and analysis, libraries and locations, and Foundation Center publications. Searchable links to over 160 sources of private, commercial, and corporate funding. Ranks foundations by assets and total giving.

The HistoryNet: Where History Lives on the Web

http://www.thehistorynet.com

Contains an archive of different topical areas, including eyewitness accounts, historic travel, and people profiles. Links to history magazines on the Internet and sponsors daily quizzes and factoids. Sponsored by the Cowles History Group.

Horus' Web Links to History Resources

http://www.ucr.edu/h-gig/horuslinks.htm

This Web page is designed to experiment in Internet history teaching and research. Contents include histories of specific countries, times, and places; areas of history; online services about history; Web tools; and searching hints. Hosted and supported by the University of California, Riverside, Department of History.

HyperHistory Online

http://www.hyperhistory.com/online_n2/History_n2/a.html

A 3,000–year timeline is available to access over 2,000 files with relevant maps, biographies, and brief histories of people, places, and events. The People section reaches from 1000 B.C.E. to the present for over 800 individuals in science, culture, religion, and politics. The History section displays timelines for major civilizations. The Events section continually grows on the site, ranging from 1790 to the present.

Intellectual Property Law

http://www.cs.utexas.edu/users/ethics/prop_rights/IP.html

Connects visitors to numerous topics including patents, trademarks, copyright, general intellectual property law, other resources on the Internet, and publications.

Internet Scout Project

http://scout.cs.wisc.edu/

Published every Friday on the Web and by e-mail, this site provides valuable information about new electronic and online resources free of charge. Subject report areas include social sciences; science and engineering; business and economics; and the site's general weekly report. Librarians and educators contribute reviews of useful and not-so-useful pages. Searchable archives.

Locating U.S. Corporation Records Online: A Directory of State Web Sites and Secretaries of State Contact Information

http://www.internet-propsector.org/secstate.html

Links to state Web sites that provide information on corporations within selected states. Databases for U.S. nonprofit companies in some states are available. Links to state home pages and secretaries of state. Locator provides a search engine to browse through over one million entries.

U.S. Copyright Office

http://www.loc.gov/copyright

The purpose of the U.S. Copyright Office is to "promote the Progress of Science and useful Arts, by securing for limited Times to Authors and Inventors the exclusive Right to their respective Writings and Discoveries" (U.S. Constitution, Article I, Section 8). This site describes how to file for a copyright, what can be copyrighted and the terms of a copyright and also includes information on the Digital Millennium Copyright Act, legislation, and publications.

Glossary

ActiveX: This is a Microsoft technology used on the Internet. ActiveX controls can be downloaded from the Internet. These controls are "activated" by the Web browser and perform a variety of different functions, allowing users to view Microsoft word documents via the Web browser, play animated graphical effects, and display interactive maps. As the name suggests, ActiveX controls make the Web page "active"; and they provide the same functions as Java Applets.

alias: A name used in place of a "real" name. Aliases are often shorter or cleverer than a person's real name.

animated GIF file: A special type of GIF File. A collection of GIFs, presented one after the other, with each picture slightly different from the previous one, gives the impression of a video.

applet: An applet is a brief program written in the Java programming language that can be used only as part of a Web page.

ASCII (American Standard Code for Information Interchange): This is a way of formatting data so that it can be read by any program, whether DOS, Windows, or Mac.

BBS (bulletin board system): This term usually refers to small, dial-up systems that local users can call directly.

bit: A bit is the smallest unit of information understood by a computer. A bit can take a value of 0 or 1. A byte is made up of eight bits, which is large enough to contain a single character. A kilobyte is equivalent to 1,024 bytes. A mega-

byte is equivalent to 1,024 kilobytes. A gigabyte is equivalent to 1,024 mega-
bytes.

browser: A program used to access the World Wide Web. The most popular browsers—Netscape and Mosaic—allow users to interact audiovisually with the
World Wide Web.

client: A synonym for Web browser or browser.

DNS (Domain Name System): DNS is the system which locates addresses on
the WWW. A DNS error message given by a browser means the address it is
looking for cannot be found.

document: On the WWW, a document can be either a file or a set of files that
can be accessed with a Web browser.

download: The process of getting a file or files from a remote computer—that
is, a computer other than the one on a user's desk or local area network.

e-mail (electronic mail): Sending typed messages and attachments through an
electronic mail network.

encryption: A method of converting data into "unreadable code" so that prying
eyes cannot understand the content.

FAQ (frequently asked questions): A FAQ is a document that contains answers to the most frequently asked questions about a given topic.

file: A file is a collection of data stored on a disk or other storage device under a
certain name.

flame: The practice of sending negative or insulting e-mail.

FTP (file transfer protocol): FTP is a tool for moving files from another computer site to a user's local service provider's computer, from which they can
be downloaded.

GIF (graphic interchange format): A set of standards for compressing graphic
files so that they occupy less space in a computer's memory or on a storage
device. CompuServe and Unisys developed GIF.

gopher: An older method of navigating the Internet developed at the University of Minnesota (where the mascot is the Golden Gopher). It displays information and links to documents, but is not graphics-based and is more
difficult to use than the World Wide Web. The World Wide Web is rapidly
replacing Gopher.

hits: This is Internet slang for both the number of times a site is accessed by a
user and for the number of sites found when using any Web search engine.

H-Net (The Humanities Network, or Humanities Online Initiative): H-Net
is an organization dedicated to exploiting the potential of electronic media
for history. It is supported by the National Endowment for the Humanities,
the University of Illinois–Chicago, and Michigan State University. H-Net
sponsors discussion lists, Web sites, book reviews, conferences, and other
activities.

home page: A home page is the designated beginning point for accessing a WWW site.

hypermedia: Computer-generated displays that combine text, images, and sound.

hypertext: Data that provide links to other data, allowing a user to move from one resource to another.

HTML (Hypertext Markup Language): This is the computer language used to construct documents on the World Wide Web. Most home pages are written in HTML.

http (hypertext transfer protocol): This is a method of coding information that enables different computers running different software to communicate information. It permits the transfer of text, sounds, images, and other data.

icon: A graphic image that is used to represent (and usually activate) a file or program.

Internet: The Internet refers to the worldwide network of computers that is linked together using the Internet protocol TCP/IP.

Java: A programming language developed by Sun Microsystems that allows programmers to create interactive applications that can be run within Web browsers on any type of computer. Java programs are referred to as applets.

JavaScript: A programming language for developing Internet applications. A Web browser interprets JavaScript statements embedded in an HTML page to create interactivity.

JPEG (Joint Photographic Experts Group): The standard format for compressing graphic files so that they occupy less space in a computer's memory or on a storage device.

Kbps (kilobits per second): The unit used to measure how fast data is transferred between devices on a network. One kilobit is 1,024 bits.

LAN (local area network): A group of computers connected together by cable or some other means so that they can share common resources.

link: A connection point that takes a user from one document to another or from one information provider to another.

listserv: A computer that serves a discussion group by processing, distributing, and storing messages and files for all members of the list.

log in: The process of gaining access to a remote computer system or network by typing the user's login name and password.

login name: The name used for security purposes to gain access to a network or computer system.

MPEG (Moving Pictures Expert Group): The standard format for compressing video images so that they occupy less space in a computer's memory or on a storage device.

netiquette: Etiquette for the Internet.

network: A group of interconnected computers.

page: Either a single screen of information on a Web site or all of the information on a particular site.

PDF (Portable Document Format): A file type developed by Adobe Systems to allow the preservation of complex formatting and symbols.

POP (Post Office Protocol): A standard for exchanging e-mail between a user's computer and an Internet access provider.

RAM (random access memory): RAM is the memory that a computer uses to temporarily store and manipulate information. RAM does not hold information after the computer is turned off.

RealAudio: Software that allows sound files to be transmitted from the Internet back to the user's computer in streams, allowing the experience of immediate and simultaneous playing.

service provider: Any organization that provides connections to the Internet.

SLIP/PPP (serial line internet protocol/point to point protocol): This is a connection which enables a home computer to receive TCP/IP addresses. To work with the World Wide Web from home, via a modem, a SLIP or PPP connection is necessary.

SMTP (Simple Mail Transfer Protocol): An accepted standard used extensively on the Internet to allow the transfer of e-mail messages between computers.

snail mail: A term that e-mail users employ to describe the traditional mail or post office service.

spam: To send e-mails to people who did not ask to be sent that information. Spamming is usual done as bulk e-mailing to promote a product.

TCP/IP (Transfer Control Protocol/Internet Protocol): Essentially this is the most basic language on the Internet. The rules of TCP/IP govern the sending of packets of data between computers on the Internet and allow for the transmission of other protocols on the Internet, such as http and FTP.

Telnet: An Internet protocol that enables a user to log on to a remote computer.

T-1 line: A leased Internet line connection. The speed at which data can be transmitted is 1.45 megabits per second on a T-1 line.

UNIX: Like DOS or Windows, UNIX is an operating system run by most of the computers that provide access to the Internet.

URL (uniform resource locator): This is the address for an Internet site.

Usenet: A network of newsgroups dedicated to thousands of different topics.

Web bot: A search engine that obtains its information by starting at a specified Web page and visiting each Web page that has a link to it. Web bots are used by large search engines such as Yahoo! to create their database. Also called spider, bot, and robot.

Web browser: A program used to access the WWW. The most popular browsers—Netscape and Mosaic—allow users to interact audiovisually with the World Wide Web.

Winsock: A program which runs in the background on a Windows-based personal computer, allowing the user to make a SLIP/PPP connection to the Internet and to use TCP/IP.

WWW (World Wide Web): An Internet service that enables users to connect to all of the hypermedia documents on the Internet. The Web is like a network within the Internet.

Zip: Zip (or zipped) files are files that have been compressed by a software package to reduce the amount of space that the data take up. This type of file is popular on the Internet because smaller files can be sent faster. To create or open a Zip file, a user needs a special software package such as WinZip or PKUNZIP. The .zip extension indicates a Zip file.

About the Editors
and Contributors

Guido Abbattista is Full Professor of Modern History, University of Trieste, Italy. His field of research is eighteenth-century political and historical culture in Europe and North America. Among his recent publications are *La rivoluzione americana* (Roma, 1998); "*Imperium* e *libertas*: repubblicanesimo e ideologia imperiale all'alba dell'espansione europea in Asia, 1650–1780," in *Studi settecenteschi*, n. 20, 2000, pp. 9–49; "Risorse elettroniche e telematiche per gli studi di Storia moderna," in *Memoria e Ricerca*, n. 5, January–June 2000, pp. 205–215; and "'Quand a commencé leur sagesse'? il *Journal des Sçavans* e il dibattito su antichità e civiltà della Cina (1754–1791)," in *Saggi in onore di Antonio Rotondò*, a cura di L. Simonutti, Firenze, Olschki, 2001, pp. 593–625 (forthcoming). He is currently a member of the team working on the critical edition of G.-T. Raynal, *Histoire philosophique et politique des établissements des Européens dans les Deux Indes* (1770–1780) (Oxford, Voltaire Foundation), and is writing a book on the Europeans in Asia in the early modern age. He is coeditor of the journal *Storia della Storiografia* and founder and editor of *Cromohs*, an electronic journal of the history of modern historiography (http://www.cromohs.unifi.it) with an electronic library of historiography and methodology (http://www.eliohs.unifi.it).

Susanna Betzel is a bookseller and freelance writer with a particular interest in revolutionary France. She is currently working on her second novel about the

French Revolution and hopes soon to have *Keystone of the Terror*, her translation of the memoirs of the executioner of Paris, published by a university press.

Samuel E. Dicks holds a doctorate from the University of Oklahoma and has been a member of the history faculty at Emporia State University, Kansas, since 1965. He is the publication director of *Teaching History: A Journal of Methods*, and edits its Internet Web site. In addition to courses in ancient and medieval history, he also teaches historiography and an introductory class in genealogy.

Bambi L. Dingman is a freelance writer from New Jersey. She has been the French and Indian War editor for *Smoke and Fire News*, an internationally recognized living history newspaper, and has also written for *Recreating History Magazine*. She currently serves as the Regimental Adjutant for the 7th Vermont Infantry Regiment as part of the Web-based project Vermont in the Civil War.

Kenneth R. Dvorak is the Secretary-Treasurer of the American Association for History and Computing and a doctoral candidate in American culture studies at Bowling Green State University, Ohio. He is the codirector of two nationally honored Web sites—America in the 1890s and 1890s Bowling Green, Ohio, and he has written numerous articles that have appeared in the *Journal of Film and History*, the *Journal of Popular Culture*, and the *Journal of American Culture*.

Susan Ferentinos is associate editor of the *OAH Magazine of History*, published by the Organization of American Historians, and a Ph.D. candidate in U.S. history at Indiana University. She holds an M.A. in history and an M.L.S., with a concentration in special collections.

Mary Anne Hansen is an Assistant Professor at Montana State University Libraries. She has authored numerous articles and presented papers at several scholarly conferences, including the Association of College and Research Libraries Biennial Conference.

James E. Jolly is a doctoral student and Adjunct Professor of American History at Middle Tennessee State University.

Ken Kempcke received his M.A. in American studies from Purdue University and his M.L.S. from Indiana University. He is currently the Social Science Reference Librarian and Coordinator of Library Instruction at Montana State University, Bozeman.

Andrew E. Kersten has taught at the University of Wisconsin, Green Bay, since 1997. He earned his B.A. at the University of Wisconsin, Madison, and he received the M.A. and Ph.D. in United States history from the University of Cincinnati. He has published in the *Queen City Heritage*, *The Michigan Historical Review*, and *The Missouri Historical Review* and has contributed to several anthologies. He is currently working on a book-length study of President Franklin D. Roosevelt's Fair Employment Practice Committee.

Leo E. Landis is Curator of Agriculture at Henry Ford Museum and Greenfield Village in Dearborn, Michigan. He launched the Web site for the editorial office of *Agricultural History* in October 1995. He often provides content for the museum's Web site (http://www.hfmgv.org) and is working toward a Ph.D. in agricultural history from Iowa State University. His research interests are Midwestern agriculture and social and cultural history. He is author of *Building Better Roads: Iowa's Contribution to Highway Engineering*.

Tracy Penny Light is a Ph.D. candidate in the Department of History at the University of Waterloo, Ontario, Canada, and currently holds a Teaching Fellowship at the University's Centre for Learning and Teaching Through Technology. Her research areas include Canadian and women's history and the improvement of student learning through the use of new instructional technologies, in the discipline of history specifically and across the disciplines generally. She teaches in these areas and also develops workshops and coordinates programs for instructors on a wide array of instructional design issues.

Margaret M. Manchester is Assistant Professor of History and Director of the American Studies Program at Providence College, Rhode Island.

Robert M.S. McDonald is Assistant Professor of History at the United States Military Academy, West Point. A specialist in the Revolutionary and early national periods of U.S. history, he holds degrees from the University of Virginia, Oxford University, and the University of North Carolina at Chapel Hill, where he received his Ph.D. He is currently at work on a book about Thomas Jefferson's public image between 1776 and 1826.

Scott A. Merriman is a doctoral candidate in modern American history at the University of Kentucky. He has previously taught history at the University of Cincinnati, Northern Kentucky University, and Thomas More College. He is also a coauthor of *The History Highway: A Guide to Internet Resources*, coeditor of *The History Highway 2000: A Guide to Internet Resources*, coeditor of *History.edu: Essays on Teaching with Technology*, and an associate editor for the *Journal of the Association for History and Computing*. He has contributed to the *Register of the Kentucky Historical Society*, *Historical Encyclopedia of World Slavery*, *American National Biography*, and *Buckeye Hill Country*.

Martin V. Minner is a Ph.D. candidate at Indiana University who specializes in urban history and photographic history. His current research is on civic politics and cultural memory in Newark, New Jersey. He is also a technical communication consultant and has worked in software development and computer publishing.

Charlene Mires is Assistant Professor of History at Villanova University. She received her M.A. from the University of Pennsylvania and her doctorate from Temple University. She has published widely on American culture and material culture and serves as the project coordinator for the Centennial Exhibition of 1876 Project (http://www.villanova.edu/~his2998cm/).

Jessie Bishop Powell is completing her M.L.S. at the University of Kentucky, where she holds an M.A. in English. Her primary research interest is the economic situation of Appalachian libraries in Eastern Kentucky.

Edward Ragan is currently a Ph.D. candidate at Syracuse University, where he is studying early American and native American history. His dissertation explores Anglo-Indian relations in Virginia. Through his research, he has become involved with Virginia's Indians in their efforts to gain federal recognition.

J. Kelly Robison is an American Studies Fellow and the Academic Computing Specialist at the Center for U.S. Studies, Martin-Luther University Halle-Wittenberg, Wittenberg, Germany. He holds a Ph.D. in American history from Oklahoma State University and an M.A. in American history from the University of Montana. His research and teaching focus is the history of the American West and Native America, with a special emphasis on the Spanish Borderlands and cross-cultural acculturation. He is also interested in the use of computer technology in teaching and researching history. He is a consulting editor for the *Journal of the Association for History and Computing* and is a member of the Executive Board of the American Association for History and Computing.

Anne Rothfeld is an Information Specialist at the University of Maryland, Baltimore. She earned her M.A. in library science from the Catholic University of America, concentrating in special collections and archives. Previously she was the Archivist Technician at the U.S. Holocaust Memorial Museum in Washington, D.C.

Dennis A. Trinkle is the Tenzer University Professor in Instructional Technology and the Associate Coordinator of Information Services and Technology at DePauw University. He received his B.A. from DePauw University and his M.A. and Ph.D. from the University of Cincinnati. He also serves as the Executive Director of the American Association for History and Computing (http://www.theaahc.org). He has published broadly on technology, teaching, and history. His recent books include *The History Highway: A Guide to Internet Resources*; *Writing, Teaching, and Researching History in the Electronic Age*; *History.Edu: Essays on Teaching with Technology*; and *The History Highway 2000*.

Susan Tschabrun is Reference and Electronic Resources Librarian at California State University, San Bernardino. She holds a Ph.D. in history from University of Wisconsin, Madison, and an M.L.S. from UCLA. She is currently the project director for a Getty-funded grant to catalog and digitize the holdings of the Center for the Study of Political Graphics, an educational archive of domestic and international political and protest posters in Los Angeles. Other projects include work on a set of multimedia learning modules to teach history majors information competency skills and coauthorship of the Web site Africa Research Central: A Clearinghouse of African Primary Sources.

Laura Winninghoff is the Evening Circulation Librarian at the Law Library at Indiana University, Bloomington. She has also worked in the Curatorial and Collections Departments of the Houdini Historical Center and the Children's Museum of Indianapolis and has taught history and English at Notre Dame Girls Academy in Chicago. Her research interests include the interaction of museum visitors and Web-based exhibits. She earned her M.L.S. and M.A. in history at Indiana University, Bloomington.

Alexander Zukas is Associate Professor of History at National University in San Diego. He received his Ph.D. in history from the University of California, Irvine, in 1991. He has written on European working-class and gender history, innovative approaches to the teaching of world history, and the use of music and theater to teach historical subject matter. His publications include the articles "Lazy, Apathetic, and Dangerous: The Social Construction of Unemployed Workers in the Late Weimar Republic," *Contemporary European History* (forthcoming); "Cyberworld: Teaching World History on the World Wide Web," *The History Teacher* (August 1999); "Age of Empire," *Radical History Review* (Winter 1997); and "Different Drummers: Using Music to Teach History," *Perspectives* (October 1996). He is currently working on articles about teaching world history courses on the Internet, the phenomenology of teaching online, Karl Korsch's Marxism, unemployed workers in the Ruhr region of Germany during the Weimar Republic, and the ecology of the Ruhr from 1850 to 1930. He serves as Director of the Institute for Community and Oral History of the Center for Cultural and Ethnic Studies at National University.

Index